ADAPTATION AND
EVOLUTION IN
COLLECTIVE SYSTEMS

ADVANCES IN NATURAL COMPUTATION

Series Editor: **Xin Yao** (University of Birmingham, UK)

Assoc. Editors: **Hans-Paul Schwefel** (University of Dortmund, Germany)
Byoung-Tak Zhang (Seoul National University, South Korea)
Martyn Amos (University of Liverpool, UK)

ADAPTATION AND EVOLUTION IN COLLECTIVE SYSTEMS

Advances in Natural Computation – Vol. 5

Akira Namatame

National Defense Academy, Japan

World Scientific

NEW JERSEY · LONDON · SINGAPORE · BEIJING · SHANGHAI · HONG KONG · TAIPEI · CHENNAI

Published by

World Scientific Publishing Co. Pte. Ltd.

5 Toh Tuck Link, Singapore 596224

USA office: 27 Warren Street, Suite 401-402, Hackensack, NJ 07601

UK office: 57 Shelton Street, Covent Garden, London WC2H 9HE

British Library Cataloguing-in-Publication Data
A catalogue record for this book is available from the British Library.

ADAPTATION AND EVOLUTION IN COLLECTIVE SYSTEMS
Advances in Natural Computation — Vol. 5

ISBN-13   978-981-256-856-4
ISBN-10   981-256-856-5

Printed in Singapore

This book is dedicated to those
who have made my academic-life exciting.

Preface

It is thought that ants in an ant colony do not know exactly how the ant colony where they live should be built. Each ant has certain things that it does in coordinated association with other ants, but no ant designs the colony. How the colony of ants works collectively in the manner it does remains a mystery. However, an important clue to the answer to this question may be found by looking at interactions among ants.

Many organisms form collectives that strongly affect the behavior of individuals. Familiar examples include the schooling behavior of fish and the flocking behavior of birds. Collective behavior emerges from traits of individuals. Collectives emerge from relatively simple traits of individuals, and these traits give rise to individual behaviors that form the collective. Collectives can be treated as an additional level of organization between the individual and the population.

For the last decade, attempts have been made to develop some general understanding, and ultimately a theory of systems that consist of interacting agents. It is common to call these systems *collective systems* because it is difficult to reduce aggregate behavior to a set of properties characterizing the individual components. Interactions produce properties at the aggregate level that are simply not present when the components are considered individually.

In his book, titled *The Wisdom of Crowds*, Surowiecki (2004) explores an idea that has profound implications. A large collection of people are smarter than an elite few, no matter how brilliant they are and or how much better they are at solving problems, fostering innovation, coming to wise decisions, even predicting the future. His counterintuitive notion, rather than crowd psychology as traditionally understood, suggests new insights regarding how complex social and economic activities are organized. He explains the *wisdom* of crowds emerges only under the right conditions, which are (1) diversity, (2) independence, (3) decentralization, and (4) aggregation.

On the other hand, the fact that selfish behavior may not achieve full efficiency has been well reported in the literature. Recent research efforts have focused on quantifying the loss of system performance due to selfish and uncoordinated behavior. The degree of efficiency loss is known as the *price of anarchy*. We need to design systems so that selfish individual behaviors need not degrade the system performance.

In this book, a collective system, or simply a *collective*, is modeled as a collection of autonomous decision-making entities, called *agents*. A collective refers to any complex system of interacting agents, together with performance measures by which we can rank the behavior of the entire system. Collective systems include a collection of diverse and mutually adaptive agents pursuing varied and often conflicting interests. The collective systems are situated between a few agents in game theoretic systems, a few hundred agents in multi-agents systems, and a larger scale of agents in typical economic and social systems.

The mission of collective evolution is to harness the collective systems of selfish agents and to serve to secure a sustainable relationship in an attainable manner so that desirable properties can emerge as *collective intelligence*. Of particular interest is the question as to how social interactions can be restructured so that agents are free to choose their own actions while avoiding outcomes that none would have chosen.

Darwinian dynamics based on mutation and selection form the core of models for evolution in nature. Evolution through natural selection is understood to imply improvement and progress. If multiple populations of species adapt to each other, the result is a co-evolutionary process. The problem to contend with in co-evolution based on the Darwinian paradigm, however, is the possibility of an escalating arms race with no end. Competing species might continually adapt to each other in more and more specialized ways, never stabilizing at a desirable outcome.

In biology, the gene is a better unit of selection by which to represent individuals. However, the collective evolutionary process is expected to compel agents towards ever more refined adaptation and evolution, resulting in sophisticated behavioral rules. The persistence and sustainability of the collective system in turn depends on its persistent collective evolution.

Hardware developments will soon make possible the construction of very-large-scale models, for instance, models that contain one million to 100 million agents. It has been argued that the main impediment to creating empirically relevant agents on this scale is our current lack of understanding of the realistic behavior of agents. This bottleneck, i.e., what rules to write for agents, is the primary challenge facing the agent research community. The approach of collective evolution is very much at the forefront of this issue.

As is usual in the case of any book, the author is deeply indebted to several people. My friends and colleagues, the authors of the books and papers to which I have referred herein, have contributed to this book in many ways. I would like to thank those colleagues who provided stimulating academic interactions through debate and dialog through readings, including Professors Yuji Aruka, Robert Axtell, David Green, Dirk Helbing, Taisei Kaizoji, Thomas Lux, Robert MacKay, Hidenori Murakami, Frank Schweitzer, Bernard Walliser, and Xin Yao. I would also like to Associate Professors Hiroshi Sato and Masao Kubo, my many wonderful students at the National Defense Academy, Japan, who provided a quiet retreat from the pressures of teaching and administration during the editing of this book.

Above all, there is my family. My wife Kazuko and our daughters Aya and Kaori have all supported me and tolerated my bringing my work home with me. I would also like to thank Mr. and Mrs. Russell and Lynn Phillips who taught me how to write a thesis when I was a student at Stanford University 30 years ago. Since my college years, they have observed my progress, but I have struggled with speaking and writing in my second language. Finally, I would like to thank all of you who will take the time to read this book. I hope that you will learn as much from reading this book and as I have learned through its writing.

Akira Namatame

Contents

Chapter 1

Introduction to Collective Systems

A collective system is a large system of adaptive agents, where each agent has her own utility function to optimize, along with global performance measures of the full system. The envisioned objective is to study the mechanism of inducing desirable collective outcomes. This aim is quite novel, since a collective of agents needs to establish coordinated and synchronized behavior from the bottom up. In this chapter, we provide a survey of approaches to the study of collective systems.

1.1 Collective Outcomes of Interacting Agents

Billions of people make billions of decisions everyday about many things. It often appears that the aggregation of these unmanaged individual decisions leads to a desired outcome. It is amazing that economic and social activities generally work well in this way without any authority. Adam Smith characterized this fact by stating that an *"unseen hand"* brought about coordination among self-interested individual economic activities. The unseen hand is observed behind many market activities. This principle also works as a basic mechanism for allocating limited resources to people who need them.

People constantly interact with each other in different ways and for different purposes. Somehow these individual interactions produce some coherence at the aggregate level, and therefore, aggregation may generate structure and regularity. The individuals involved may have a very limited view of some part of the whole system but their activities are coordinated to a large degree and produce a desirable outcome at the aggregate level.

However, there are other systems for which it is difficult to understand how they work or to find out better ways to make them work. For instance, many economic and social systems often produce inefficient outcomes at the aggregate level in a way that the individuals who comprise the system need not know anything about or even be aware of it. When the system results in some undesirable outcome, we often think about whether it is due to the members who comprise the system. We tend to observe the resulting outcome as corresponding to the intentions of the members who compromise the system.

There is strong interest in many fields to answer the following questions. How do interacting individuals with micro-motives produce the aggregate outcome? How do we identify the micro-rules of agents that produce some regularities of interest at the macroscopic level? There has been no natural methodology for systematically studying these issues.

Most of our social activities are substantially free of centralized management, and although we may care how it all comes out in the aggregate, our own decisions and behaviors are typically motivated by self-interest. Therefore, in examining collective behavior, we shall draw heavily on the individual decisions. It might be argued that understanding how individuals make decisions is sufficient to understand most parts of the collective system. Although individual decisions are important to understand, they are not sufficient to describe how a collection of agents arrives at specific decisions. These situations, in which the decision of an agent depends on the decisions of others, are situations that usually do not permit any simple summation or extrapolation to the aggregate (Schelling,1978). To make this connection, we usually have to look at the system of interactions among agents.

We usually ascribe human behaviors as if they are oriented toward a goal. Peoples have preferences and pursue their own goals, or maximize comfort as well as minimize effort embarrassment. We might characterize these behaviors as *purposive behaviors*. Economists argue that much of individual private consumption is also dependent upon other peoples' consumption. We often behave by reacting to others. Therefore, what we also have is a mode of *contingent behavior* that depends on what other people are doing (Schelling, 1978). For example, each person's enjoyment of driving a car is inversely related to others' enjoyment if too many peoples drive. Everybody becomes stuck in congested traffic in this case. This is a kind of social congestion and the problem is that there is no way of knowing what others will do. When we are in a mode of contingent behavior, the resulting collective behavior is often volatile and far from desirable.

It is not easy to tell from collective phenomena just what the motives are behind individuals and how strong they are. For instance, consider a traffic jam again. It is not easy to capture the properties of a traffic jam at the aggregate level without describing what individual drivers do. Each of these drivers is different, and the characteristics of their driving behavior become the rules in the model. When we run this model we can reproduce a traffic jam, but this time we need to watch closely how the individual drivers interact with each other and we can inject to see how these interactive behaviors among drivers would affect the visible properties of the traffic jam (Resnick, 1999)(Bonabeau, 2002).

Therefore, we have to look closely at agents who are adapting to other agents. In this way, the behavior of one agent affects the behaviors of the other agents. How well agents accomplish what they want to accomplish depends on what other agents are doing. What makes this kind of interactive situation interesting and difficult is that the aggregate outcome is what has to be evaluated, not merely how agents behave within the constraints of their own environments.

How well they do for themselves in adapting to environments is not equivalent to how satisfactory a social environment they collectively create for themselves. There is no presumption that the self-serving behavior of agents should lead to collectively satisfactory results. If our problem is that there is too much traffic, we are also part of the problem. If we raise our voice to make ourselves heard, we add to the noise level that other people are raising their voices to be heard over.

Our complex systems often result in the features of *emergent properties*, which are properties of the system that separate components do not have. These emergent properties, we find, are the result of not only the behavior of individual agents but the interactions between them as well. For instance, what drivers do on the road depends on what other drivers do. This can not be explained without looking at how the agents behave and interact with each other to make up the whole. Resulting traffic jams are counterintuitive phenomenon that we could only predict with the framework of the collective system of interacting agents.

We can observe many collective phenomena viewed as *emergence* that has arisen from billions of small-scale and short-term decisions of interacting agents. Viewing complex systems as a collective of interacting agents means adopting a new scientific approach that shifts from *reductionism* to *connectionism*.

With the view of reductionism, every phenomenon we observe can be reduced to a collection of components, the movement of which is governed by the deterministic laws of nature. In such reductionism, there seems to be no place for novelty or emergence. The basic approach with the view of reductionism is the rational choice model. The rational choice theory posits that an agent behaves to optimize her own utility produces relevant and plausible prediction about many aggregate phenomena.

However, there are many critics of approaches based on the *rational choice model*. The problem of the rational choice model is that it assumes agents who are sufficiently rational. Goals and purposes of agents are also often related directly to other agents or they are constrained by an environment that consists of other agents who are pursuing their own goals.

When a society or organization faces some complex problems, the typical reaction is to fall into *"centralized thinking"* (Watts, 2001). A small coherent group of experts decide what to do based on the characteristics of the problem, and execute rules and everyone else then simply follows these rules. However, introducing additional rules can serve only to make the problem worse. This is because it is usually centralized thinking behind these local rules, so the effect of new local rules being added to existing local rules is quite strong. Without modeling the process of the chains of reactions, it would be very hard for a human brain to predict this pathological collective behavior.

To understand this paradox, we need to take a look at the problem of *"decentralized thinking"* (Resnick, 1999). What should be clear is that combining the many different individuals involved at a single point is almost certain not to succeed in delivering the kind of essential functionality. Some other kind of connectionism is required.

1.2 The Study of Collective Systems

A collective system is modeled as a collection of autonomous decision-making entities, called agents. In this section, we provide the definition and a survey of approaches to collective systems. A collective system, or just simply a collective, means any complex system of interacting agents, together with performance measures by which we can rank the behavior of the entire system (Tumer and Wolpert, 2004). Collective systems include a collection of diverse and mutually adaptive agents pursuing varied and often conflicting self-interests.

Many organisms form aggregations that have strong effects on individual behaviors. Familiar examples include schools of fish and flocks of birds. Auyang (1998) defines the term *"collective"* for such aggregations. According to Auyang, the defining characteristics of a collective are as follows. Interactions among individuals making up a collective are strong, that is internal cohesion is strong while external interactions are weak. Furthermore, collectives have their own characteristics and processes that can be understood independent of the individuals that compromise them.

Another defining characteristic of collectives in ecological systems is that collectives exist for longer or shorter times than do the individuals making up the collective. Collectives can be treated as an additional level of organization between the individual and the population (Grim, 2005). Individuals belonging to a collective may behave very differently from individuals alone, so different traits may be needed to model in individuals that are not in a collective.

The behavior of a collective emerges from traits of individuals. A school of fish is an example of modeling a collective as emerging from relatively simple traits of individuals, and these traits give rise to individual behaviors that form the collective. Representing a collective explicitly does not mean that individuals are ignored. Instead, a collective can also be represented by the manner in which individual behaviors affect the collective and how the state of a collective affects individual behaviors. For instance, individuals make decisions as to when to disperse, and this affects the formation and persistence of the collective, while these individual decisions are based in part on the state of the collective. Therefore, the collective system can only be understood by modeling individuals and the aggregate, as well as the link between them.

We use the term *collective system* when it is impossible to reduce the overall behavior of the system to a set of properties characterizing the individual agents. Interaction between agents is also important consideration that produces emergent properties at the aggregate level that are simply not present when the components are considered individually. Another important feature of collective systems is their sensitivity to even small perturbations. The same action is found to lead to a very broad range of responses, making it exceedingly difficult to perform prediction or to develop any type of experience of a typical scenario.

At the basic level, a collective system consists of agents and the relationships between them. Agents may execute various behaviors that are appropriate for the system they represent. Each agent individually assesses her situation and behaves on the basis of a set of local and idiosyncratic rules. Repetitive and competitive interactions between agents are a feature of a collective system and require the power of computers to explore the collective dynamics, which are not obtainable through pure mathematical modeling and analysis.

An agent is described by a number of fundamental components including, (1) a private utility function, (2) the drive to optimize the private utility function, (3) a set of possible actions, (4) the rule that generates an action in an attempt to optimize her utility or adapt to others, and (5) information and memory about history. In addition, (6) agents may be capable of learning or evolving, allowing new behavioral rules to emerge.

The collective systems are situated between a few agents in game theoretic systems, a few hundred agents in multi-agents systems, and a larger scale of agents in typical economic and social systems. Hardware development will soon make possible the construction of very large-scale models. Therefore, we may obviate the need for small-scale multi-agent systems. It will be argued that the main impediment to creating empirically relevant agents on this scale is our current lack of understanding of the realistic behavior of agents. Therefore, the bottleneck of what rules to decide for agents is also the primary challenge for researching collective systems (Axtell and Epstein, 1999).

The performance of the collective system, which consists of many interacting agents, should be described on two different levels: the microscopic level, where the decisions of the individual agents occur, and the macroscopic level, where the collective behavior can be observed. Understanding the role of the link between these two levels also remains a challenge (Schweitzer, 2002).

There are two related theoretical issues in the study on collective systems. One is the effect of interactions among agents in determining macroscopic outcomes. The other issue is how to design the micro-rules of agents that produce a desirable outcome at the macroscopic level.

Tumer and Wolpert (2004) propose two different perspectives for the study of collective systems: analysis, or the *forward problem*, and design, or the *inverse problem.*

(1) The forward problem focuses on how the localized attributes of a collective (the properties of agents) induce global behavior of interest and determine system performance.

(2) The inverse problem arises when we wish to design a system to induce a desirable outcome.

It is generally believed that ants in an ant colony do not know exactly how to build the ant colony in which they live. Each ant has certain things that it does, in coordinated association with other ants, but there is no ant that designs the whole colony. No individual ant knows whether there are too few or too many ants exploring for food. Why the colony of ants works collectively as it does, and as effectively as it does, remains a mystery. An important factor in understanding such behavior is the interactions among ants (Bonabeau, 1999).

Economists may not like the idea of comparing the economy to an ant colony. They are no doubt convinced that such organizations are in some sense optimal, but they are not convinced that the optimality is achieved in the same way as it is in a market. Thus, if we ask most economists to describe the basic question that concerns them, they answer that they are trying to understand the equilibrium of the market and whether it entails an efficient use of limited resources (Kirman, 2001).

Most of these are activities in which an agent's behavior is influenced by others, or in which agents care about the behavior of others. Or, they both care and are influenced by trying to obtain an equilibrium. An equilibrium is a stable situation in which some motion, or activity, or some adjustment, or response, has ceased, resulting in some stagnation in which several items that have been interacting and adjusting to each other are at last adjusted and are *in balance*.

Equilibrium is a central concept in the study of social systems as well as in the study of physical collective phenomena. In physical systems, equilibrium results from a balancing of forces. In a physical system, particles are in equilibrium when they do not deviate from a given position or stable trajectory. In a collective of agents, their behaviors are typically motivated toward their own interests. Therefore, in a collective of agents, equilibrium is a balancing of intentions. That is, individuals' intentions are in equilibrium when no one wants to deviate from her intended behavior given the intentions of others (Young, 2005).

However, it is widely observed that an equilibrium situation is not usually efficient at the macro level. The fact that selfish behavior at equilibrium may not achieve full efficiency is well documented in the literature. While all agents understand that the outcome is inefficient, acting independently cannot manage the collective with respect to what actions to take or how to decide these actions.

Yet there is also the problem of explaining how disparate individual activities are coordinated, as in the case of ants and other social insects. The solution must apply equally well to other collective systems. The forward problem arises in the study of some previously existing field such as complex theory. The fundamental problem lies in determining how the combined actions of many agents lead to coordinated behavior on a global scale. Approaches in existing research fields may provide valuable insight into some aspects of studying the forward problem of collective systems. However, these approaches fall short of providing suitable methodologies for dealing with heterogeneity in agents and their interactions.

Agent interactions also occur on structured networks. Yet the development of tools for modeling, understanding, and predicting dynamic agent interactions and behavior on complex networks lags behind. Even recent progress in complex network modeling has not yet offered any capability to model dynamic processes among agents who interact on a global scale, as in small-world or scale-free networks. Computational modeling of dynamic agent interactions on structured networks is important for understanding the sometimes counter-intuitive dynamics of such loosely coupled agent systems of strategic interactions.

Given a collective system, there is also an associated *inverse problem* or a *design problem*, with respect to configuring or modifying each agent so that in the pursuit of their own interests, the agents also optimize the global performance. Solving this kind of inverse problem may involve determining and modifying the internal models of agents as well as the method of interactions between agents.

We should also consider the degree of freedom that each agent should have. Here, there are two basic approaches: top-down and bottom-up approaches. With the top-down approach, the designer may have the freedom to assign the private utility functions of the agents. With the bottom-up approach, agents may have the freedom and incentive to modify their private utility functions. In either case, the focus is on guiding collective systems toward desirable outcomes.

The agent wishes to optimize her own utility, and the system designer wishes to implement a decentralized algorithm for optimizing the collective performance. However, excessive pollution or social congestion problems are the most commonly recognized examples of a break between individual optimization and collective efficiency. Therefore, the inverse problem is concerned with how the private utility functions of agents can be redesigned so that their selfish behaviors give rise to a desired collective outcome. If the collective system can be designed, we need design it so that selfish behaviors of agents need not degrade the system performance, by providing a carefully chosen decentralized mechanism that can be implemented at the agent level.

The inverse problem is a high priority for the study of collective systems. The investigation of the inverse design problem also comes up in the study of already existing fields, such as learning in games and multi-agent systems. However, these approaches are basically based on so-called equilibrium analysis and, therefore, they fall short of providing suitable methodologies for solving the inverse problem.

1.3   The Price of Anarchy in Collective Systems

The fact that selfish behavior may not achieve full efficiency has been well known in the literature. Therefore, it is important to investigate the loss of collective welfare due to selfish and uncoordinated behavior. Recent research efforts have focused on quantifying this loss for specific game environments. The resulting degree of efficiency loss is known as the *price of anarchy* (Roughgarden, 2005). The investigation of the price of anarchy provides a foundation for the design of collective systems with robustness against selfish behaviors. We may need to design systems such that selfish behaviors of individuals need not degrade the system performance.

Social interactions in which people's behavior is influenced by the behaviors of others, or in which people care about the behaviors of others, are analyzed in the context of *collective action*. In this section, I demonstrate that there are a host of collective action problems that share the same general structure and that make agent interaction problematic whenever they arise.

An *externality* is an unexpected side-effect of the social activities of some individuals on seemingly unrelated people. An externality also occurs when individuals care about the choices of others, and each individual's choice affects the choices of others. There are basically two types of social activities with externalities: *strategic compatibility* and *strategic complementarity*. With strategic compatibility, individual payoffs increase with the number of people taking the same action. Instead, with strategic complementarity, payoffs are better if the actions of people are distributed.

Many collective action problems can be investigated through the underlying *social games*. Game theory studies the interaction between human beings and provides a way of modeling strategic interactions, situations in which the consequences of agents' actions depend on the actions taken by the others, and each agent knows who is involved in the same game. The outcome of a conventional game is a set of actions taken by all involved agents. On the other hand, social games are a way of modeling social interactions in which each agent may not know who is involved.

1.3.1 Collection action with strategic compatibility

The study of collective action began with Olson (1965). In his book, there are rich discussions about how different factors, such as instrumental and social incentives, are embodied as the payoff structures in a collective action problem. Consider the provision of a *public good* for individuals. In contrast to private goods, public goods are non-excludable in consumption, and the nature of the public enables an individual to have a free ride. Olson analyzed this problem in terms of the size of the group for which the public good is provided. Olson found that unless the number of individuals in the group is quite small, or unless there is coercion or some other special device to make individuals act in their common interest, self-interested individuals will not act to achieve collective interest, and simply attempt to gain a free ride.

Free riding is a very frequent phenomenon in everyday life. Economists use public goods games to calculate optimal taxes and subsidies. These exercises rest on the assumption that agents will free ride on others, hence leading to a social inefficiency. An effective approach to handle the problem of free riding is to use external enforcement. However, an alternative approach has emerged that investigates the exact circumstances under which efficient collective outcome is possible in the absence of external enforcement.

However, rather than exploring the possibility that various types of games coexist, most collective action problems focus on analyzing cases in which the collective action can be interpreted as a type of dilemma game. In general, human interaction is characterized by a mixture of conflict and consensus.

Let us consider situations in which N agents are identically situated by presenting a binary choice problem with externalities. That is, each agent's payoff, whichever way she makes her choice, depends on the number of agents who choose one way or the other. The typical situation is the interaction with strategic compatibility, where the increased effort by some agents leads the remaining agents to follow suit, which produces *multiplier effects*.

We formally consider this situation by specifying the payoff function of each agent with the following two strategies:

$$S_1 : \text{Disclose her private knowledge,}$$
$$S_2 : \text{Does not disclose.} \tag{1.1}$$

Each agent receives a benefit in proportion to the number of agents to disclose by choosing S_1, which is denoted by n $(0 \leq n \leq N)$. The payoff function of each agent is defined as follows:

$$U(S_1) = a(n/N) - c,$$
$$U(S_2) = b(n/N). \tag{1.2}$$

If an agent discloses her knowledge, she receives some proportional benefit $a(n/N)$ minus some cost c due to disclosure. Even if she does not disclose her knowledge, she can receive some benefit $b(n/N)$ from the contribution of other agents as the *spillover effect*.

Interdependent decision making problems involving N agents are called *N-person games*. We simplify an *N-person game* considering a population of N agents, each with a binary choice between S_1 and S_2. In addition, for any agent the payoff for choosing either S_1 or S_2 depends on how many other agents choose S_1 or S_2. This social game can be analyzed in the following two cases.

<Case 1> $b > a - c$: In this case, the payoff to S_2 is greater than that to S_1. Therefore, the rational choice of each agent is S_2 without considering the choices of the other agents. In game theory, this is defined as a dominant strategy. When this condition holds for all agents, no agent will trade, and this results in the sharing of no common knowledge. This case is known as the *N-person prisoner's dilemma game* (NPD) or the *social dilemma*.

It may not be surprising that the result of local optimization by many agents with conflicting interests does not possess any type of global optimality. In the language of game theory, this means that an equilibrium situation arising from individual rationality can be *Pareto-inefficient*, and thus the outcome can be more efficient, that is, some are better off while no one is worse off. In game theory, the most canonical example of Pareto inefficiency of selfish behavior is the social dilemma. There are many problems involving the clash of individual and collective interests, including the energy crisis problem, various problems related to the conservation of scare natural resources, and a range of problems arising from environmental pollution.

Game theory suggests two alternative solutions to social dilemmas. One solution is to introduce external enforcement. In this case, the payoff structure is altered in such a way that the defecting person incurs some penalty. The other solution is to repeat the game in a way that, from the standpoint of the players, looks like it is being played infinitely many times. The evolutionary paradigm is also built on this type of analysis. It should be noted that the analysis of repeated games is also a very fertile area of study with respect to collective systems.

<Case 2> $b < a - c$: It is easy to recognize that there are other collective action problems with a very different structure from that of the social dilemma. Under the condition of Case 2, we have two stable solutions: an all-S_1 choice and an all-S_2 choice.

The payoff is maximum at $n/N=1$, when all agents choose S_1, and they can enjoy the highest externality, which is better for all agents. On the other hand, if the proportion of agents who disclose their knowledge is relatively low (less than $c/(a-b)$), it becomes rational to choose S_2. If this condition holds for all agents, no agent will disclose her knowledge, and they encounter the same situation as the social dilemma.

In this case, with multiple equilibria, the problem involves not only how to get a concerted choice, but also how to achieve the best equilibrium. If many agents choose S_2, no agent is motivated to choose the inferior choice S_2 unless a sufficient number of agents switch beyond the intersection of the two payoff functions in (1.2). Therefore, the ratio at the intersection provides a crucial mass parameter for the selection of the efficient equilibrium.

It is enough merely to get agents to make the right choice at the beginning. If the ratio of agents that choose the superior strategy (S_1) is greater than that of the intersection point of $U(S_1)$ and $U(S_2)$, then all agents will self-enforce to choose S_1. In this sense, a certain threshold appears. If the initial ratio of the agents choosing S_1 exceeds this threshold, they can induce other agents to shift to a superior choice. The inverse is also true. If many agents stick to an inefficient choice, then all agents follow the same path to an undesirable outcome.

1.3.2 Collection action with strategic complementarity

The fact that selfish behavior need not produce a socially optimal outcome was well known before the advent of game theory. Pigou (1920) proposed a route selection problem in which individuals independently need to travel from the same source to destination. Suppose that there are two highways between two locations. One of which is broad enough to accommodate all traffic that appears without congestion, but is poorly graded and surfaced. While the other is a much better road, but is narrow and quite limited in capacity. Assuming that all individuals aim to minimize the driving time, we have good reason to expect all traffic to follow the better road, and therefore, the better road will be completely congested.

The route selection problem is commonly used for the prediction of traffic patterns in transportation networks that are subject to congestion. We formulate the route selection problem as follows. There are two alternative choices, *Route A*, using a private vehicle, or *Route B*, using a public train to commute to the same destination. Let us suppose that the required time if an agent chooses public transportation, the train (Route

B), is 40 minutes, which is constant regardless of the number of agents on the train. On the other hand, the required time for an agent who chooses a personal vehicle (Route A) is an increasing function of the number of agents who choose the same route, as depicted in Figure 1.1 (Dixit and Nalebuff, 1991). If a large number of agents are free to choose either of the two choices, they will tend to distribute themselves between the two routes in such proportions that the transportation time will be the same for every agent on both routes. As more agents use personal vehicles (Route A), congestion develops, until at a certain point there is no difference between routes.

Knight (1924) developed the idea of traffic equilibrium. He gave a simple and intuitive description of a postulate of the route choice under congested conditions. Wardrop (1952) clarified two basic principles that formalize the notion of *user equilibrium* and *system optimal*. The latter is introduced as an alternative behavior postulate of the minimization of the total travel costs.

Wardrop's first principle is that the journey times in using two routes are equal and are less than those that would be experienced by a single vehicle on any unused route. Each user non-cooperatively seeks to

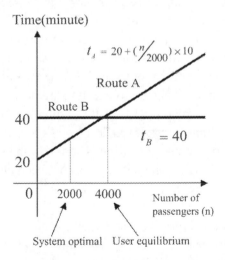

Figure 1.1 The vertical axis represents the estimated traveling time, and the horizontal axis represents the number of agents that use private vehicles (Route A)

minimize her cost of transportation. This principle of route choice, which is identical to the notion postulated by Knight, became accepted as a sound and simple behavioral principle to describe the spreading of trips over alternate routes due to congested conditions. The traffic flows that satisfy this principle are usually referred to as *user equilibrium*, since each user chooses the route that is the best. Specifically, a user-optimized equilibrium is reached when no user can lower her transportation cost through unilateral action.

On the other hand, the system optimal conditional is characterized by Wardrop's second principle, which is the equilibrium at which the average journey time is minimum. This implies that each user behaves cooperatively in choosing her own route to ensure the most efficient use of the entire system. Traffic flows satisfying Wardrop's second principle are generally known as *system optimal*. This second principle may require that users cooperate fully or that a central authority controls the transportation system.

User equilibrium is realized at the intersection in Figure 1.1. However, the system optimal condition is achieved at $n=2,000$, which is half of user equilibrium. In much of the transportation science literature, *Nash equilibrium* is called *user equilibrium*, and *Pareto-efficient outcome* is called system optimality.

Can the power of centralized control improve over the selfish outcome? We suppose that we can choose who chooses what, and assigning half of the commuters to each of the two alternative choices. The commuters who are assigned to the train are no worse off than in the previous outcome. On the other hand, the commuters that are allowed to drive now enjoy lighter road traffic conditions and arrive at their destination at half of the previous time. Therefore, the state of affairs has improved for half of the commuters and has not been changed for the rest of the commuters. The problem of equity or fairness may arise with regard to who should be better off.

A solution to this kind of problem may invoke the intervention of an authority that finds the system optimal condition and imposes the desired behavior on agents. While such an optimal solution may be easy to find, the implementation of a desired solution becomes difficult to enforce in many practical situations.

1.4 Review of the Literature

The emerging research field of collective systems represents a fundamentally new scientific approach to sharing compared to existing approaches. Collective systems are situated between a few agents in game-theoretic systems, among a few hundred agents in multi-agents systems, and among a greater number of agents in typical social systems. Some relevant research fields provide a partial solution to the study and design of collective systems. In particular, game theory, multi-agent systems, complex systems, and evolutionary systems are fields that grapple with some of the issues encountered in the field of collective systems. What is needed for exploring new research fields is to survey the basic concepts in related fields and to clarify where they fall short of providing suitable methodologies for the study of collective systems.

<Agent-based modeling> The approach of agent-based modeling is the main tool in many research fields. With agent-based modeling, we can describe a system from the bottom up, from the point of view of its constituent units, as opposed to a top-down approach, where we look at the properties at the aggregate level without worrying about the system's components and their interactions. The novelty in agent-based modeling, compared to what physicists call micro-simulation, is that we are dealing with modeling collective systems, where the components of the system are agents or human beings with adaptive and evolving behavior.

It is generally not possible to conclude for an agent-based model that a particular attribute will give an agent an absolute advantage over time, or that a particular behavioral rule is optimally configured for an agent in an absolute sense (Epstein and Axtell 1996). In principle, using agent-based tools, a modeler can permit attributes and rules to vary and evolve over time. These variations could be the result of innate or external forces for change, or they could result from deliberate actions undertaken by agents. We also relax assumptions to permit endogenous adaptation or learning. This raises an interesting nature-nurture modeling issue: namely, which attributes and rules of agents should be viewed as part of their core maintained identities and which attributes and rules should be permitted to vary in response to environmental influences? Moreover, this issue arises at both the individual and collective levels. How much variation in behavioral rule should agent to be permitted to exhibit over time, and how much variation should be permitted across all agents?

<Multi-agent systems> Today we face many challenges with respect to designing large-scale systems consisting of multiple autonomous agents. Research on multi-agent systems is intended to provide both principles for construction of complex systems involving multiple agents and mechanisms for the coordination of many agents. The most important reason is that some domains require multiple agents. In particular, if there are different people with different goals and proprietary information, then a multi-agent system is needed to handle their interactions.

An agent-based model is extended to the study of multiple agents and their interactions. We specify how multiple agents interact, and then observe the properties that occur at the macro level. The connection between micro-motivation and macro-outcomes will be developed in which agents are instantiated to interact according to fixed or evolving local rules.

An important characteristic to consider when designing a multi-agent system is whether the agents are stable or evolving. Because of the inherent complexity of the problem domain, there is a great deal of interest in using machine learning techniques to help handle this complexity. Of course agents with learning capabilities can be particularly useful in dynamic environments, but when agents are allowed to learn or evolve into other agents, it is not guaranteed that the outcome will be desirable.

Agents are both heterogeneous and versatile. As a result of both behavioral heterogeneity and versatility, small differences in agents can make large differences in collective outcomes. Heterogeneity turns up repeatedly as a crucial factor in collective systems. But the situation is not always as simple as saying that heterogeneity is desirable and homogeneity is not good. The basic question remains: what is the proper balance between heterogeneity and homogeneity? When heterogeneity is significant, we need to be able to show the gains from heterogeneity.

However, the analysis of a collective system of heterogeneous agents becomes difficult and is often intractable.

Another interesting problem is that agents are very homogeneous in the beginning. Differences in behavior and strategy use evolve endogenously as the collective system runs. Agent heterogeneity becomes a changing feature of the collective systems that can then be studied. Unlike some approaches in the previous research, we are primarily interested in the problem in which the preferences, and even the identities of the agents, can evolve over time, rather than situations in which the agents and their preferences are fixed.

<*Complex systems*> Complex systems deal with systems that are composed of many interacting particles. Complex systems often result in features, self-organization and emergent properties, which are properties of the system that the separate parts do not have. Therefore, the emerging system outcome is extremely hard to predict.

Axelrod and Cohen (2001) propose three methods by which to harness the complexity based on variation, interaction and selection. The term *harnessing complexity* means deliberately changing the structure of a system in order to increase some measure of performance. Variation in a population of agents and actions of agents provides the raw material for adaptation. However, we need to select the proper balance between variety and uniformity. The mechanism that deals with interactions fits into two types: external and internal. The external mechanism is a way to modify the system from outside. On the other hand, the internal mechanism is a way to change the interaction patterns that are driven by the components of the system.

Selection is based on natural selection in evolutionary biology. The selection mechanism is important as the fundamental means by which agents and actions should be eliminated and replaced. While natural selection provides an important paradigm for how an evolving system can work, it also has a serious disadvantage compared with collectives, where we are interested in achieving desired adaptation and evolution. Furthermore, there are two approaches to selection: selecting at the agent level and selecting at the strategy level. Selection at these two levels can work very differently. Determining whether selection is at the agent level or strategy level depends on the performance measures. Using fine-grained and short-term measures of success can help individual learning by providing focused and rapid feedback. Such narrow and prompt measures of success can also be used to evaluate who is successful and who is not.

However, our challenge in collective systems in dealing with the overall performance or long-term measures, using fine-grained measures of success (individual utilities) can easily be misleading. In collective systems, individual measures need to be appropriately correlated, so that agents can generally use strategies that are mutually beneficial. The importance of interaction may not be understood if selection is done at the agent level.

<Complex adaptive systems> How does self-organization work? This is a huge question that humans may never answer completely. Evidently something intrinsic in the manifestation of the reality that humans perceive may spontaneously produce spatial, temporal, or functional structures by means of self-organization, the principles of which are searched in a variety of disciplines, ranging from physics, chemistry and biology, to medicine, psychology and sociology.

Complex adaptive systems proposed by Holland (1995) mainly concern self-organization and emergence in complex large-scale behaviors from the aggregate interactions of less complex agents. An ant nest serves as a typical example. The individual ant has a stereotyped behavior, and almost always dies when circumstances do not fit the stereotype. On the other hand, the collective of ants, the ant nest, is adaptive, surviving over long periods in the face of a wide range of hazards. It is much like an intelligent organism constructed of relatively unintelligent parts (Bonabeau, 1999).

The process of self-organization can be accelerated and deepened by increasing variation, for example by adding noise to systems. Collective systems may have several equilibrium outcomes. To adapt to a changing environment, the systems need a sufficiently large variety of possible equilibrium states to cope with likely perturbations. Given this variety, the most adequate configurations are selected according to the fitness defined for the system. The basic method is then to define an appropriate fitness function that distinguishes better outcomes from worse outcomes, and then create a system in which the components (agents) vary relative to each other in such a way as to discover behavioral rules with higher fitness. This is also a challenging issue in the study of collective systems.

<*Evolution*> Evolution is based on the concept of natural selection that supports the survival of more successful strategies or individuals. In general, an evolutionary process combines two basic elements: A *mutation* mechanism that provides variation and a *selection* mechanism that favors some variations over others. Agents with higher payoff are at a productive advantage compared to agents who use strategy with lower payoff. Hence, the latter decrease in frequency in the population over time by natural selection.

It is not surprising that many scientists are exploring a new unified theory of evolution by merging learning in game theory and evolutionary game theory with modern biological evolution theory. This new theory attempts to explain all kinds of evolutionary processes. Its methods and models in fact cover not only biological evolution of organisms but also the evolution of animal and human behavior in their societies.

There may be two competing approaches in dealing with evolution in collective systems: the microscopic model based on individual learning and the macroscopic model based on system evolution. Instead of drawing a distinction between models of learning and evolution, it is easier to make a distinction between models that describe adaptive behavior at the individual level and those that describe adaptive behavior at the aggregate level.

<*Co-evolution*> If we observe the natural world, species do not evolve in isolation, but rather, they have, to varying degrees, an evolutionary history of interactions with other species. Much of the diversity and specialization observable within the natural world is due to *co-evolution*.

Like biological systems, many socio-economic systems can be modeled as a co-evolutionary system containing many interactive agents, each reciprocally evolving in response to adaptations in the others. If multiple populations of agents are adapting to each other, then the result is a co-evolutionary process. If we use the standard definition of co-evolution, there must be two populations, with each reciprocally evolving specific adaptations and counter-adaptations in response to the other. Co-evolution is defined as an evolutionary change in a trait of the individuals in one population in response to a trait of the individuals of a second population, followed by an evolutionary response by the second population to the change in the first.

Co-evolution is a holistic, synergetic and complex evolutionary flow that cannot be split up into components. Co-evolution rests not only on mutually coupled interactions, but also on our desire to realize better outcomes by solving mutual conflicts or overcoming competition. However, the problem to contend with in co-evolution is the possibility of an escalating *arms race* with no end. Competing agents might continually adapt to each other in more and more specialized ways, never stabilizing at a desirable behavior. This is an example of the problem of sub-optimization. Optimizing by each individual does not lead to optimal performance for the collective system as a whole.

<*Evolutionary dynamics* > The term *evolutionary dynamics* often refers to systems that exhibit a time evolution in which the character of the dynamics may change due to internal mechanisms. Such models are of course interesting for studying systems in which variation and selection are important components. Evolutionary dynamics are described by equations of motion that may change in time according to certain rules that can be interpreted as mutation operations.

For a species, survival is a necessary goal in any given environment. On the other hand, for a collective system, both purpose and environment need to be specified by the designers or agents who compromise the system. If certain aspects of the world can be set by design, one can explore through intensive experimentation, in which designs tend to induce desirable outcomes when other aspects of the world are permitted to exhibit realistic degrees of plasticity. Alternatively, exploiting the growing power of evolutionary algorithms, one can deliberately induce evolution as a means of discovering improved design configurations.

One important area of research on collective systems lies outside the conventional evolutionary approach based on the Darwinian paradigm of natural selection. Co-evolution also concerns cooperation within in and between species. For instance, in symbiosis, competition is suppressed because the long-term benefits gained from cooperation outweigh short-term competitive advantages. A mathematical framework to model co-evolutionary dynamics in such non-Darwinian systems has been developed (Crutchfield and Schuster, 2003).

<Individual optimization and collective efficiency> We might expect collective behavior to be closer to the optimal behavior if we typically assume rational behavior at the individual level. Adam Smith's conclusion that collective efficiency arises from the individual pursuit of self-interest may be more general than it appears. The connection between individual rationality and collective efficiency, between optimization by individuals and optimality in the aggregate, has been studied in some domains. Regarding this issue, the traditional approaches usually assume that aggregate efficiency requires individual optimization.

Collective behavior may be rational, whereas that of the individuals may not be so. Gode and Sunder (1993) show that *market efficiency*, a key characteristic of market outcomes, is largely independent of variations in individual behavior under classical condition. They showed that market efficiency is achievable in double auction markets even if agents act randomly within their budget constraints. They performed a series of experiments with humans and computational agents who take decisions on a random basis. They referred to these agents as *zero intelligence* agents. In their experiments, they obtained a remarkable collective efficiency with these agents in that by simply applying a budget constraint to the zero intelligent agents, the efficiency in such a market is almost equal to the efficiency in markets with profit motivated humans.

Their results suggest that the achievement of high levels of collective efficiency under classical conditions may place minimal demands on individual rationality, no maximization and not even bounded rationality is necessary. Perhaps the main issue then is not how much rationality there is at the micro level, but how little rationality is sufficient to generate macro-level patterns in which most agents are behaving as if they were rational (Axtell, 2003). We seek an alternative methodology that leaves room for the improvement of the collective system through learning as a substitute for *individual rationality*. Adaptation and evolution may affect the dynamics of a collective system and lead it to evolve to a more efficient outcome.

<Individual learning and social learning> One important issue is the level at which learning is modeled. The two basic possibilities are the individual level and the collective level. Various studies to clarify an essential difference between *individual learning* and *social learning* have been performed. Vriend (2000) and Arifavoric (2004) make these two learning processes more precise. They consider a population of agents who produce homogeneous goods in an oligopoly market. Each firm learns the proper production level the generic algorithm. The first is as a model of social (or population) learning. Each individual agent in the population is characterized by an output rule, which is a binary string of fixed length, specifying simply the agent's production level. The measure of success is simply the profits generated by each rule. The underlying idea is that firms look around, and tend to imitate, and re-combine rules of other firms that appeared to be successful. The more successful these rules were, the more likely they are to be selected for this process of imitation and re-combination.

The second way is to use a model of *individual learning*. Instead of being characterized by a single output rule, each individual agent now has a set of rules in mind. In each period, only one of these rules is used to determine its output level to the market. The rules that were more successful recently are more likely to be chosen. In individual learning, instead of examining how well other agents with different rules did in previous periods, each agent checks how well it did in previous periods when it used these rules itself.

They showed that the individual learning model converges close to the Nash equilibrium output level, whereas the social learning model converges to the competitive equilibrium output level, where no firm gains profit. The difference to modeling learning between these two approaches is often neglected, but they claim that for a general class of games this difference is essential.

1.5 Evolutionary Design of Desired Collective Systems

This book deals with an important question. In collective systems where many agents are all adapting to each other and the collective outcome is extremely hard to predict, what actions should agents take? When there are a huge number of agents, and numerous interactions, a great deal of learning is an attempt to imitate the success of other agents, the resulting collective outcomes are hard to predict. There are also curious questions about how complex systems work and how they can be made to work better. However, no natural method has been proposed for systematically studying these issues. We need to identify and redesign the microscopic rules of agents that produce desirable outcomes at the macroscopic level.

The emerging research field of collective systems represents a fundamentally new scientific approach. In dealing with the above problem we de-emphasize traditional scientific goals such as optimization, equilibrium analysis, and control, in favor of appreciating the importance of emergence, self-organization, diversity, adaptation and evolution.

A collective system is characterized as a system that consists with many learning agents who adapt to other learning agents. A collective system consists of individuals who are learning about a process in which other members are also learning. Learning the true state of the system is therefore quite unlike learning the values of parameters that govern a physical process, for example, or even the parameters that describe a social process that is external to the observer (Young, 2005). When the observer is a part of the system, the act of learning changes the point to be learned. It is therefore unclear whether there behavioral rules of any degree of complexity that can solve this problem consistently. It is also unclear whether the problem can be solved using fixed learning models that bear some resemblance to actual learning behavior in human. Therefore, in order to investigate the performance of a collective system of adapting or evolving agents, we need to explore a new method beyond the conventional equilibrium analysis that emphasizes the dynamic and evolving aspects of the system.

The priority for a desirable collective outcome is stability, which is to be crudely modeled using the idea of equilibrium of the system. However, the condition of stability is not enough, and we need other criteria, efficiency and equity. In the field of economics, efficiency means that nothing gets wasted. This follows Pareto-optimality in taking the absence of waste to be equivalent to the requirement that nobody can be made better off without someone else being made worse off (Binmore, 2001). Efficiency represents the measure of the desirability of collective at the macro level. On the other hand, equity stands for the measurement of the desirability at the micro level.

As shown in Figure 1.2, given a collective system, there is an associated inverse design problem, i.e., how to configure or modify the components (agents) of the system so that in their pursuit of their own interest, they also optimize the global performance. Solving this inverse problem may involve determining and modifying the number of agents and how they interact with each other and what degree of freedom each agent has.

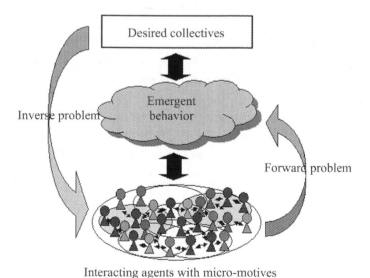

Figure 1.2 The forward and inverse problems of a collective system

In this book, we develop a game-based approach for designing collective systems. For studying frequency-dependent natural selection, game-theoretic arguments are more appropriate than optimization algorithms. This allows the design of agents that have the ability to correct and improve agents' behavioral rules. We also propose a flexible learning paradigm that allows agents to identify situations in which their behavioral rules fail or can be enhanced and to respond by initiating learning processes of successful agents.

Agents interact with each other in complex ways, and linked agent behaviors are highly nonlinear. However, we investigate the situations in which they succeed in organizing themselves into a coherent behavior and produce desirable outcomes through a simulation study. In particular, we focus much of the hidden knowledge of the mysteries of collective behavior of linked learning agents.

Learning agents play the underlying game repeatedly by starting off with a small set of sample rules to be tested. Individual learning then involves, (1) assignment of a rating to each of the rules on the basis of experience, and (2) invention of new rules to replace those rules that end up with a low rating. The rating of a rule is merely the average of the payoffs received when it is used against the opponent. The genetic algorithm uses these ratings as fitness and generates new rules accordingly. Evolutionary learning also follows numerous rules that are causally dependent on previous interactions and on their stored rules. There is no social learning such as imitation or exchange among agents.

However, in the standard model of individual learning, agents are viewed as being genetically coded with a strategy and selection pressure favors agents that are fitter, i.e., whose strategy yields a higher payoff against the average payoff of the population. Natural selection operates on the local probability distribution of strategies within the repertoire of each individual member. An individual's ability to survive and grow is based on advantages that stem from core competencies that represent evolution.

The envisioned research object is quite novel since it requires harmonic and synchronized interactions among self-interested agents. An important aspect of collective evolution is the learning strategy adapted by individuals. In this book, the concept of *collective evolution* can be extended beyond the boundaries of a single agent. Collective evolution is valuable in a social context because it can help to expose new behavioral rules and spread them to other agents who cannot effectively make the proper choice. Each agent is modeled to learn the coupling rule rather than a specific behavior.

Collective evolution also provides a microscopic foundation that is missing in evolutionary approaches. To be sure, we do not see collective evolution as a potential replacement for evolutionary theory, but I argue that they may provide necessary complements, or can be seen as capacities that evolved during evolution to increase the learning efficiency of the individual.

Agents constantly improve their behavioral rules. As such, an important requirement for an efficient behavioral rule is that it should be robust. That is, it may not to be replaced by other rules. Significantly, if a rule achieves both efficiency and equity then it is robust. Our framework synthesizes the principle of collective learning and the mechanism of collective evolution into a coherent approach to the design of the desired collectives. It also provides a device for channeling the complexity of collective systems into manageable and desirable change. Collective evolution is also a driving force for building networks of sustainable interaction that foster stability, efficiency, and equity in collectives of selfish agents.

1.6 Outline of the Book

The foundations of this book lie in three distinct fields: computer science, game theory, and complex theory. These three traditions have made important contributions to this discussion and to the mechanisms proposed to solve the problem of collective action. These traditions will be the subject of this book.

From computer science come insights about collective systems with many agents that can be designed to work together and adapt to each other. Two areas of computer science are important. First, there is the rapid growth of multi-agent systems, which has led computer science into deeper analyses of what it takes for systems of many agents to work together by establishing efficient coordination. Second, there is the field of evolutionary computation, which has fostered an engineering approach to evolution and adaptation. With an engineering approach, one asks how systems can be designed to become more effective over time. By making evolution an engineering problem, evolutionary computation has shed light on how collective system can evolve to a desirable outcome.

Game theory provides insights into how agents can choose actions to maximize their utilities in the presence of other agents who are doing the same thing. A primary question in the recent study of game theory is how each individual should learn in the context of many learners.

Complex systems deal with systems composed of many interacting particles. Complex systems often result in features, self-organization and emergent properties, which are properties of the system that the separate parts do not have. Therefore, the emerging collective outcome is extremely hard to predict. The generation of collective systems with advantageous behaviors beyond our manual design capability requires long-term incremental evolution with continuing emergence.

This book provides some fundamental and common problems for studying adaptation and evolution in collective systems and highlights the benefits and shortcomings of the many related fields. This book also provides some of the essential questions that need to be addressed if the new research field of collective systems is to mature into a new *collective science*.

In Chapter 2, we review the basic concepts of game theory and evolutionary games. Game theory is devoted to the logic of rational decision-makings in social contexts. It is about what happens when self-interested agents interact. The outcome is explained by the concept of equilibrium. Evolutionary game theory, instead, assumes that the game is repeated many times and asks which strategies can survive in the long run.

In Chapter 3, we formulate social games in which there are a large number of agents, each of which faces a binary decision problem with externalities. The outcome depends on the strategy choices of all agents. Fortunately, in certain strategic situations, interactions among many agents can be analyzed by decomposition into the underlying 2x2 games.

In Chapter 4, we consider a global adaptation model of heterogeneous agents. We obtain the relationship between agents' heterogeneous micro-motives and the macroscopic behavior. In particular, we characterize the gains from heterogeneity of agents.

In Chapter 5, we characterize the gains from heterogeneous interactions by formulating knowledge trading in a population. The main concern is in what circumstances knowledge trading can be accelerated by self-interested agents.

Chapter 6 presents a comparative study of two adaptive populations, one in a global environment, and the other in a spatial environment. We also show that the gain from heterogeneity depends on the type of interaction and the location of heterogeneous agents.

In Chapter 7, we study a model in which agents can select partners with whom to interact. An agent needs to select her neighbors to interact with and faces a tradeoff between joining a neighborhood where most agents share her preference or another neighborhood where they have different preferences than hers. Unlike some approaches in these fields, we are primary interested in the problem in which the preferences and even the identities of the agents can evolve over time, rather than situations in which the agents and their preferences are fixed.

In Chapter 8, we deal with social congestion problems. Dispersion games provide a simple model for understanding the mechanisms behind many paradigms for all types of congestion that may arise when we need to utilize limited resources. We introduce a new adaptive model based on the give-and-take strategy, in which agents yield to others if they gain, and otherwise randomize their actions.

In Chapter 9, we explore an alternative learning model, coupled learning, and focus on coupling dynamics that may change in time according to coupled behavioral rules. We show that collective learning of coupling behavioral rules serves to secure desired outcomes by establishing sustainable relationships.

In Chapter 10, we consider another type of social interaction in which agents should be dispersed. In particular, we focus on the emergence of synchronized behavioral rules that sustain efficient and equitable outcomes. Collective evolution reconciles individual-based evolution and leads to socially desirable outcomes.

Chapter 2

Introduction to Game Theory and Evolutionary Games

In this chapter, we review the basic concepts of game theory and evolutionary games. Game theory is devoted to the logic of rational decision-making in a social context and is concerned with what happens when multiple self-interested agents interact. The outcome is explained by the concept of equilibrium. A Nash equilibrium is a combination of strategies that provide the best outcome for each party, and no party can obtain a better payoff by unilateral deviating from their strategy. Evolutionary game theory, instead, assumes that the game is repeated many times and asks which strategies can survive in the long-run.

2.1 Classification of Games and Nash Equilibrium

A game is any interdependent situation in which at least two agents interact. There are situations in which the agents' payoffs are identical or completely opposed. The former situations are classified as *pure coordination games*, and the latter are classified as *zero-sum* or *constant-sum games*. On the other hand, games in which the agents' payoffs are neither identical nor opposed are called *mixed-motive games* (Schelling, 1978). This term focuses on the complex strategic properties that motivate the agents to partly cooperate and partly compete with other agents. An agent in a mixed-motive game has to contend with both the internal conflict causing the mixed-motive and the external conflict arising from interaction with the other agents.

There is a rich collection of literature and theoretical analyses on two-person games. In this section, we classify 2x2 (two-person, two-strategy) mixed-motive games into a few categories and examine the basic characteristics of strategic interactions. Consider the situation in which two self-interested agents face a binary decision problem having with two strategies, S_1 and S_2. The payoffs of each agent depend on the outcome of the other agent's choice, as shown in Table 2.1.

This matrix defines the general payoff matrix of a *symmetric 2x2 game*. The game is *symmetric*, because the game is identical from each agent's point of view. If the payoff values further satisfy the condition, $b = c$, then it is defined as a *doubly symmetric 2x2 game*.

The choice of an action is called a *strategy*. A self-interested agent is rational in the sense that the agent chooses an optimal strategy based on a guess or on the anticipation of the other agent's choice. Therefore, each agent considers her payoff and chooses the best strategy to optimize payoff. *Nash equilibrium* is defined as any profile of strategies in which each agent's strategy is the best response to the strategies of the others.

There are at least two reasons that Nash equilibrium is important. The first is that if a game has a kind of solution that is common knowledge among the agents, then it must be in equilibrium. If it were not, some agents would have to believe that it is rational for them not to make their best response to what they know. But it is not rational not to behave optimally. The second reason is that equilibrium matters are more important. If the payoffs in a game correspond to how fit agents are, then evolutionary processes that prefer more fit agents to less fit agents will not work when they are in equilibrium, because all of the survivors will be as fit as possible in order to be in the social contexts.

Table 2.1 Payoff matrix of a 2x2 game

Agent 1 \\ Agent 2	S_1	S_2
S_1	a a	c b
S_2	b c	d d

Another interesting question is this. Under what circumstances can a population of self-interested agents realize a desirable collective outcome without explicit communication or cooperation. Here, we define concepts of individual rationality and collective rationality.

Definition 2.1 *The strategy for each agent to maximize her payoff is defined to be individually rational.*

It should be irrational for each agent to deviate from her individually rational strategy as long as the other agents stick to their strategy. A formal solution when self-interested agents interact is Nash equilibrium, a combination of strategies that are the best against one another.

Definition 2.2 *A set of strategies satisfying the conditions of the individual rationality of all agents is defined as a Nash equilibrium. In other words, if no agent can improve her payoff by a unilateral change in strategy, such a pair of strategies is defined as a Nash equilibrium.*

No one can obtain a better payoff by deviating unilaterally from a Nash equilibrium. However, there is another solution concept, which is referred to as *efficient equilibrium*.

Definition 2.3 *A set of strategies in which if no agent can improve her payoff without lowering the payoff of the other agent is defined to satisfy collective rationality.*

Definition 2.4 *A set of strategies is defined as being in efficient equilibrium (Pareto-efficient) if it maximizes the summation of the payoffs of all agents.*

Consider two agents that face a binary decision with the payoff matrix in Table 2.1. If an agent chooses either strategy S_1 or S_2, we define such a definitive choice as *a pure strategy*. If an agent chooses S_1 with some probability x and S_2 with remaining probability *1-x*, we define such a probabilistic choice as *a mixed strategy*, which is denoted as $x=(x, 1-x)$.

When an agent chooses the mixed strategy $e_1=(1, 0)$ or $e_2=(0, 1)$, she is said to choose pure strategy S_1 or S_2 respectively.

Each agent is assumed to choose an optimal strategy based on the guess or anticipation of the other agent's strategy. If both agents are assumed to be so knowledgeable as to correctly guess or anticipate, the other agent's strategy, their best responses are the same, since they face a symmetric game with the same payoffs.

Suppose the other agent chooses a mixed strategy $y=(y, 1-y)$. The expected payoffs $U(e_i, y)$ of choosing the pure strategies e_i, $i = 1, 2$, are

$$U(e_1, y)=(a-b)y+b,$$
$$U(e_2, y)=(c-d)y+d. \qquad (2.1)$$

The difference in expected payoffs when she chooses e_1 or e_2 is

$$U(e_1, y)-U(e_2, y) = (a+d-b-c)y+d-b. \qquad (2.2)$$

A symmetric 2x2 game in Table 2.1 is classified into four categories depending on the payoff values. We obtain both a Nash equilibrium and an efficient equilibrium of a game in each category.

(1) **Dilemma Game:** $(c > a > d > b, 2a > b + c)$

Suppose two agents face binary decisions to choose either S_1 (Cooperate) or S_2 (Defect). We consider the case in which the payoff values satisfy:

(i) $\quad c > a > d > b,$ and (ii) $2a > c + d.$

Both agents evaluate the payoffs associated with each strategy and choose the best one, which is the same in this symmetric game. The first (i) inequality implies for any mixed strategy $y=(y, 1-y)$,

$$U(e_2, y) > U(e_1, y) \qquad \forall y. \qquad (2.3)$$

Therefore, if both agents seek their individual rationality, they choose $(S_2, S_2) =$ (Defect, Defect) and the sum of payoffs of both agents is $2d$. On the other hand, the sum of payoffs of both agents is $2a (= a + a)$ if they choose S_1, and $b + c$ if one agent defects and the other cooperates. Therefore, the second condition (ii) implies that $(S_1, S_1) =$ (Cooperate, Cooperate) satisfies the condition of collective rationality.

These two conditions create the tension in dilemma between individual and collective interests. The two agents benefit if they establish mutual cooperation. However, self-interested agents may be motivated to defect if they seek individual rationality.

(2) **Coordination Game:** $(a > c, d > b)$

The necessity for coordination may arise when contributions of many participants are necessary to produce a common good that everyone may value highly. We consider the situation in which the payoff values satisfy $a > c$ and $d > b$. In this case, there is some y at which the expected payoffs of an agent from choosing S_1 and S_2 are indifferent. Two expected payoffs in (2.1) can be equated at

$$ay + b(1 - y) = cy + d(1 - y). \qquad (2.4)$$

Such y is obtained as

$$y = (d - b)/(a + d - b - c) \equiv \theta. \qquad (2.5)$$

The expected payoffs in (2.1) of choosing pure strategy $S_1 (e_1)$ or $S_2 (e_2)$ satisfy the following inequalities:

$$\begin{aligned}
U(e_1, y) &> U(e_2, y) \quad if \quad y > \theta, \\
U(e_1, y) &< U(e_2, y) \quad if \quad y < \theta, \qquad (2.6)\\
U(e_1, y) &= U(e_2, y) \quad if \quad y = \theta.
\end{aligned}$$

Therefore, if the other agent is more likely to choose $S_1 (e_1)$, an agent also chooses S_1, on the other hand, if the other agent is more likely to choose $S_2 (e_2)$, she also chooses S_2. If the other agent chooses the mixed strategy $y = (\theta, 1-\theta)$, then she is indifferent with respect to the two strategies.

Since the payoff matrix in Table 2.1 is symmetric, the optimal strategies are the same for both agents. Therefore, the coordination game has two pure Nash equilibria of (S_1, S_1) and (S_2, S_2), and one mixed Nash equilibrium (θ, θ), where $\theta = (\theta, 1-\theta)$. Among these three equilibria, the most preferable efficient equilibrium, defined as the *Pareto-dominance*, is (S_1, S_1), which dominates the other two equilibria. There is another equilibrium concept besides Pareto-dominance, which is defined as *risk-dominance*. If the other condition, $a + b < c + d$, is also satisfied, then the equilibrium (S_2, S_2) becomes risk-dominate (S_1, S_1).

Coordination games have multiple equilibria with the possibility of coordinating on different strategies. This problem is known as *miscoordination*. The traditional game theory does not address how agents know which equilibrium will actually be realized when a game has multiple equally plausible equilibria. Game theory is also unsuccessful in explaining how agents should learn in order to shift to a better equilibrium.

(3) *Dispersion Game:* ($c > a$, $b > d$)

Coordination is mainly being considered in a context in which agents can achieve a common interest by taking the same action. Therefore, a more frequently studied class of games is the class of coordination games in which both agents gain payoffs when they choose the same action. A complementary class that has received relatively little attention is the class of games in which agents gain payoffs only when they choose the distinct action. These situations are formulated as *dispersion games*.

Some discussions of coordination and dispersion games have focused on the two-agent case. In this case, the coordination game and the dispersion game differ only by the renaming of one agent's strategies. However, with arbitrary numbers of agents the two games diverge. While the generalization of the coordination game to multiple agents is quite straightforward, that of the dispersion game is more complex. We discuss *multi-person dispersion games* in Chapter 8 and Chapter 10.

There is a mixed strategy that equates the expected payoffs of each agent in (2.1). The two expected payoff functions can be equated at

$$ay + b(1-y) = cy + d(1-y). \tag{2.7}$$

Such y is obtained as

$$y = (b-d)/(b+c-a-d) \equiv \theta \tag{2.8}$$

The expected payoffs to an agent for choosing pure strategy S_1 (e_1) or S_2 (e_2) satisfy:

$$\begin{aligned}
U(e_1, y) &> U(e_2, y) \quad if \quad y < \theta, \\
U(e_1, y) &< U(e_2, y) \quad if \quad y > \theta, \\
U(e_1, y) &= U(e_2, y) \quad if \quad y = \theta.
\end{aligned} \tag{2.9}$$

That is, if the other agent is more likely to choose S_1, she will choose the other strategy S_2. On the other hand, if the other agent is more likely to choose S_2, she chooses S_1. If the other agent chooses the mixed strategy y, she is indifferent with respect to the two strategies. Therefore, the dispersion game has two pure Nash equilibria (S_1, S_2) and (S_2, S_1), and these are non-equivalent, each one assigning different payoffs to each agent. There is also one mixed Nash equilibrium (θ, θ), where $\theta = (\theta, 1-\theta)$. Under this mixed Nash equilibrium, both agents gain the same expected payoff.

(4) *Hawk-Dove Game*

We have a special case of dispersion games. The two-person game with the payoff matrix in Table 2.2 is known as the *Hawk-Dove game*. Let us suppose that there are two possible behavioral types: one escalates the conflict until injury or sticks to display and retreats if the opponent escalates. These two behavioral types are described as "*hawk*" and "*dove*".

The payoff corresponds to a gain in *fitness v*, while an injury reduces fitness by c, and we assume $c > v$. If a hawk meets a hawk, they fight until one is seriously injured. The fitness of the winner is increased by v, and that of the loser is reduced by c, so that the expected fitness is $(v-c)/2$, which is negative since the cost of the injury exceeds the prize of the fight. If a dove meets a dove, they engage in threatening display, but flee when confronted with real danger, and therefore, each expected fitness is $v/2$. If a hawk meets a dove, the dove runs away, and the hawk wins the

Table 2.2 Payoff matrix of the Hawk-Dove game

Agent 1 \ Agent 2	S_1 (Hawk)	S_2 (Dove)
S_1 (Hawk)	$(V-C)/2$ $(V-C)/2$	0 V
S_2 (Dove)	V 0	$V/2$ $V/2$

contested resource of value v.

The expected payoffs of an agent choosing from S_1 (Hawk) or S_2 (Dove) if the other agent chooses a mixed strategy $\mathbf{y} = (y, 1\text{-}y)$ are

$$U(e_1, y) = (v - c)y/2 + v(1 - y),$$
$$U(e_2, y) = v(1 - y)/2. \tag{2.10}$$

There is a mixed strategy that equates the expected payoffs, and such y is obtained as

$$y = v/c \equiv \theta . \tag{2.11}$$

The expected payoffs in (2.10) to an agent choosing pure strategy S_1 (e_1) or S_2 (e_2) satisfy:

$$U(e_1, y) > U(e_2, y) \quad if \ \ y < \theta,$$
$$U(e_1, y) < U(e_2, y) \quad if \ \ y > \theta, \tag{2.12}$$
$$U(e_1, y) = U(e_2, y) \quad if \ \ y = \theta.$$

Therefore, if the other agent is more likely to choose S_1 (Hawk), she will choose S_2 (Dove). On the other hand, if the other agent is more likely to choose S_2, she chooses S_1. The Hawk-Dove game also has two pure Nash equilibria of (S_1, S_2) and (S_2, S_1), each assigning different payoffs to each agent. There is also one mixed Nash equilibrium $(\boldsymbol{\theta}, \boldsymbol{\theta})$, where $\boldsymbol{\theta} = (\theta, 1\text{-}\theta)$, and under this mixed strategy agent gains the same expected payoff.

In the context of symmetric games with the payoff matrix given in Table 2.1 or Table 2.2, let us suppose a pair of the mixed strategy $(\boldsymbol{x}, \boldsymbol{y})$ constitutes a Nash equilibrium. A Nash equilibrium $(\boldsymbol{x}, \boldsymbol{y})$ is defined as *symmetric* if $\boldsymbol{x}=\boldsymbol{y}$, that is, both agents use the same mixed or pure strategy. All three Nash equilibria of a coordination game are symmetric; however, only the mixed equilibrium is symmetric for the dispersion game and the Hawk-Dove game.

Strategic interactions between two agents who have two strategies are formulated as 2x2 games with the payoff matrix in Table 2.1. This payoff matrix with the four parameters can be transformed into the equitable payoff matrix in Table 2.3 with the two payoff parameters. Subtracting c from a ($\alpha = a - c$), and b from d ($\beta = d - b$), we obtain the payoff matrix in Table 2.3. With this transformation, a symmetric game becomes a doubly symmetric game. We will see the payoff matrices in Table 2.1 and Table 2.3 have the same Nash equilibria.

Suppose the other opponent chooses mixed strategy $\mathbf{y}=(y,\ 1\text{-}y)$ in the payoff matrix in Table 2.3. If an agent chooses pure strategy S_1 (e_1) or S_2 (e_2), her expected payoffs are obtained as

$$U(e_1, y)=\alpha y,$$
$$U(e_2, y)=\beta y. \tag{2.13}$$

(1) Dilemma Game: $(\alpha < 0,\ \beta > 0)$

In this case, two expected payoffs in (2.13) satisfy

$$U(e_2, y) > U(e_1, y) \quad \forall y . \tag{2.14}$$

Therefore, the payoff matrix in Table 2.3 has a unique Nash equilibrium (S_2, S_2), which is the same as the Nash equilibrium of Table 2.1.

(2) Coordination Game: $(\alpha > 0,\ \beta > 0)$

The two expected payoffs in (2.13) when an agent chooses S_1 (e_1) and S_2 (e_2) are equated at the point,

$$y= \beta /(\alpha + \beta)=(d\text{-}b)/(a + d - b - c)= \theta , \tag{2.15}$$

and we have the following relation:

$$\begin{aligned} U(e_1, y) &> U(e_2, y) \quad if \ \ y > \theta, \\ U(e_1, y) &< U(e_2, y) \quad if \ \ y < \theta, \\ U(e_1, y) &= U(e_2, y) \quad if \ \ y = \theta. \end{aligned} \tag{2.16}$$

Table 2.3 Normalized payoff matrix in Table 2.1

Agent 1 \ Agent 2	S_1 (y)		S_2 (*1-y*)	
S_1		α		0
	α		0	
S_2		0		β
	0		β	

Therefore, the payoff matrix in Table 2.3 has the same three Nash equilibria as the payoff matrix in Table 2.1.

(3) *Dispersion Game:* ($\alpha < 0$, $\beta < 0$):

In this case, the two expected payoffs in (2.11) are equated at the point
$$y = \beta / (\alpha + \beta) = (b-d)/(b + c - a - d) = \theta \qquad (2.17)$$
Then, we have the relation:
$$\begin{aligned} U(e_1, y) &> U(e_2, y) \quad \text{if} \quad y < \theta, \\ U(e_1, y) &< U(e_2, y) \quad \text{if} \quad y > \theta, \\ U(e_1, y) &= U(e_2, y) \quad \text{if} \quad y = \theta. \end{aligned} \qquad (2.18)$$

Therefore, the dispersion game with the payoff matrix in Table 2.3 has the same three Nash equilibria as the payoff matrix in Table 2.1.

2.2 Correlated Equilibrium

In this section we will look at a different concept of equilibrium, *correlated equilibrium*. We start with an example of the asymmetric coordination game, which is also known as the *battle of sexes game*.

Two agents (a man and a woman) who have two strategies play the game of the payoff matrix in Table 2.4. It is easy to see that both (S_1, S_1) and (S_2, S_2) constitute pure Nash equilibria, since if one agent chooses pure strategy S_i, $i=1,2$, the best response of the other is to choose the same strategy. Under these two Nash equilibria with pure strategies, the pair of payoffs for both agents are $(2,1)$ and $(1,2)$, respectively.

Table 2.4 Asymmetric coordination game

Man \ Woman	S_1 (Baseball)	S_2 (Soccer)
S_1 (Baseball)	2 1	0 0
S_2 (Soccer)	0 0	1 2

There is another Nash equilibrium with mixed strategies. That consists of a man choosing S_1 with probability *2/3* and S_2 with probability *1/3*, and a woman choosing S_1 with probability *1/3* and S_2 with probability *2/3*. In this case the expected payoffs to both are *(2/3, 2/3)*, which are lower than that of the pure Nash equilibria, because both the man and the woman can receive *1* at the worst outcomes in the pure Nash equilibria.

Now, we consider a situation in which a third party flips a fair coin, and based on the outcome of the coin toss, both the man and the woman are advised as to what they should do. For example, if the coin shows heads, both agree to choose S_1, and when the outcome is tails both agree to choose S_2. This type of game is defined as play with *correlated strategies*. It is important to note that no one has any incentive to deviate from the agreement. The advantage of following such advice is that the pair of expected payoffs *(1.5, 1.5)* is higher compared to that of *(2/3, 2/3)* from the mixed Nash equilibrium.

Similarly, we consider the Hawk-Dove game in Table 2.5. In this case, the worst outcome occurs when both agents choose hawk. There are two pure Nash equilibria, *(Hawk, Dove)* and *(Dove, Hawk)* and with payoffs *(12,0)* and *(0,12)* to both agents, respectively, and these equilibria are Pareto-efficient. A mixed Nash equilibrium occurs when both agents choose *"Hawk"* and *"Dove"* with probabilities *0.4* and *0.6*, respectively. This mixed Nash equilibrium has an expected payoff of *3.6* to each agent, which is not Pareto-efficient equilibrium. Now, let us consider a correlated equilibrium. As before, a third party tells both agents what to do based on the outcome of the following probability: *(Dove, Dove)* with *1/3*, *(Dove, Hawk)* with *1/3*, and *(Dove, Hawk)* with *1/3*.

Table 2.5 Example of the Hawk-Dove game

Agent 1 \ Agent 2	S_1 (Hawk)		S_1 (Dove)	
S_1 (Hawk)		-9		0
	-9		12	
S_2 (Dove)		12		6
	0		6	

Therefore, the third party tries to avoid the worst case *(Hawk, Hawk)*. We note that the third party only tells the agents what they are supposed to do, and does not reveal whether the other agent deviates from the third party's instruction. Therefore, if the third party tells Agent 2 to be *"Hawk"*, then Agent 2 has no incentive to deviate. This is because Agent 2 knows that the outcome must be *(Dove, Hawk)* and that Agent 2 will obey the instruction.

Next, let us consider the case when Agent 2 is told to *"Dove"*. Then, Agent 2 knows that the outcome must be either *(Dove, Dove)* or *(Hawk, Dove)* each happening with equal probability. Agent 2's expected payoff on choosing *"Dove"* conditioned on the fact that Agent 2 is told to *"Dove"* is *3*. Under this instruction, *6* is the payoff when Agent 1 is also *"Dove"*, i.e., the outcome is *(Dove, Dove)* and *0* is the payoff that Agent 2 receives when Agent 1 chooses *Hawk*, since the outcome is *(Hawk, Dove)*. If Agent 2 decides to deviate, by choosing *Hawk* when told to choose *Dove*, the expected payoff is *1.5*. So, this expected payoff by deviating is lower than the payoff *3* on obeying the instruction. Therefore, Agent 2 does not deviate. Since the game is symmetric, Agent 1 also has no incentive to deviate from the instruction. In the case of this correlated equilibrium, the expected payoff for each agent is *6*, which is higher than the expected payoff *3.6* of the mixed Nash equilibrium. Therefore, the payoffs of both agents can be made be improved by correlating their independent strategy-choices.

For obtaining correlated equilibrium, we need to find a probability distribution on the set of all possible outcomes. Let S be the set of strategy combinations of both agents. Let $U_i(S)$ be the payoff to agent i, i=1,2, when a pair of strategies $S=(S_1, S_2)$ is followed by both agents, and let $p(S)$ denote the probability with which the third party observes the outcomes, $S=(S_1, S_2)$, in which case, Agent 1 is told to choose strategy S_1 and Agent 2 is told to choose strategy S_2. To ensure that correlated equilibrium results, no agent should have a motivation to deviate from the instruction S by the third party. So, if both agents are told to choose S_i, $i = 1,2$, then the other strategy for that agent should have no better outcome. Thus, the expected payoff of choosing the informed strategy is at least as great as the expected payoff when each agent alone switches to the other strategy.

Asymmetric coordination games such as the battle-of-sexes game in Table 2.4 and the *Hawk-Dove* game in Table 2.5 have two pure equilibria in which both agents gain different payoffs, resulting in asymmetric pure equilibria. However, both agents gain the same payoff at the mixed equilibrium, which is sub-optimal compared with pure equilibria. This raises many issues. In particular, we need to find a better solution to overcome the tradeoff between efficiency and equity.

How can we motivate a particular choice when there is no sufficient reason for preferring one of two or more indistinguishable outcomes?

Since there is no way to choose between the pure equilibria, one solution is to select the mixed equilibrium. For instance, in the context of the *Hawk-Dove* game, agents can increase their expected payoff by tossing a coin ahead of time, and the loser may agree to swerve (dove), and the winner will not swerve (*hawk*). This kind of treatment will increase the expected payoffs for both agents.

We could also introduce the concept of *a joint strategy* that specifies a rule for each agent to follow. The rule of the joint strategy specifies strategy choices for both agents, and an equilibrium is defined as the joint strategies such that no agent has any incentive to depart from it. We can also define a *randomized joint strategy*, which randomizes between pure joint strategies. When both agents choose mixed strategies, it is characterized as randomized joint strategies that randomize between pure joint strategies. Then, the question is whether we can find an *efficient rule* of the joint strategy choice that specifies a plan for each agent so that the Pareto-efficient outcome is obtained. We may need to find some mechanism for achieving Pareto-efficiency using, (1) an external device, such as signals, or an authorization device, or (2) learning. We discuss this issue in Chapters 9 and 10.

2.3 Interaction Structures

The interaction structure specifies who affects whom. The importance of interacting with the right people is often stressed, which is sometimes stated as *"It's not what you know, but who you know that matters"*. Therefore, it is important to consider with whom an agent should interact.

In order to describe the ways of interaction, the *random matching model* is frequently used. There are also a variety of interaction models, depending on how agents meet, and what information is revealed before interaction.

(1) *Global interaction model*

When all agents are modeled to interact with all other agents in the same population, the model is referred to as a *global interaction model*. The global interaction model becomes equivalent to the random matching model, in which each agent is assumed to interact with a randomly chosen agent from the population.

(2) *Random interaction model*

The *random interaction model* is treated as follows. As shown in Figure 2.1, two agents who are randomly chosen from the same population are matched and play a 2x2 game. In each round, all agents are randomly matched. At the end of each round each agent observes only the play in her own match. The way an agent acts now will influence the way her current opponent plays in the next round, but the agent is unlikely to be matched with her current opponent or anyone who has met the current opponent for a long time.

An important assumption of the random interaction model is that agents receive knowledge of the current strategy of the population. Let us suppose that at the end of the round, the population aggregates are

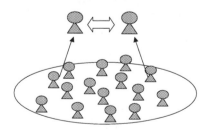

Figure 2.1 A random interaction model

announced. If the population is large, each agent has little influence on the population aggregates, and consequently little influence on future play, so agents have no reason to depart from myopic behavior. Therefore, agents choose their optimal strategy based on aggregated information concerning what the other agents of the same population have chosen in the past. This aggregate information is defined as the *population strategy*. Each agent calculates her expected payoffs and chooses the best response to this population strategy.

(3) *A local interaction model*

There are many situations in which a spatial environment becomes a more realistic representation, since interactions in real life rarely happen on such a macro-scale as assumed in the global interaction model. Spatial interaction is generally modeled through the use of the two dimensional (2D) grid in Figure 2.2 with each agent inhabiting each cell of the lattice on the grid. Interaction between agents is restricted to nearest neighboring agents. Each agent chooses an optimal strategy based on local information about what her neighbors will choose. However, the consequences of their choices may take some time to have an effect on agents with whom they are not directly linked.

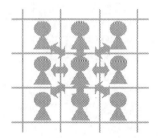

Figure 2.2 Local matching

(4) *A small-world network model*

Complex networks describe a wide range of systems in nature and technology and can be modeled as a network of nodes in which the interactions between nodes are represented as edges. Recent advances in understanding these networks revealed that many of the systems show a small-world structure. Watts and Storogatz (1998) introduced *a small-world network* architecture that transforms from a nearest neighbor coupled system to a random coupled network by rewiring the links between the nodes. Two parameters are used to describe the transition.

The mean path length L, which specifies the global property of the network, is given as the mean of the shortest path between all pairs of vertices. In contrast, the clustering coefficient C characterizes the local property of the system and can be calculated as the fraction of the connections between the neighbors of a node divided by the number of edges of a globally coupled neighborhood, averaged over all vertices. Probability results in a random coupled network with a short mean path length and a low clustering coefficient.

For instance, consider a one-lattice model in which each node is coupled with its nearest neighbors, as shown in Figure 2.3. It has a large mean path length and a high clustering coefficient. If one rewires the links between the nodes with a small probability, then the local structure of the network remains nearly intact, while maintaining the clustering coefficient contrast. In contrast, due to the introduction of shortcuts by the rewiring procedure, the mean path length becomes strongly reduced. Networks with these properties are called *small-world networks*.

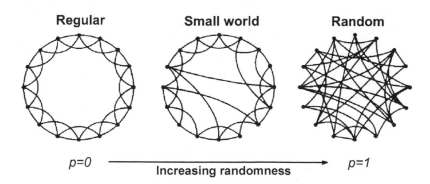

Figure 2.3 A small-world network model. Illustration of a one-lattice model

2.4 Learning in Games

The traditional assumption in game theory is that agents are rational in the sense that agents maximize their own payoffs, and all agents who are involved commonly know this. Rationality means to respond optimally to others' decisions. Thus, the rational decision making process is purely *forward-looking*. Such a forward-looking model that involves *deliberate decision-making* is defined as a *rational-choice model*, which requires well-defined preferences and unlimited information for all agents.

The reason for the dominance of the rational-choice approach in game theory is not that it is realistic. Theoretically, it is quite understandable to confront the rational-choice approach. There may even exist situations in which agents know very little about their decision environments, so that all what they can do is repeat past decisions. The real advantage of the rational-choice assumption is that it often allows deduction.

An alternative to the assumption of a rational choice model is some form of adaptation. The adaptation may be at the individual level, through learning, or may be evolution at the population level, through survival of more successful individuals. Either way, the consequences of adaptive processes are often very hard to deduce when agents following their own adaptive rules interact with each other.

Recently, more general notions have been introduced, which allows bounded rationality. This means that we combine the ideas of (1) how agents cognitively perceive their decision environment and update their cognitive model in the light of new information and (2) how previous successful feedback leads to adaptation. Work on learning in game theory started with descriptive motivation in mind. That is, its main goal is to show that agents who follow simple learning rules for updating their strategy would eventually adopt an optimal strategy that corresponds to Nash equilibrium (Fudenberg and Levine, 1998) (Young, 2005).

The basic research agenda in game theory is also to explore non-equilibrium explanations in games, to view equilibrium as the long-run outcome of a dynamic adaptive process of learning. In other words, the outcomes of the games should be interpreted as steady states of an underlying dynamic learning process. A variety of learning models have been studied. Many adaptive mechanisms have been discussed in the literature on learning, and they are classified as follows.

(1) *Reinforcement learning*

Reinforcement is an empirical principle that states that the higher the payoff from taking an action in the past, the more likely it will be taken in the future. In *reinforcement learning models*, agents are taken to behave quite primitively, simply reacting to positive or negative stimuli. Reinforcement learning models reflect the simple mechanism whereby the propensity for an agent to choose a strategy is positively related to the amount of satisfaction historically associated with it. Agents tend to adopt actions that yielded a higher payoff in the past and to avoid actions that yielded a low payoff. Although the payoff is related to an agent's choice behavior, only the agent's own payoffs matter, and not those of others.

A more complicated version of reinforcement learning is based on the principle of probabilistic choice. That is, the probability of selecting a strategy at present increases with the payoff that resulted from taking that strategy in the past. This general principle underlying reinforcement learning can be formulated in a variety of ways. Subsequently, a more complex analysis turns to models in which agents are postulated to behave in a substantially more involved fashion, i.e., they entertain expectations on future interactions at the current interaction and react optimally to them.

Within such a class of learning models, they range from *shortsighted agents*, who behave without deliberate calculation, to *forward-looking agents*, who attempt to understand their environment in a dynamic fashion. If they repeatedly play the same game against each other, forward-looking agents consider the possibility that their current play may influence the future play of their opponent.

(2) *Best-response learning*

In most game theoretic models, agents are assumed to have perfect knowledge of the consequences of their choices. In this learning model, agents are assumed to adopt a strategy that optimizes their expected payoff given what they expect the other (or others) to do. An important assumption of best-response learning is that they receive knowledge of the current strategy of their opponent.

Alternatively, they may know the strategy distribution of the population and can calculate their best-response strategy based on information about what the other agents have done in the past. In this learning model, agents choose the best replies to the current strategy population and may gradually learn the strategy population at a Nash equilibrium.

(3) *Evolutionary learning*

Evolutionary learning is based on the concept of natural selection that supports the survival of more successful strategies or individuals. Agents with higher payoff are at a productive advantage compared to agents who use strategies with a lower payoff. Hence, the latter decrease in frequency in the population over time by natural selection.

In the standard model of evolutionary learning, agents are viewed as being genetically coded with a strategy and selection pressure favors agents that are fitter, i.e., agents whose strategy yields a higher payoff against the average payoff of the population. The idea of using a genetic algorithm to create complex strategies has been developed by many researchers.

(4) *Social learning*

Learning also occurs in the social contexts in which an agent learns some behavioral patterns or acquires knowledge as a consequence of observation of or interaction with other agents. For instance, an agent may learn the behavior of others, especially behaviors that are popular for yielding a high payoff. The term *social learning* is a general term that represents learning that is influenced socially, in contrast to instances of *individual learning* in which a behavioral pattern or knowledge acquisition is not influenced by interaction with other agents. In general, evolutionary learning is very slow with regard to proliferating a superior rule. However, social learning may be fast, because the transmission of a superior rule from one agent to another is very fast.

However, this term should be distinguished from *imitation*, which describes one psychological process that can result in social learning. Imitation refers to instances whereby the observation of the behavior of another individual allows an individual to reproduce the same behavioral pattern. The term imitation is not a synonym for social learning, since it is possible to imitate without learning anything. Imitation is just one of several processes that can be result in social learning (Laland, 2002).

The basic question a learning model must address is what agents know before the game starts, and what it is that they are learning. Depending on these details, i.e., the length of an agent's memory or their assumed knowledge on the payoff structure, many different versions of best-response learning models also arise.

Most learning theory abstracts from repeated game considerations by explicitly or implicitly relying on a model in which the incentive to try to alter the future play of opponents is sufficiently small so as to be negligible. There are two levels of sophistication in this type of forward-looking learning. One is simply to forecast how opposing agents will play. If two agents are repeatedly matched against each other, they ought to consider the possibility that their current strategy may influence the choice of the future strategies of the opponent. There are several ways of modeling the learning of an opponent's strategy.

A closely related issue is how much rationality to attribute to the agents. The true challenge is then to describe how the best bounded rational agents rely on past results to improve their outcomes on how they predict the consequences of certain decision alternatives based on some simple learning models. With the above learning models, we basically try to understand how various learning models lead to a Nash equilibrium.

On the other hand, we also have to seek the proper models in which agents consciously try to improve the collective outcome. In this sense, we can look at learning models for behavioral rules. We are especially interested in learnable rules in the sense that agents try to obtain a better outcome. Rules that do poorly are not likely to be used, and agents will seek a better behavioral rule. We discuss this issue in Chapter 9 and Chapter 10.

2.5 Evolutionary Games

In many applications, it is of interest to know which strategies can survive in the long run. While the concept and techniques of game theory have been used extensively in many diverse contexts, they have been unsuccessful in answering this key question. In this section, we present the basic model of evolutionary games that may remedy the shortcomings of game theory.

One of the variations involves iterated games. The standard interpretation of game theory is that the game is played exactly once between fully rational individuals who know all the details of the game, including each other's preference concerning outcomes. Evolutionary game theory, instead, assumes that the game is repeated in a large population of agents. Two agents who are randomly drawn from a population play the underlying game. That is, we focus on a population of agents who are assumed to undergo identical pair-wise interaction, which is formulated as a 2x2 game (Weibull, 1996).

An evolutionary model starts with a description of the aggregate behavior of a population. An example of this approach is *replicator dynamics* (RD), which postulates that the fraction of the population playing a strategy increases if the payoff (or fitness) received from that strategy is above the average payoff of the population. Although the RD was originally motivated by biological evolution, it can be derived from various sorts of game theoretic models. One such model is the *stimulus-response model*, which postulates that a strategy that performs well is reinforced and so is more likely to be played in the future. An alternative model is the *imitation model*, in which an agent mimics other more successful agents. The imitation model is also similar to a model of social learning, where agents are trying to learn what strategy is best from other agents.

More precisely, we consider a population whose members are randomly matched in pairs to play the underlying 2x2 game. An evolutionary selection process operates over time on the strategy distribution of the population. From a theoretical viewpoint, there are two basic related questions.

(1) What reasonable features should be postulated on the dynamics of the strategy distribution in a population?

(2) Under what conditions does the strategy distribution converge to equilibrium of the underlying game?

Research on the above issues have been attracted a great deal of attention from many researchers, from the viewpoint of evolution. In essence, evolutionary game theory builds upon the simple idea that any non-optimal behavior should eventually be weeded out of the population by the pressure of *natural selection*. Thus, rather than invoking agents' rational choices, some criterion of long-run survivability is used. There are a number of interesting scenarios, in which such an evolutionary approach is able to explain the selection of the specific equilibrium based on multiple Nash equilibria of the underlying game. This property is known as a *refinement of Nash equilibria*.

In general, an evolutionary process combines two basic elements: a *mutation* mechanism that provides variety, and a *selection* mechanism that favors some varieties over others. A key concept in evolutionary games is that of an *evolutionarily stable strategy*. Such a strategy is robust to natural selection. Suppose all agents are genetically programmed to apply the same incumbent strategy. Now inject a small proportion of agents who are also programmed to adapt some other strategy (often referred to as a *mutant strategy*). The incumbent strategy is said to be *evolutionarily stable* if there exists an invasion barrier such that if a proportion of agents adapting the mutant strategy falls below this barrier, then the incumbent strategy earns a higher payoff than the mutant strategy.

Evolution is modeled as a dynamic process. As a first step, however, it is useful to study it from a static viewpoint and ask what kind of configurations can be suitably conceived as a stable point of evolutionary dynamics. The first equilibrium concept in evolutionary games is the *evolutionarily stable strategy* (ESS), which is proposed by Smith and

Price (1982). It is known that the aggregate behavior of a population tends toward a Nash equilibrium, and this property is said to satisfy the condition of *evolutionary stability*. The criterion of evolutionary stability generalizes Darwin's notion of *survival of the fittest* from an exogenous environment to a competitive environment, where the fitness of a given strategy depends on the strategies of others.

The evolutionary stability requires that a small number of agents who adopt some alternative strategy do not do as well as the agents who stick to the incumbent strategy. Consequently, agents who adopt the prevailing strategy have no incentive to change their strategy, since they do better than those who choose the mutant strategy, and the latter has an incentive to return to the incumbent strategy. However, the evolutionary stability property does not explain how a population of agents may arrive at such an equilibrium. Instead, it asks whether a strategy is robust to evolutionary pressures.

Let us suppose that the underlying game is symmetric with $S=(S_1, S_2)$ being the common strategy set for all agents. The underlying game has the payoff matrix shown in Table 2.3. The question implicitly posed by the ESS concept can be formulated as follows. Can the originally monomorphic population be permanently invaded by a small number of alternative agents who adopt a different strategy?

Suppose that a number of agents who choose a different mixed strategy $y = (y, 1 - y)$ (mutant strategy) appear in a large population of agents, all of whom are programmed to choose the same mixed strategy $x = (x, 1 - x)$ (incumbent strategy). Let the proportion of agents in the population who choose a mutant strategy y be ε. Since they are randomly matched against each other, the expected payoff earned by an agent for choosing the incumbent strategy x is

$$(1 - \varepsilon)U(x, x) + \varepsilon U(x, y) = U(x(1 - \varepsilon)x + \varepsilon y). \tag{2.19}$$

Similarly, the expected payoff earned by an agent for choosing the mutant strategy y is

$$(1 - \varepsilon)U(y, x) + \varepsilon U(y, y) = U(y, (1 - \varepsilon)x + \varepsilon y). \tag{2.20}$$

A strategy x is defined as *evolutionarily stable* if the following inequality holds for any mutant strategy y ($\neq x$)

$$U(x,(1-\varepsilon)x+\varepsilon y) > U(y,(1-\varepsilon)x+\varepsilon y). \tag{2.21}$$

If the expected payoff (Darwinian fitness) of an agent adopting the mutant strategy y is smaller than that of agents adopting the incumbent strategy x, then that mutant cannot invade the population. Such a strategy is defined as evolutionarily stable.

Definition 2.5 *A (mixed) strategy x is defined as an evolutionarily stable strategy (ESS) if it satisfies*

$$U(x,(1-\varepsilon)x+\varepsilon y) > U(y,(1-\varepsilon)x+\varepsilon y). \tag{2.22}$$

Since ε is assumed to be small, (2.22) implies the condition (i) or (ii),

(i) $U(x,x) > U(y,x)$ $\qquad\qquad \forall y\,(\neq x),$ $\qquad\qquad$ (2.23)

(ii) If $U(x,x) = U(y,x)$, then $U(x,y) = U(y,y)$. $\qquad\qquad$ (2.24)

The above ESS concept induces a symmetric Nash equilibrium of the underlying game, since condition (2.23) simply reflects this. In addition, an ESS must also satisfy condition (2.24). Therefore, the ESS notion is stronger than Nash equilibrium, and it can be regarded as a refinement of Nash Equilibrium. This brings us to an important question of the existence of an ESS.

When the underlying game has a symmetric payoff matrix in Table 2.3, the ESS is obtained as follows.

(1) **Dilemma Game**: If the underlying game is a prisoner's dilemma game, the pure strategy $S_2(e_2)$ is the unique ESS.

(2) **Coordination Game**: If the underlying game is a coordination game, two pure strategies $S_1(e_1)$, $S_2(e_2)$ and one mixed Nash strategy $\theta = (\theta,\ 1-\theta)$ are ESS, where $\theta = \beta / \alpha$, are all ESS.

(3) **Dispersion Game**: If the underlying game is a dispersion game, the mixed Nash strategy $\theta = (\theta,\ 1-\theta)$, where $\theta = \beta / \alpha$, is the unique ESS.

(4) **Hawk-Dove Game**: If the underlying game is a Hawk-Dove game with the payoff matrix shown in Table 2.2, the mixed Nash strategy $\theta = (\theta,\ 1-\theta)$, where $\theta = 1 - v/c$, is the unique ESS.

The criterion of evolutionary stable equilibrium (ESS) highlights the role of mutations. It is also of interest to know which strategies can survive in the long run. Evolutionary dynamics highlight the role of selection. We now take a dynamic approach to the study of evolution by characterizing the dynamic aspect of evolutionary games. In particular, we ask the following question: Do any reasonable dynamics exist that would lead a population of agents to an ESS in the long-run?

We focus on evolutionary dynamics formulated as the replicator dynamics (RD) model. We will observe that a Nash equilibrium is a stable point of the RD model. The model of RD starts with a description of the aggregate behavior of a population of agents. The fraction of the population choosing a specific strategy increases if the payoff received from that strategy is above the average payoff of the population.

Let $x \in [0, 1]$ denote the proportion of agents choosing pure strategy $S_1(e_1)$. The current strategy distribution of the population at time t is denoted as $x(t) = \{x(t), 1 - x(t)\}$, which is defined as the *strategy distribution* of the population. The RD model describes the growth rates of the strategy distribution. Since we consider a population of agents who play with two strategies, the RD model is governed by the equation in which the function $x(t)$ denotes the percentage growth rate of strategy $S_1(e_1)$. The expected payoff to an agent choosing $S_1(e_1)$ is $U(e_1, x(t))$, and the average payoff of the population is $U(x(t), x(t))$. Since we assume that greater payoff (fitness) yields greater reproductive success, the percentage growth rate of $x(t)$ is described as

$$\dot{x}(t) = \{U(e_1, x(t)) - U(x(t), x(t))\}x(t). \qquad (2.25)$$

The above dynamics is defined as the replicator dynamics (RD) of a single population. From (2.13), we can derive

$$U(e_1, x) - U(x, x) = (1 - x)\{U(e_1, x) - U(e_2, x)\}$$
$$= \{(\alpha + \beta)x - \beta\}x(1 - x). \qquad (2.26)$$

Then, the dynamics in (2.25) is in the form of

$$\dot{x}(t) = \{(\alpha + \beta)x - \beta\}x(t)(1 - x(t)). \qquad (2.27)$$

The stability of the RD in (2.27) is then determined depending on the signs of the payoff values α and β.

(1) **Dilemma Game**: For any initial value $x(0)$, the RD converges to $x=0$, where all agents choose $S_2(e_2)$.

(2) **Coordination Game**: If the initial value $x(0)$ is greater than $\theta = \beta/(\alpha+\beta)$, the RD converges to $x=1$, where all agents choose $S_1(e_1)$. On the other hand, if that the proportion is smaller than θ, the RD converges to $x=0$, where all agents choose $S_2(e_2)$.

(3) **Dispersion Game** and **Hawk-Dove Game**: For any initial value $x(0)$, the RD converges to $x = \theta$ and the proportion θ of the population chooses $S_1(e_1)$, and the rest of the agents choose $S_2(e_2)$.

Figure 2.4 represents the phase diagrams of the RD depending on the underlying game. If the underlying game is a coordination game, then evolution from all initial conditions other than the mixed equilibrium leads to one of the pure equilibria of the game, and which equilibrium is reached is determined by the side of the mixed equilibrium on which play begins. However, for a dispersion game and a Hawk-Dove game,

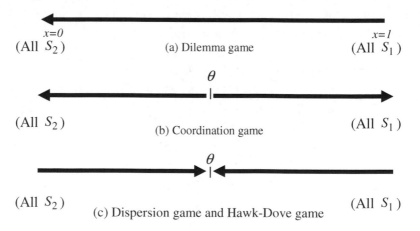

Figure 2.4 Basins of attraction of replicator dynamics

evolution from all interior population states leads to the unique mixed equilibrium $x^* = (\theta, 1-\theta)$.

By definition, the ESS concept is restricted to the analysis of monomorphic configurations, i.e., situations in which *all* agents in the population adopt the *same* strategy. Naturally, the evolutionary performance of the strategy must be tailored to some global assessment of the payoff induced across all of the individuals that adopt it. For simplicity, the ESS concept identifies such global performance with the corresponding average payoff. Thus, in view of the large-population scenario, the evolutionary stability is linked to the *identical* payoff faced by all agents.

However, diversity is also an important feature of most interesting evolutionary environments. Therefore, the checks and balances afforded by a suitable degree of heterogeneity are crucial to understanding the evolutionary stability of the situation. However, the heterogeneity must be introduced explicitly into the framework if the problem is to be suitably modeled. We will discuss this issue in Chapter 4.

In order to extend the generality of our approach, it is also worth the effort to allow for the possibility that several *distinct* populations interact. Thus, let us suppose that there are several distinct populations, the members of which interact according to a certain underlying game. In fact, in order to avoid unnecessary notational burden, let us simply posit that there are just two populations of agents. We will discuss this issue in Chapter 5.

2.6 Relation between Learning and Evolution

The standard assumption of game theory is that the game is played exactly once between fully rational individuals who know all the details of the game, including each other's preferences concerning outcomes. In this case, rationality means that agents maximize their own payoffs and react optimally to others' decisions.

In many real contexts, agents can seldom hope to understand the underlying game, which in turn leads them to adopt different approach. In these situations, agents can repeat strategies that worked well in the past. A very different reaction is to substitute forward-looking deliberation, which is also referred to as the *shadow of the future*, for pure adaptation to past results, which is referred to as the *shadow of the past*. This approach is also characterized as adaptation based on a behavioral strategy that is acquired based on past success or failure.

The origins of evolutionary game theory lie in biological models of natural selection. They treat agents as automata, merely responding to changing environments without deliberating on other agents' decisions. Agents are genetically programmed to adopt a certain strategy. Then, evolution is driven by differences in their reproductive success. In essence, evolutionary game theory builds upon the simple rule that any non-optimal behavior should eventually be weeded out of the population by the pressure of competition and better-suited behavior. Thus, rather than invoking agents' reasoning ability to discipline behavior, the criterion of long-run performance and survival is used.

In most game theoretic models, agents calculate their best strategy based on information about what other agents have done in the past. Then, agents gradually learn the equilibrium strategy. However, it is easy to see that there is no general way to guarantee that agents will behave in an efficient manner. This is due to the fact that although a pair of strategies is efficient, performing them may be irrational for one agent or both agents, as illustrated in the dilemma game. Game theory and evolutionary games are not able to provide answers explaining how agents should behave in order to overcome an inefficient equilibrium situation.

Many inconsistencies within game-theoretical models and the evolutionary models emerged. We need to explore models that provide a micro foundation that is missing in evolutionary approaches. The combined approach may provide a necessary complement, which can be seen as capacities that evolved during evolution to increase the learning efficiency of the individual.

It is also not surprising that many scientists are exploring a new unified theory of evolution by merging game theory and evolutionary game theory with modern biological evolution theory (Nowar and Sigmund, 2004). This new theory attempts to explain all kinds of evolutionary processes. Its methods and models cover not only biological evolution of organisms, but also the evolution of animal and human behavior in their respective societies. Evolutionary models explore changes in the global frequency distribution of strategies across a population. In contrast, models of learning operate on the local probability distribution of strategies within the repertoire of each individual member.

When agents are driven by their conscious choices, rather than natural selection, we need to describe how agents learn. Although sometimes learning and evolution may occur simultaneously, the former usually proceeds much more quickly than the latter. Agents can quickly switch to preferred strategies, but the change in the strategy distribution is driven by gradual turnover in the population.

Baldwin (1896) proposed the idea that individual lifetime learning has an influence on evolution, an idea that is known as the *Baldwin effect*. This idea explains the relationship between learning and evolution, particularly in regard to benefits and costs in learning. The Baldwin effect occurs in two steps. In the first step, lifetime learning gives agents the chance to change their phenotypes. If the learned traits are useful to the agents and result in increased fitness, they will spread in the population in the next generation. This step implies synergy between learning and evolution. In the second step, if the environment is sufficiently stable, then the evolutionary path finds innate traits that can replace learned traits, because of the learning cost. This step is also known as *genetic assimilation*. Through these two steps, learning can accelerate the genetic acquisition of learned traits.

Hinton and Nowlan (1987) developed the first computational model to evaluate the Baldwin effect. Ackley and Littman (1991) showed that learning and evolution together are more successful than either alone in a collection of agents. Most of these studies have assumed that environments are fixed and investigate the first step of the Baldwin effect.

Suzuki and Arita (2003) have investigated dynamic environments and how learning can affect the course of evolution in dynamic environments. They used the Iterated Prisoner's Dilemma (IPD), in which phenotypic plasticity is introduced into strategies. They conducted computational experiments in which phenotypic plasticity was allowed to evolve. They considered a population of agents involved in an IPD. All genes were set randomly in the initial population. A round robin tournament was conducted between individuals and can be changed by noise (mistake) with some probability. The game was played for several rounds, and the total score of each agent was regarded as a fitness value. A new population was generated by roulette wheel selection according to the scores, and mutation was performed on a bit-by-bit basis with some probability.

They showed how learning can affect the course of evolution. A drastic mode transition happens at the edge between the first and second steps of the Baldwin effect in dynamic environments where the optimal solution changes dynamically, depending on the interactions between individuals. They showed that the implicit cost of learning yields the evolution of the potential region that the population could reach through the learning process on the fitness landscape. They interpreted the Baldwin effect through the meta-strategy generated during evolution and analyzed the property of this meta-strategy.

2.7 Design of Learning and Evolving Agents

There is no doubt that agents learn from their past successful and unsuccessful attempts, from iterating social interactions and from improving and adapting behaviors. A variety of learning models have been studied with little concern for the extent to which the models do a good job of learning. We believe that agents may tend not to use learning models that do poorly. First, we must determine what types of learning models agents may use and what they know during learning. Are they learning about how to choose the best response strategy, or are they learning how to play?

We believe that for most purposes proper models involve neither full rationality nor extreme stimulus-response models. We will simplify matters by assuming that agents know the extensive form of the game and their own payoff. However, they may or may not know their opponents payoffs. We can imagine how learning agents might move toward a desirable outcome. However, in principle, we could fold this evolutionary element into a meta-learning that includes both the short-term learning and long-term evolution.

We endow agents with some learning capability and describe the evolutionary dynamics that magnifies tendencies toward better situation. By incorporating consideration of how agents learn into evolutionary models, we not only make them more realistic, but we also enrich the aggregate behavior that can emerge. It is also important to determine how a population of learning agents moves toward an efficient equilibrium in an imperfect world as they evolve.

A few researchers have tackled the design problem of learning agents. Learning agents may be modeled to adapt their strategy choices with certain rules. Agents might observe only the history of their own payoffs and strategies and might discover new strategies by experimentation. The genetic algorithm model of learning attempts to explore such a setting. However, agent design has not clarified how to think about learning.

The most important question faced in market design, for instance, lies in the representation and structure of the agents. Agents can vary from simple agents, who behave only considering constraints, to sophisticated learning models. Given that there are many ways to process past data, there must be as many ways to construct learning agents. This leaves some open questions about evolutionary dynamics with only a limited amount of new speciation. Agents may be modeled as adapting their strategies. This allows for the possibility of agents to learn how to overcome inefficiencies. An interesting feature is that agents are very homogeneous in their abilities at the start. Differences in behavior and strategy evolve endogenously as the system runs. Agent heterogeneity becomes a changing feature of the system that can then be studied.

Young (2005) investigates the performance of a system that is composed of other learners. He provides a framework emphasizing the amount of information required to implement different learning types of learning models. He proved that a learning procedure that satisfies certain criteria of convergence to Nash equilibrium may not exist.

Shoham (2003) classified the following agenda of leaning in the environment of multiple agents. The first agenda is descriptive and asks how humans learn in the context of other learners. The name of the game here is to show experimentally that a certain formal model of learning agrees with peoples' behavior. This is a key concern for game theory, since a successful theory would support the notion of Nash equilibrium, which plays a central role in the game theory.

The second agenda is how to design learning agents. In this case, we can easily imagine situations in which agents are implemented with different learning models. This is also a basic design problem of distributed systems. A central designer may control multiple agents, but will not design and implement the same learning rules for them. Instead each agent is endowed with a different learning rule that will be improved over time. Then, the choice of a learning model becomes a basic issue to be considered. We need to view the designer's choice of learning models as a fundamental decision that should follow normative criteria.

The other research agenda is prescriptive and asks how agents should learn in the context of other learners. In this case we may not be able to obtain optimal learning models for them. Instead, we assign a learning rule to each of them so that they may converge to a desired situation. In this case the question of how best to learn is different from the issue of how best to behave.

Tennenholtz (2002) introduced the concept of *efficient learning equilibrium* (ELE), a normative approach to learning in multi-agent settings. In ELE, the learning algorithms themselves are required to be in equilibrium. In addition, the learning algorithms must arrive at a desired value after polynomial time, and deviation from the prescribed ELE becomes irrational after polynomial time. The following are the requirements:

(1) **Individual Rationality**: The learning models themselves should be in equilibrium. It should be irrational for each agent to deviate from its learning model, as long as the other agents stick to their learning models.

(2) **Efficiency**: Deviation from the learning models by a single agent while the others stick to their learning models will become irrational, in the sense that it will lead to a situation in which the deviator's payoff is not improved after many stages. If all agents stick to their prescribed learning models, then the expected payoff obtained by each agent will be

close to the value it could have obtained in a Nash equilibrium. The agents known the game from the outset.

A set of learning algorithms satisfying the above properties for a given class of games is said to be an *Efficient Learning Equilibrium* (ELE). They proved the existence of an ELE, where the desired value is the expected payoff in a Nash equilibrium. They also introduced the concept of a *Pareto-ELE*, where the objective is the maximization of the sum of all agents' payoffs.

Tennenholtz proved the existence of an ELE and of a Pareto-ELE in repeated games. The idea of equilibrium of learning models can be viewed similarly. We can search for learning models such that it will be irrational for each agent to deviate from its current model assuming the other agents sticks to their models, regardless of the state of the game. Both ELE and Pareto-ELE provide new basic tools for learning in multi-agent settings.

Another unique approach is a design approach (Shoham, 2003). Let us consider the existence of some correlation device that provides the agents with a learning model to use and suggested payments to be made. This correlation device is not a designer who can enforce behaviors or payments and docs not possess any private knowledge or aim to optimize private payoffs. Suggested payments are just part of the learning model, and it is up to the agents to decide whether to make them. This is proof that the learning models are in equilibrium and suggests that these payments will actually be executed by self-interested agents.

We may ask what the best learning model is for a given agent for a fixed class of the other agents facing the same situations. The model thus retains the design stance of engineering, asking how to design an optimal or effective learning agent for a given environment. This is precisely because it adopts the optimal agent design approach and does not consider the equilibrium concept to be central or even necessarily relevant.

The essential divergence between the equilibrium approach and the design approach lies in the attitude towards bounded rationality, a largely unsolved problem. In contrast, the design approach embraces bounded rationality as the starting point, and only adds elements of learning when appropriate. The result is fewer elegant theorems in general, but perhaps a greater degree of applicability in certain cases.

In general, this applies to situations with complex strategy spaces, and in particular to multi-agent learning settings. We especially need to focus on the behavior rules that provide the guidance to choose their actions. This means that agents are trying to realize a better relationship, rather than to receive a good payoff. We discuss this issue in detail in Chapter 9 and Chapter 10.

Chapter 3

Social Interactions and Social Games

In this chapter, we formulate social games in which there are a large number of agents, each of which faces a binary decision problem with externalities. The outcome depends on the strategy choices of all agents. Fortunately, in certain strategic situations, interactions among multiple agents can be analyzed by decomposition into underlying 2x2 games.

3.1 Social Interactions with Externalities

In this section, we demonstrate that there are a host of problems that share the same general structure with externalities and that make social interactions problematic whenever they arise.

The question of how it is possible for a collection of independent individuals to achieve both their own goals as well as their common goal has been addressed in many fields. The key element that distinguishes a common goal from an individual goal is that the former requires a kind of collective action. By a common goal, we mean a goal that is achievable by collective action that requires explicit cooperation.

Coordination is different concept from cooperation, which does not assume the existence of the common goal shared by all members. Coordination is necessary in order to achieve individuals' goals more efficiently. The essence of the collective system is that it is the individuals who are making the decisions, not the collective. Therefore, we need to cope with the collective system by attempting to stack the deck in such a way that individuals have selfish incentives to do the collectively desirable thing.

Undesirable outcomes that no one would have chosen may occur when social interactions of agents leads to a result that is not *optimal*. This problem is often referred as a *coordination failure*. The reason that uncoordinated activities of agents who pursue their own ends often produce outcomes that all would seek to avoid is that each agent's action affects the others and these effects are often not included in the optimization process made by other agents. These unaccounted for effects on others are called *externalities*.

Externality in economic activities, for instance, causes a good or a service to have a value for a potential customer that is dependent on the number of customers already owning that good or using that service (Cooper, 1999). One consequence of externality is that the purchase of a good by one individual indirectly benefits others who own the good. For example by purchasing one particular type of the mobile phone, a person makes other users of the same type more useful. This kind of side-effect is known as a *positive externality*. There is another type, known as a *negative externality*, which occurs when the by-product is viewed as having a social cost. For instance, when we drive a car we create air pollution. This air pollution can have harmful effects on others. Although we do not usually account for this in the costs of driving, other people pay the costs of dealing with air pollution.

An *externality* is usually considered to be an unaccounted side effect of activities by some agents on other unrelated agents. An externality also occurs when individuals care about others' choices and each individual's choice affects others' choices. For instance, when deciding which movies to visit, which new technologies to adopt or which job candidates to select, we often have little information with which to evaluate the alternatives. Therefore, we rely to the recommendation of friends or simply select the choice that most people have selected. Even when we have access to plentiful information, we often lack the ability to make sense of it and rely on the advice of trusted friends or colleagues.

An externality also occurs in other social interactions when a decision causes benefits all of the costs to other individuals. In other words, the individual does not bear the entire gain or loss brought about by his or her action. For instance, consider the provision of a public good for a collective of individuals. In contrast to private goods, public goods are non-excludable in consumption. The public-good nature of a lighthouse, for instance, enables each individual to have a free ride. It is not always individuals' incentives to abstain from certain activities that cause social dilemma problems. Sometimes, it is the individual activities themselves that have a harmful effect on the common interest, which suggests the implicit agreement to abstain from these activities (Olson, 1965). Air-pollution is another typical example. Although everybody can be made better off by an appropriate agreement controlling everyone's pollution level, individuals have an incentive to free ride in the absence of enforcement.

We distinguish two types of externalities: *strategic compatibility* and *strategic complementarity*. If social interactions are characterized to have strategic compatibility, agents' payoffs increase with the number of agents who take the same action. In contrast, if social interactions are characterized to have strategic complementarity, things are better off if agents distribute themselves among the possible actions. But even if everyone prefers to be mixed, it often turns out that most agents begin to take the same action. The problem of coordination failure arises in both contexts of social interactions with externalities.

Social interaction with externalities raises two basic questions, a positive question and a normative question. The first question concerns how the outcome actually comes to exist, and the second question concerns what the desired outcome should look like. The producers of externalities do not have an incentive to take into account the effect of their actions on others, and the outcome will be inefficient. This may make the problems of externalities too complex to deal with.

3.2 Binary Decisions with Externalities

From the perspective of a social planner, social interactions with externalities will result in an outcome that is not socially optimal. In this section, we illustrate some problems of inefficiency by considering binary decisions with externalities.

We consider a population of N agents, each faces a binary choice problem between S_1 and S_2. For any agent, the payoff for choosing S_1 or

S_2 depends on how many other agents also choose S_1 or S_2. Here, we consider social interactions in which agents are identically situated in the sense that every agent's outcome, which ever way she makes her choice, depends on the number of agents who choose on way or the other.

The payoff to each agent is given as an explicit function of the actions of all agents, and therefore she has an incentive to pay attention to the collective decision. However, the binary decision itself can be considered to be a function of solely the *relative* number of other agents who are observed to choose one alternative over the others. This class of binary decision problems is referred to as *binary decisions with externalities*.

As simplistic as it appears, a binary decision framework is relevant to surprisingly complex outcomes. Both the detailed mechanisms involved in binary decision problems and the origins of the externalities can vary widely across specific problems. The relevant binary decision problem frequently exhibits a *threshold* nature. Agents display inertia in switching outcomes, but once their personal threshold has been reached, the action of even a single neighbor can tip them from one state to another.

We now formulate some binary decision problems with externalities. A typical example is the situation in which the increased effort by some agents leads the remaining agents to follow suit, which causes *multiplier effects*. In this case, each agent receives a high payoff if she selects the same action as the majority.

Example 3.1 *<A network formation problem>* We consider a population of N agents in which each agent periodically has to make a decision as to whether to join the network or separate from it. If more agents join the network, then they receive a higher payoff. Intuitively, it is enough to accept that an agent's rational decision depends on the other agents directly linked with her. This interdependence with externality in decision may in turn influence the decisions of the others.

Here, each agent has the following two strategies:

S_1: joins the network,

S_2: separates from the network. (3.1)

Two assumptions that simplify the analysis further are that the payoff function is *symmetric*, that is to say, it is the same from every agent's point of view, and that every agent's payoff function is linear with respect to the number of agents choosing one of the choices. That is, an agent's payoff function is directly proportional to the number of agents selecting one of the choices.

The payoffs to each of the agent choosing S_1 or S_2 are given as

$$U(S_1) = a(n/N) - c \,,$$
$$U(S_2) = b(n/N) \,.$$

(3.2)

where n/N $(0 \le n/N \le 1)$ is the proportion of agents of choosing S_1.

The above payoff functions are depicted in Figure 3.1. The payoff for joining the network is an increasing function of the agents who make the same decision. Any agent who chooses S_1 or S_2 gains if some agents that previously chose S_2, shift and choose S_1, since both payoff functions are rising to the right. Therefore the collective maximum can occur at the right extremity, where all agents choose S_1.

The optimal strategy of each agent is obtained in the two cases depending on the relations among the payoff values, a, b, and c.

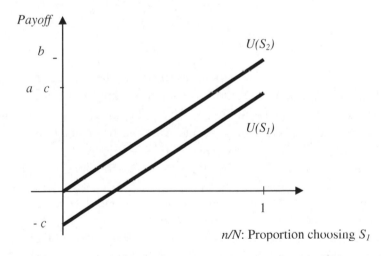

Figure 3.1 The $U(S_1)$ and $U(S_2)$ functions indicate the payoffs to an agent choosing S_1 or S_2 when the proportion of agents who choose S_1 is n/N

<Case1> $b > a - c$: In this case, the payoffs of an agent choosing from S_1 or S_2 satisfy

$$U(S_2) > U(S_1) \qquad \forall n / N .\tag{3.3}$$

Therefore, the rational choice is S_2 without regarding the others' choices. In game theory, S_2 is defined as a *dominant strategy*. In this case, no agent will add to the networks, and this situation is known as a *social dilemma*. There are several social and economic problems involving the clash of *individual optimality* and *collective optimality*.

Game theory suggests two alternatives for solving social dilemma problems. One of them is to introduce enforcement. For instance, the payoffs are altered in such a way that a non-cooperative agent incurs some penalty. The other option is to repeat the binary choice problems. It should be noted that the analysis of repeated games has been very fertile for the study of social dilemmas (Axelrod, 1987).

<Case 2> $b < a - c$: The expected payoff to an agent choosing S_1 or S_2 is shown in Figure 3.2. In this case, the two lines showing the expected payoffs intersect at $c / (a - b)$, and they satisfy:

(i) $U(S_1) < U(S_2)$ if $n / N < c / (a - b)$,

(ii) $U(S_1) > U(S_2)$ if $n / N > c / (a - b)$.
$$\tag{3.4}$$

The collective payoff is maximum at *n/N=1*, when all agents choose S_1. However, when the proportion of agents joining the network is less than the value at the intersection $c / (a - b)$, it begins to be rational for an agent to choose S_2. When this condition holds, no agent will join the network, and they encounter the same social dilemma problem.

In Case 2, we have two stable solutions, an all-S_1 choice and an all-S_2 choice. The former situation enjoys the highest externality and is better for all agents. When there are multiple solutions, one for each extremity, the problem is to obtain a collaborative choice.

Since the two payoff functions have the same slope, there is no ambiguity about which solution is superior. If many agents choose S_1, no agent is motivated to choose the inferior S_2 unless enough others do so, which switches the intersection of the two payoff functions. Therefore, the ratio at the intersection becomes a *crucial value* for the selection of the efficient outcome. It is enough merely to get agents to make the right choice at the beginning. If the ratio of agents who choose S_1 is greater than the critical value, $c/(a-b) \equiv \theta$ at the intersection, all agents may self-enforce to choose S_1. Therefore, the initial ratio (*threshold*) is vital and if it exceeds this threshold, it can induce all other agents to shift to a superior choice without any central authority.

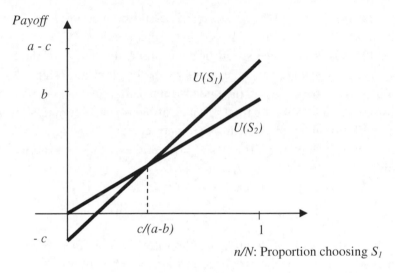

Figure 3.2 The vertical coordinate represents the payoff functions $U(S_1)$ and $U(S_2)$. These functions indicate payoffs to an agent choosing S_1 or S_2 when the proportion of agents who choose S_1 is n/N

Example 3.2 <*A competitive route selection problem* (1)> Example 3.1 illustrates the situation in which the increased effort by some agents leads the remaining agents to follow suit. On the other hand, there are opposite situations where agents may receive a high payoff if they select the distinct strategy as the majority does.

We now reformulate the competitive route selection problem discussed in Chapter 1. For a collection of N agents, there are two choices, either to use a private car (S_1 or Route A in Figure 1.1) or a public train (S_2 or Route B) to commute to the same destination.

S_1: uses a private car,

S_2 : uses the train.   (3.5)

If more agents use private cars to commute, congestion develops and the required time to commute increases in proportion to the number of agents who use cars. However, even if a large number of agents choose the train, the required time for them to commute is constant, as illustrated in Figure 1.1.

The payoff for each strategy S_i, $i=1,2$, could be measured in terms of its inverse travel time $1/T(S_i)$. We have the relation $1/T(S_1)=V(S_1)/L$, where $V(S_1)$ is the average speed of a car and L the length of the route. We can approximate the average speed by the linear relationship: $V(S_1) = V_{max}(1- n/N)$, where V_{max} is the speed limit, n is the number of agents who use cars, and N is the total number of agents who commute. Then, the payoffs to an agent for using a private car or for using a train, the inverse of traveling time (benefit) minus time (cost), are defined as follows:

$$U(S_1) = a(1 - n/N),$$

$$U(S_2) = b.$$ (3.6)

In this case, the payoff to an agent choosing S_1 is defined as a linearly decreasing function of the proportion of agents who choose $S_1(n/N)$, as shown in Figure 3.3. On the other hand, the payoff to an agent who chooses S_2 is constant, regardless of the choices of the others. User equilibrium based on individual optimality is reached at the intersection, which is achieved at $n/N=a/(a+b)$. However, the collective maximum (system optimal) is achieved at $n/N=a/2(a+b)$, which is half of the value at the user equilibrium.

In this situation, the choice of S_1 benefits those who make the opposite choice, S_2, and the choice of S_2 benefits those who choose S_1. Each agent non-cooperatively seeks to maximize her own payoff, and a Nash equilibrium (user equilibrium) is achieved when each agent chooses the route that is the best for all agents. Specifically, a Nash equilibrium is achieved when no agent may improve her utility through unilateral action. Therefore, a Nash equilibrium is achieved at the intersection, which is given at $n/N = a/(a + b)$.

However, this Nash equilibrium at the intersection is not at collective maximum. Any agent choosing S_1 or S_2 gains if some agents who previously chose S_1 instead choose S_2. Since the slope of the payoff function of S_1 is shaper than that of the payoff function of S_2, if fewer agents than the ratio at the intersection choose S_1, then the agents who eventually choose S_2 will increase more than the agents who switch from S_1 to S_2 decreases.

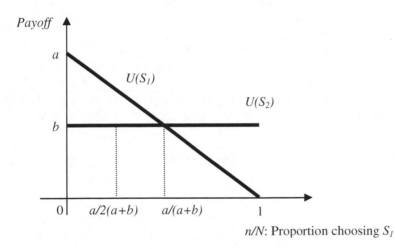

Figure 3.3 The functions $U(S_1)$ and $U(S_2)$ indicate the payoffs to agents choosing S_1 or S_2 as a function of the proportion of agents choosing S_1, i.e., n/N

Example 3.3 <*A competitive route selection problem* (2)> We consider another route selection problem with a different payoff function. The payoffs to an agent choosing from S_1 or S_2 are given

$$U(S_1) = a(1 - n/N),$$

$$U(S_2) = b(n/N). \tag{3.7}$$

The payoff for choosing S_1 is given as a linearly decreasing function of the proportion of agents choosing S_1, which is illustrated in Figure 3.4. We notice a difference between the two payoff schemes, in that only one curve slopes up to the right in Figure 3.3, whereas two curves having slopes of opposite sign appear in Figure 3.4. In Section 3.4, we will show that the collective efficiency is achieved at $n/N=0.5$.

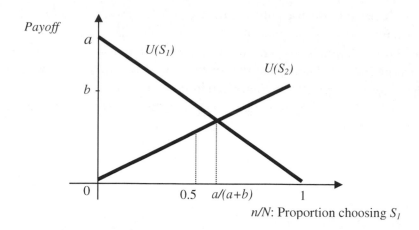

Figure 3.4 The vertical coordinate represents the payoff functions $U(S_1)$ and $U(S_2)$. These functions indicate payoffs to an agent choosing S_1 or S_2 when the proportion of agents who choose S_1 is n/N

Example 3.4 <*A market entry problem*> Market entry games are often used to understand how competitive firms implicitly coordinate their self-interested market entry decisions. Market entry games are modeled to simulate a situation in which a newly emergent market opportunity may be fruitfully exploited by no more than a fixed number of firms.

When too many entrants wish to exploit a new market opportunity, a problem arises regarding how many entries should be coordinated. Without coordination, too many firms may decide to enter and consequently will result in a much worse situation. Conversely, when they are fully aware of the consequences of excessive entry, firms may be reluctant to enter, or no firm may try to exploit the market in the first place.

We formulate a market game with a collection of N agents. Some integer N_c ($1 < N_c < N$), representing the capacity of the market, is publicly known. Each agent i must decide independently whether to enter the market (S_1) or stay out of it (S_2). The payoff for each strategy is given as

$$U(x) = \begin{cases} v + r(N_c - n) & \text{if decides to enter } (S_1) \\ v & \text{if decides to stay out } (S_2) \end{cases} \qquad (3.8)$$

where $x = (x_1, x_2,.., x_n)$ is the vector of all agents' decisions, x_i, $x_i \in \{S_1, S_2\}$, is a decision of agent i, n is the number of entrants ($0 \leq n \leq N$), and v and r are positive constants (Duffy and Hopkins, 2002).

Note the similarity between the route choice in Example 3.2 and the market entry problem if we compare the payoff schemes in Figure 3.3 and Figure 3.5, in which one payoff function slopes up to the right and the other is constant. We have a stable Nash equilibrium at the intersection of the two payoff functions. If more than N_c agents choose S_1, then the choice of S_2 will be better, and agents will switch from S_1 to S_2 until the two functions are equivalent in value. On the other hand, if fewer agents choose S_1, then the choice of S_1 will be the more attractive choice, and agents will switch from S_2 to S_1 until the advantage of the payoff disappears.

Therefore, a Nash equilibrium is reached at the intersection at $n/N = N_c/N$. However, this equilibrium is not at collective maximum. The collective maximum is achieved at $N_c/2N$, which is a half of the value of a Nash equilibrium.

Market entry problems typically admit a large number of Nash equilibria (Ochs, 1998). Given this multiplicity of equilibrium outcomes, a question arises as to which type of equilibrium agents are likely to coordinate upon. In addition, there is no support for convergence to equilibrium on either the collective or individual level.

If collective efficiency does not occur at the intersection and it is achieved by lowering the frequency of entry, there is a payoff difference between choice S_1 and choice S_2. Since the collective occurs to the left of the intersection, agents who choose S_2 gain less than those who choose S_1. This is very different from the Nash equilibrium at the intersection, at which all agents receive the same payoff. This raises another problem of equity.

Some compensation may be necessary, or agents may need to take turns, in order to solve this problem. If an inefficient S_2 choice has become established, no one will choose S_2 unless she expects others to do so. There are many situations in which no one is willing to be the first to switch and everyone waits for the others to switch. Therefore, they become trapped at an inefficient Nash equilibrium at the intersection.

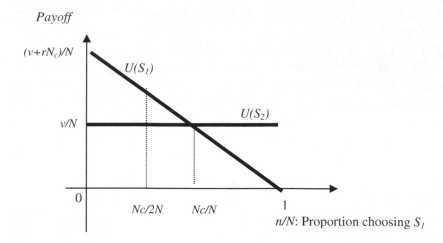

Figure 3.5   The function $U(S_1)$ shows the payoff to an agent who chooses S_1, and the function $U(S_2)$ shows the payoffs to an agent who chooses S_2 when the proportion of agents choosing S_1 is n/N

3.3 Decomposition to Pair-wise Interactions

In the previous section, we addressed some examples of binary collective decision problems with externalities. There is extensive literature and many theoretical results on two-person games, however, literature and theoretical results on multi-person games remains sparse. In general, multi-person games become analytically difficult to treat if the number of agents becomes large. However, multi-person games illustrated in the previous section can be decomposed into two-person games by treating them as the interaction between an individual and the collective. By decomposition into 2x2 games, we can treat multi-person games from a single agent's viewpoint (Colman, 1999).

Let us consider the network formation game with the payoff functions described by (3.2). We assume that the agents interact with each other with the payoff matrix shown in Table 3.1. The expected payoffs to an agent choosing from S_1 or S_2 are given as

$$U(S_1) = (a - c)(n / N) - c(1 - n / N) = ap - c ,$$

$$U(S_2) = bp .$$
$$\tag{3.9}$$

Therefore, the payoffs for choosing S_1 or S_2 become the same as those given in (3.2). As we showed in Chapter 2, the linear transformations of the payoff matrix do not affect the Nash equilibrium. By subtracting b from a-c, subtracting 0 from $-c$, and then dividing all payoffs by $\theta = c/(a-b)$, we obtain the payoff matrix in Table 3.1, which is strategically equivalent to the payoff matrix in Table 3.2.

Similarly the route selection problem in Example 3.3, in which an agent's payoff functions are given in (3.3), can be decomposed into the payoff matrix of Table 3.3. By dividing all payoffs by $\theta = a/(a+b)$, we obtain the payoff matrix in Table 3.3, which is also strategically equivalent to the payoff matrix in Table 3.4.

Note the similarity between the competitive route choice in Example 3.2 and the market entry problem, in which one payoff slopes up to the right and the other is constant. The market entry problem formulated as a multi-person game can be also decomposed into a two-person game, in which each agent has the payoff matrix in Table 3.5.

Table 3.1 Decomposition of the payoff function in Figure 3.2 into a 2x2 game

Own choice \ Collective choices	S_1 (p)		S_2 (1-p)	
S_1		$a - c$		b
	$a - c$		$- c$	
S_2		$- c$		0
	b		0	

Table 3.2 Transformed payoff matrix $(\theta = c/(a-b))$

Own choice \ Collective choice	S_1 (p)		S_2 (1-p)	
S_1		$1-\theta$		0
	$1-\theta$		0	
S_2		0		θ
	0		θ	

Table 3.3 Decomposition of the payoff function in Figure 3.5 into a 2x2 game

Own choice \ Collective choice	S_1 (p)		S_2 (1-p)	
S_1	0	0	0	b
S_2	b	a	0	0

Table 3.4 Transformed matrix in Table 3.2 ($\theta = a/(a+b)$)

Own choice \ Collective choice	S_1 (p)		S_2 (1-p)	
S_1	0	0	θ	$1-\theta$
S_2	$1-\theta$	θ	0	0

Table 3.5 The decomposed payoff matrix of a market entry game

Own choice \ Collective choice	S_1		S_2	
S_1	0	0	$v/(N-N_c)$	v/N
S_2	v/N	$v/(N-N_c)$	v/N	v/N

3.4 Compound Social Games

In the previous section, we observed that multi-person games involving social interaction by many agents could be decomposed into two-person games by treating them as the interaction between an individual and the collective. We can also examine this property in the opposite sense. The payoff function to each agent in social games is defined by the composition of the underlying 2x2 games. We define multi-person games having this property as *compound social games*.

The theory of compound games was first suggested by Colman (1999). Compound games apply to multi-person games in which the underlying two-person games are symmetric in the sense of being the same from every agent's viewpoint. Furthermore, the payoff resulting from one of the two choices is a linear function of the number of the other agents who choose one of the choices.

In compound games, it does not make any difference whether each agent interacts with all the others or whether each encounters a randomly chosen opponent. Each agent's payoff depends the agent's choice and all others' choices. In this case, each agent's payoff depends her choice and the strategy distribution of the population.

Suppose that agents repeatedly play the underlying game with the payoff matrix in Table 3.6. When the proportion of agents choosing S_1 is $p\varepsilon$ [0, 1], the expected payoffs of an agent who adopts either S_1 (e_1 with the mixed strategy representation) or S_2 (e_2) are

$$U(e_1, p) = (a-b)p + b ,$$

$$U(e_2, p) = (c-d)p + d .\tag{3.10}$$

Therefore, the payoff functions of an agent are a linear function of the proportion of agents p who choose S_1.

We now define the following *indifference function*:

$$I(p) = U(e_1, p) - U(e_2, p)$$

$$= (a+d-b-c)p + b-d\tag{3.11}$$

Table 3.6 Payoff matrix of a decomposed social game

Choice of other agents / Own choice	S_1 (p)	S_2 ($1-p$)
S_1	a	b
S_2	c	d

This function is equal to the expected payoff of both strategies at the strategy distribution $p=(p, 1-p)$ of the population. The derivative of this indifference function, $L=a+d-b-c$, measures the marginal change in each strategy's relative payoff when the number of agents choosing the same strategy increases. That is, this derivative measures the degree to which acting in concert benefits the agents when aggregate behavior of the population is $p=(p,1-p)$.

Compound social games are classified into the following types depending on the payoff values, a, b, c and d :

(i) Compound dilemma games: $(a > c, b > d$, or $a < c, b < d)$,

(ii) Compound coordination games: $(L > 0$: $a > c, d > b)$,

(iii) Compound dispersion games: $(L < 0$: $c > a, b > d)$,

(iv) Compound Hawk-Dove games: $(L < 0$: $a=(v-c)/2, b=v, c=0, d=v/2)$.

(1) **Compound Dilemma Games**: $(c > a > d > b)$. The *N-person Prisoners' Dilemma (NPD) game* is a multi-person decision-making involving the clash of individual and collective interests. The NPD is modeled with the following structure:

(i) Each agent faces a binary choice between two strategies: S_1 (Cooperate) and S_2 (Defect).

(ii) The strategy S_2 is dominant for each agent, that is, each agent obtains a better payoff by choosing S_2 than S_1, no matter how many of the other agents choose S_1.

(iii) The outcome if all agents choose their inferior strategy S_1 is preferable, from every agent's point of view, to the outcome if everyone chooses S_2. Since the dominant strategy S_2 is best choice for an individual, if all agents choose S_2, they collectively result in an inefficient Nash equilibrium.

The NPD is formulated as a compound dilemma game with the payoff functions shown in (3.2), which is depicted in Figure 3.6. The vertical axis represents an agent's expected payoffs, and the horizontal axis represents the proportion of agents in the population who choose S_1. In this figure, the filled dot, an all-S_2 choice at the left-extremity, indicates a Nash equilibrium, and the open dot, an all-S_1 choice at the right-extremity indicates collective efficiency. It is obvious that the right-extremity enjoys the highest externalities and is the best for all agents. If all agents seek their individual rationality, they choose S_2 and receive b. On the other hand, if all agents cooperate in choosing S_1, they receive a $(a > b)$.

However, if one agent defects by choosing S_2, and all other agents cooperate, then the defecting agent will receive c $(c > a)$. In particular, the outcome if all agents choose the inferior strategy S_1 is preferable, from every agent's point of view, to the outcome if everyone chooses S_2. However, the dominant strategy S_2 is the best choice for an individual. Therefore, no agent will be motivated to deviate unilaterally from choosing S_2.

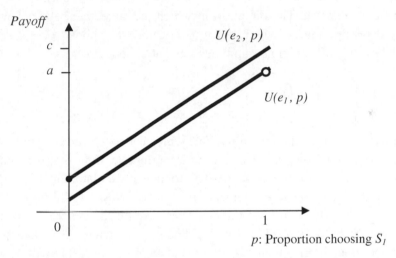

Figure 3.6 The functions $U(e_1,p)$ and $U(e_2,p)$ indicate payoffs to an agent choosing $S_1(e_1)$ or $S_2(e_2)$ as functions of the proportion of agents choosing S_1

(2) *Compound Coordination Games*: ($a > c$, $d > b$) There are many situations in which it is better to agree than to be against everyone else. On the other hand, it is better to be against everyone if no one else agrees. The payoff functions of the compound coordination game are shown in Figure 3.7. The vertical axis represents an agent's expected payoffs, and the horizontal axis represents the proportion of agents in the population who choose S_1. The payoff to an agent choosing S_1 and the total payoff to an agent choosing S_2 at their end-points are found by setting $p=1$ and $p=0$.

Compound coordination games are unlike compound dilemma games, in so far as the payoff function $U(e_2, p)$ does not dominate the function $U(e_1, p)$ across the entire region of p. As shown in Figure 3.7, we have a different case with two stable Nash equilibria at the end points on the left and right, and one unstable Nash equilibrium at the intersection point.

If only a few agents choose S_1, they will switch to S_2 if they are rational, and if most agents choose S_1, the few agents who choose S_2 will switch to S_1. Then, the tendency is always away from the intersection point. If everyone chooses S_1 or if everyone chooses S_2 then no one is motivated to switch. The direction in which the collective behavior will move depends on the initial proportion of agents who choose S_1.

The two payoff functions can be equated at the point

$$ap + b(1 - p) = cp + d(1 - p), \tag{3.12}$$

and such p is obtained as

$$p=(d-b)/(a + d - b - c) \equiv \theta. \tag{3.13}$$

In particular, the outcome in which agents choosing S_1 and S_2 split into ratios of θ and $1 - \theta$, respectively, it is preferable from every agent's point of view and none is motivated to deviate unilaterally from the status quo. Therefore, the intersection is also a Nash equilibrium. The two filled dots in Figure 3.7 indicate Nash equilibria and the open dot indicates both Nash equilibria and collective efficiency. We have two stable Nash equilibria, an all-S_1 choice and an all-S_2 choice, however, the right-extremity enjoys the highest externality and is better for all agents.

The problem then is how to achieve the most efficient Nash equilibrium. Since both curves have the same direction, there is no ambiguity about which equilibrium is superior. In this case with multiple equilibria, the problem is to obtain a concerted choice. If many agents choose S_2, then no agent is motivated to choose the inferior choice S_2 unless enough other agents switch beyond the intersection of the two payoff functions. Therefore, the ratio at the intersection provides a crucial *mass parameter (threshold)* for the selection of collective efficiency. It is enough merely to get agents to make the right choice at the beginning. If the ratio of agents who choose the superior strategy (S_1)

at the beginning is greater than the value at the intersection, all agents eventually self-enforce to choose S_1. Therefore, this threshold is viable and if the initial ratio of choosing S_1 exceeds this value, it can induce other agents to shift to a superior choice.

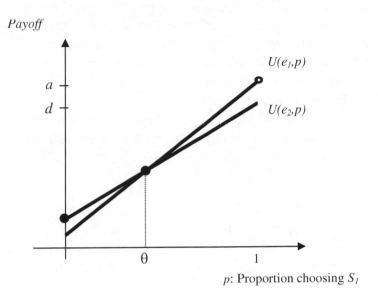

Figure 3.7 The functions $U(e_1 p)$ and $U(e_2 p)$ indicate payoffs to an agent choosing $S_1 (e_1)$ or $S_2 (e_2)$ as a function of p, the proportion of agents who choose $S_1 (e_1)$

(3) *Compound Dispersion Games*: $(c > a, b > d)$ A more frequently studied class of games is coordination games, in which agents gain high payoffs when they choose the same action. A complementary class that has received relatively little attention is games in which agents gain payoffs only when they are dispersed by choosing distinct actions. These games arc sometimes called *dispersion games*. In Chapter 2, we focused on the two-agent case, and the 2x2 dispersion games are equivalently transformed into coordination games by renaming the strategies.

However, with an arbitrary number of agents, the coordination and dispersion games diverge. While the generalization of two-person coordination games to multi-person games is quite straightforward, that of dispersion games is more complex.

The payoff functions of the compound dispersion game are depicted in Figure 3.8. The compound coordination game with the payoff functions in Figure 3.7 have two equilibria of pure strategies ($p=0$ and $p=1$) and one mixed situation, in which both strategies are used at the ratios of θ and $1\text{-}\theta$. Under this mixed population, the payoffs of all agents are equal, and under the two equilibria of pure strategies in which all agents coordinate on the same strategy. On the other hand, the compound dispersion game, in which the two functions have opposite slopes, has a unique equilibrium at the intersection of the two payoff functions, indicated by the filled dot in Figure 3.8.

The payoff at the Nash equilibrium is the same whether agents choose S_1 or S_2. The two payoff functions can be equated at the intersection

$$ap + b(1 \text{ - } p) = cp + d(1 \text{ - } p), \tag{3.14}$$

and p is obtained as

$$p = (b - d)/(b + c - a - d) \equiv \theta. \tag{3.15}$$

If the game is repeated, there will be a tendency towards a stable equilibrium with θN agents choosing S_1 and the remaining $(1 - \theta) N$ agents choosing S_2. However, such a mixed equilibrium situation is not to be efficient. We discuss this issue in Section 3.5.

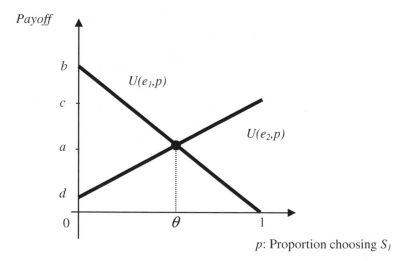

Figure 3.8 The functions $U(e_1 p)$ and $U(e\ p)$ indicate payoffs to an agent choosing $S_1 (e_1)$ or $S_2 (e_2)$ as a function of p, the proportion of agents who choose S_1

(4) ***Compound Hawk-Dove Games***: $(a=(v-c)/2, b=v, c=0, d=v/2)$. We consider a multi-person version of Hawk-Dove games. A natural way is to construct compound Hawk-Dove games in which many agents engage in a series of two-person contests with one another according to the payoff structure in Table 2.2. This is a special case of compound dispersion games with the payoff matrix in Table 3.6, where $a=(v-c)/2$, $b=v$, $c=0$, and $d=v/2$.

The compound Hawk-Dove game has a unique symmetric Nash equilibrium in the mixed population, the proportion of agents who adopt S_1('Hawk') is $\theta = v/c$ and that of agents who adopt S_2('Dove') is $1-\theta = 1-v/c$. At the Nash equilibrium of the mixed population, the expected payoff per agent is $(v/2)\{1-(v/c)\}$. However, if all agents choose S_2 ('Dove'), then each agent receives $v/2$.

Multi-person Hawk-Dove games are unlike the NPD in so far as the function of S_2 does not dominate the function of S_1 across its entire region of p, as shown in Figure 3.9. The payoff at the Nash equilibrium is the same whether the individual agent chooses S_1 or S_2. The two payoff functions are equated at the intersection

$$(v-c)p/2 + v(1-p) = v(1-p)/2, \tag{3.16}$$

and such p is obtained as

$$p = v/c \equiv \theta \tag{3.17}$$

If the game is repeated, there will be a tendency towards a stable equilibrium with $(1-\theta)N$ agents choosing S_1 and θN agents choosing S_2. However, like the compound dispersion games, this mixed Nash equilibrium is not efficient, because all agents would be better off if they chose S_2, but this outcome is not a Nash equilibrium.

As shown in Figure 3.9, we have a unique stable Nash equilibrium at the intersection (the filled dot). If more agents than the ratio at the intersection choose S_1, S_2 will be the better choice and some agents will switch from S_1 to S_2 until the two choices become equivalent. On the other hand, if fewer agents choose S_1, the choice of S_1 will be more attractive and some agents will switch from S_2 to S_1 until the payoff advantage disappears. However, this Nash equilibrium is not at a collective maximum. Any agent who chooses S_1 or S_2 gains if some agents choosing S_2 shift and choose S_1, because both payoff functions are rising to the left.

The collective maximum can occur at the left-extremity (the open dot), where $p=0$ and all agents behave as "Doves".

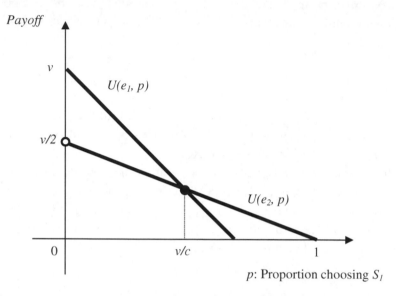

Figure 3.9 The function $U(e_1,p)$ shows the payoff to an agent who acts as a "Hawk (e_1)", and the function $U(e_2,p)$ shows the payoffs to an agent who acts as a "Dove (e_2)"

3.5 Nash Equilibrium and Collective Efficiency

A natural way to study social interactions involving many agents is to model compound social games, in which all agents engage one another in a series of two-person games according to the payoff matrix in Table 3.6. In this section, we characterize Nash equilibrium and collective efficiency in compound social games.

Definition 3.1   *There is a population of agents $G = \{i: 1 \le i \le N\}$, and each agent individually faces the binary choice problem with the two strategies S_1 and S_2. We denote the proportions of agents who choose S_1 by p and who choose S_2 by 1-p. The vector $\mathbf{p} = (p, 1- p)$ defines the strategy distribution of population $\mathbf{G}$.*

Definition 3.2 *An equilibrium situation in which if no agent can improve her payoff by unilaterally changing her strategy is defined as a Nash equilibrium. We denote the payoff of agent i as* $U(x_i, x(i))$ *when she chooses* $x_i \in \{S_1, S_2\}$ *and the remainder of the other agents choose* $x(i) = (x_1, x_2, .., x_{i-1}, x_{i+1} .., x_n)$. *The set of strategies* $(x_i^*, x^*(i))$ *is defined as a Nash equilibrium when it satisfies*

$$U(x_i^*, x^*(i)) \geq U(x_i, x^*(i)), \quad \forall x_i \in \{S_1, S_2\}, \quad \forall i \in G \qquad (3.18)$$

Definition 3.3 *The optimal situation in which no agent can improve her payoff without lowering the payoff of any other agent is defined as collective efficient (Pareto-efficient).*

We define the situation in which the summation of the payoffs of the population (or the average payoff per agent) is maximized as *collective efficiency* (or collective maximum).

Pareto efficiency (or Pareto optimality) is a central concept in game theory with broad applications in economics, engineering and the social sciences. A change that can make at least one individual better off without making any other individual worse off is called a *Pareto improvement*. An allocation of resources is Pareto efficient when no further Pareto improvements can be made. The term is named after Vilfredo Pareto, an Italian economist who used the concept in his studies of economic efficiency. If an allocation is not Pareto efficient, then it is the case that some individual can be made better off without anyone being made worse off. It is commonly accepted that such inefficient outcomes are to be avoided, and therefore, the Pareto efficient is an important criterion for evaluating social systems.

There is often more than one Pareto efficient outcome, and not every Pareto efficient outcome is regarded as *desirable*. In general, there are many Pareto efficient allocations, some of which are very bad from the point of view of *equity*, and there is no connection between Pareto efficiency and equity. In particular, a Pareto efficient outcome may be very inequitable. For example, consider a dictatorship run solely for the benefit of one person. This will, in general, be Pareto optimal because it will be impossible to raise the welfare of anyone except the dictator without reducing the welfare of the dictator. Nevertheless, most people (except the dictator) would not see this as a desirable outcome.

We obtain Nash equilibria and an efficient equilibrium outcome (collective efficiency) of compound social games with the underlying payoff matrix in Table 3.6.

Lemma 3.1 *The strategy distribution* $p^* = (p^*, 1 - p^*)$ *is a Nash equilibrium if the expected payoffs of an agent choosing* $S_1(e_1)$ *or* $S_2(e_2)$ *satisfy the following conditions:*
(i) an agent who chooses $S_1(e_1)$,

$$U(e_1, p^*) > U(e_2, p^*).$$ (3.19)

(ii) an agent who chooses $S_2(e_2)$,

$$U(e_2, p^*) > U(e_1, p^*).$$ (3.20)

Collective efficiency (Pareto efficiency) is achieved at the strategy distribution at which the average payoff per agent is maximized. We denote the average payoff per agent by $E(p)$ when the strategy distribution is $p=(p,1-p)$. Since the proportion of agents who choose S_1 is p and that of agents who choose S_2 is $1-p$, the average payoff per agent is

$$E(p) = pU(e_1, p) + (1 - p)U(e_2, p)$$
$$= (a + d - b - c)p^2 + (b + c - 2d)p + d .$$ (3.21)

In the context of the two-person symmetric game with the payoff matrix in Table 3.6, a pair of mixed strategy *(p, p)* constitutes a Nash equilibrium. A Nash equilibrium of the two-person game is defined in terms of how the payoff is affected when she switches to the other strategy when the other agent sticks to the current mixed strategy *p*.

Here, we consider the payoff to any other mixed strategy *p* and compare it with the payoff to some other strategy distribution *q* if it is switched to *q*. Since collective efficiency is defined in terms of such payoff comparisons, accordingly the strategy population *p* is defined as collective efficient if there is no such the strategy distribution *q*.

We now obtain Nash equilibria and collective efficiency for each type of compound social games with the payoff schemes depicted in Figures 3.6 to 3.9.

(1) **Compound Dilemma Games**: A compound social dilemma game has the following strategy distributions as a unique Nash equilibrium.

$$p = (0, 1) \tag{3.22}$$

The expected payoffs to an agent choosing $S_1(e_1)$ or $S_2(e_2)$ are

$$U(e_1, p) = b, \quad U(e_2, p) = d \tag{3.23}$$

Since the payoff parameters of the underlying game in Table 3.6 satisfy $d > b$, we have

$$U(e_2, p) > U(e_1, p). \tag{3.24}$$

The payoff functions of a compound dilemma game are depicted in Figure 3.6, and the values of $U(e_1, p)$ and $U(e_2, p)$ at their end-points are found by setting $p=0$ and $p=1$, respectively. Thus, if none of the other agents choose S_1, that is, if $p=0$, then the payoff to a solitary agent who chooses S_1 is b, and the payoff to an agent who chooses S_2 is d. If all of the other agents choose S_1, then the agent who chooses S_1 receives a, and a solitary agent who chooses S_2 receives c. The payoff c can be interpreted as the temptation to be the sole agent who chooses S_2. The payoff a is the reward for joint S_1 choices, and d is the punishment for joint S_2 choices. The payoff b is the payoff for being the sole agent who chooses S_1.

There remains one definitional question. How do agents behave when an agent is better off when the number of agents who choose the inferior cooperative strategy S_1 is greater. Let us consider the case in which the payoff parameters in Table 3.6 satisfy the following conditions: $c > a > d > b$ and $b + c > a + d$. For consider a collection of N agents, each of which faces a binary decision problem with the following two strategies:

  S_1: vaccinated against the disease (cooperate)
  S_2: unvaccinated (defect)

The payoffs of both strategies and also the average payoff of the population are plotted against the ratio of the agents choosing $S_1(e_1)$. Each agent, either she chooses $S_1(e_1)$ or $S_2(e_2)$, she is better off, the more there are among the others who choose inferior strategy S_1. However, as shown in Figure 3.10, the $U(e_2, p)$ curve is above the $U(e_1, p)$ curve, and each agent herself prefers to choose S_2. Figure 3.10 also shows that the advantage of the choice of S_2 *(defector)* increases with the choice of S_1

(*cooperator*). The dotted line shows the average payoff corresponding to the ratio of agents choosing S_1. At the left of the scale, every agent is choosing S_2, and the average coincides with the $U(e_2, p)$ curve. On the right hand side, every agent is choosing S_1, and the average coincides with the $U(e_1, p)$ curve.

The average payoff function takes its maximum at the middle, and the things are better off if the agents distribute themselves between the two groups, *cooperators* and *defectors*, though it is individually better to be unvaccinated (S_2). The average payoff per agent in (3.21) is maximized at

$$p^* = (2d - b - c)/2(a + d - b - c) \qquad (3.25)$$

As shown in this example, the entire population gains a higher payoff if they allow some defectors, rather than having all agents cooperate.

In Example 3.1, if the condition $b > a - c$ holds for each agent's payoff function in (3.2), then the network formation problem becomes an NPD game. In contrast, if the condition $b > 2a - c$ holds, then collective efficiency is achieved for a mixed population of cooperators and

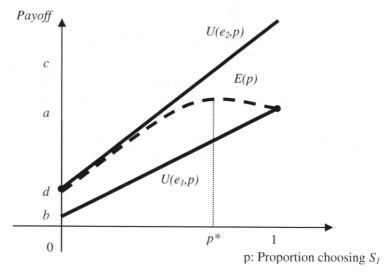

Figure 3.10 The functions $U(e_1,p)$ and $U(e_2,p)$ indicate payoffs to an agent choosing $S_1(e_1)$ or $S_2(e_2)$ as a function of p, the ratio of agents who choose S_1, as indicated by the dotted line .*Collective efficiency is achieved at* $p=p^*$

defectors. With the payoff scheme in Figure 3.6, collective efficiency ought to occur only when all agents choose S_1. In this case, all agents receive the same payoff.

On the other hand, in the case in which the payoff scheme is given in Figure 3.10, collective efficiency is achieved at $p=p^*$ with the coexistence of cooperators and defectors. In this mixed population case, however, some agents (defectors) gain more than others (cooperators). The problem is then how to maximize collective efficiency in such an inequitable situation. It may become hard to devise a scheme to split agents into two groups, in which agents in one group receive less than those in the other group. We will discuss this issue in Chapters 9 and 10.

(2) *Compound Coordination Games*: In compound coordination games with the payoff functions depicted in Figure 3.7, there are two stable Nash equilibria and one unstable Nash equilibrium as follows:

(i) $p = (1, 0)$,

(ii) $p = (0, 1)$,   (3.26)

(iii) $p = (\theta, 1-\theta)$.

The above strategy distributions correspond to the two corner points, the open dots and the filled dot and the intersection in Figure 3.7.

(i) $p = (1, 0)$: Since $U(e_1, p) = a$, $U(e_2, p) = d$, and $a > b$, the expected payoffs to an agent choosing S_1 or S_2 satisfy the inequality:

$$U(e_1, p) > U(e_2, p).$$ (3.27)

(ii) $p = (0, 1)$: Since $U(e_2, p) = d$, $U(e_1, p) = b$, and $d > c$, we have

$$U(e_2, p) > U(e_1, p).$$ (3.28)

(iii) $p = (\theta, 1-\theta)$: A Nash equilibrium is also obtained at the intersection of the two payoff functions. The expected payoffs of an agent who chooses S_1 or S_2 satisfy

$$U(e_1, p) = U(e_2, p).$$ (3.29)

To understand why this is so, consider first the point to the left of the intersection of the graph in Figure 3.7. This region represents the choice facing an agent when relatively few of the agents choose S_1 (p is small). Each agent would regret having chosen S_2 and would switch to S_1 if the games are repeated, because the $U(e_1, p)$ function is above the $U(e_2, p)$ function in this region. Thus, agents who choose S_2 will tend to change into agents who choose S_1 and the outcome will move to the right. To the right of the intersection, exactly the reverse holds. That is, agents who choose S_1 will switch to S_2 and the outcome will move to the left as p decreases.

In summary, if everyone chooses S_1 or S_2, then no one is motivated to switch. If only a few choose S_1, that is, when p is small, they will all switch to S_2 if they are rational, and if most agents choose S_1, the agents who choose S_2 will switch to S_1. The tendency is always away from the intersection point. Everyone is better off in the situation in which all agents choose S_1, compared to the situation in which all agents choose S_2. The direction in which a collective evolves depends on the initial proportion of agents who choose S_1, and an initial bias in either direction will tend to be self-reinforcing.

At the intersection, and only at the intersection, no agent will have cause for regret and none will be motivated to switch, because both strategies are equally good with regard to the indicated ratio of agents who choose S_1. Therefore, the intersection is a Nash equilibrium, and any deviation from it will tend to be self-correcting.

The average payoff per agent is

$$E(p) = pU(e_1, p) + (1 - p)U(e_2, p)$$
$$= (a + d - b - c)p^2 + (b + c - 2d)p + d \ . \qquad (3.30)$$

Therefore, the collective efficiency at which the average payoff per agent is maximized is at one of the two corner points:

$p=1$ (All agents choose S_1) if $a > d,$ $\qquad\qquad\qquad$ (3.31)

$p=0$ (All agents choose S_2) if $d > a.$ $\qquad\qquad\qquad$ (3.32)

(3) **Compound Dispersion Games**: In compound dispersion games with the payoff functions depicted in Figure 3.8, the payoff at the Nash equilibrium is the same whether the individual agent chooses S_1 or S_2. The two payoff functions can be equated at that point:

$$ap + b(1 - p) = cp + d(1 - p), \qquad\qquad\qquad (3.33)$$

and such p is obtained as

$$p = (b - d)/(b + c - a - d) \equiv \theta \tag{3.34}$$

This means that if the game is repeated, there will be a tendency toward a stable equilibrium with θN agents choosing S_1 and the remaining $(1 - \theta)N$ agents choosing S_2. More generally, it means that the agents will tend to evolve towards this mixed population. At the intersection, and only at the intersection, no agent will have cause for regret and none will be motivated to switch. Because the strategies are equally good with regard to the indicated ratio of agents who choose S_1. The intersection is therefore a unique Nash equilibrium, and any deviation from it will tend to be self-correcting.

However, this Nash equilibrium is not at collective maximum. Any agent who chooses S_1 or S_2 gains if some agents choosing S_2 shift and instead choose S_1. The collective maximum occurs to the left of the intersection. Since the slope of the payoff function S_1 is sharper than that of the payoff function of S_2, if fewer agents than the ratio at the intersection choose S_1, then the agents who choose S_1 will gain more than the agents who choose S_2 will lose. If the collective maximum does not occur at the intersection, there is a payoff difference between the choice of S_1 and the choice of S_2. For instance, if the collective maximum occurs to the left of the intersection, then the agents who choose S_2 gain less than those who choose S_1. This is a big difference from the Nash equilibrium at the intersection, at which all agents receive the same payoff.

Therefore, there is the conflict between efficiency and equity. Some compensation may be necessary or agents may need to take turns in order to solve this tradeoff problem. If some equilibrium is established, no one will change her strategy unless she expects others to do so. There are many situations in which no one is willing to be the first to switch, and every agent is waiting for the other agents to switch. Therefore, they easily become trapped at an inefficient Nash equilibrium.

The compound dispersion game has the following strategy distributions as a unique Nash equilibrium:

$$p = (\theta, 1 - \theta) \tag{3.35}$$

The expected payoffs of an agent choosing from $S_1 (e_1)$ or $S_2 (e_2)$ satisfy

$$U(e_1, p) = U(e_2, p) \tag{3.36}$$

Although the 2x2 dispersion game has three Nash equilibria, the compound social dispersion has a unique Nash equilibrium. For instance, the strategy distribution $p = (1, 0)$ is not a Nash equilibrium. The expected payoffs to an agent choosing from S_1 or S_2 satisfy

$$U(e_2, p) > U(e_1, p). \tag{3.37}$$

Since $U(e_1, p) = a$, $U(e_2, p) = c$, and $c > a$, the average payoff per agent is

$$E(p) = pU(e_1, p) + (1 - p)U(e_2, p)$$
$$= (a + d - b - c)p^2 + (b + c - 2d)p + d. \tag{3.38}$$

The collective efficiency at which the average payoff per agent is maximized is achieved at

$$p^* = (b + c - 2d)/2(b + c - a - d). \tag{3.39}$$

Therefore, if the following condition is not satisfied,

$$b = c \tag{3.40}$$

then collective efficiency is not achieved at a Nash equilibrium.

Social interaction between two agents having two strategies is also formulated as a symmetric 2x2 game with the payoff matrix in Table 3.6. Subtracting c from a ($\alpha = a - c$) and b from d ($\beta = d - b$), we obtain the payoff matrix in Table 2.2. With this transformation, we have a doubly symmetric 2x2 game. Nash equilibrium of compound social games will not be affected by this normalization. However, collective efficiency will be affected by this transformation.

(4) *Compound Hawk-Dove Games*: The expected payoffs to an agent choosing from S_1 or S_2 are

$$U(e_1, p) = vp/2,$$
$$U(e_2, p) = vp + (v - c)p/2, \tag{3.41}$$

and the two payoff functions can be equated at

$$p = 1 - v/c. \tag{3.42}$$

The average payoff per agent is

$$E(p) = pU(e_1, p) + (1 - p)U(e_2, p)$$

$$= -cp^2/2 + cp + (v - c)/2. \tag{3.43}$$

Therefore, collective efficiency is achieved at

$$p^* = 1. \tag{3.44}$$

However, the following issue remains: if the Hawk-Dove game is repeated, whether will there be a tendency toward collective efficiency, at which all agents choose S_2 (Dove) and avoid conflict? In this case, all agents receive the same payoff of $v/2$. We discuss this issue in Chapter 9.

3.6 Conflict Resolution between Collective Efficiency and Equity

A Nash equilibrium is defined as the equilibrium situation in which no agent has an incentive to change her strategy. Since each agent seeks to optimize her payoff, a Nash equilibrium is also the stable situation in which no agent improves her payoff by unilaterally changing her strategy. The payoffs of all agents should also be optimized simultaneously. On the other hand, collective efficiency is defined as the situation in which the average payoff per agent is maximized.

In the previous section, we observed that there is a conflict between a Nash equilibrium and collective efficiency in compound dispersion games. Compound dispersion games also have another qualitative difference from other compound social games. All agents come to choose the same strategy, resulting in the same payoff being received at the collective efficient outcome in dilemma games, coordination games and Hawk-Dove games. However, in dispersion games, agents must split into two groups, and the agents in one group receive a better payoff while the agents in the other group receive a lower payoff at the efficient outcome. Therefore, we also tackle the issue of inequity in dispersion games.

The equilibrium situation in which each agent uses the mixed Nash strategy seems to be fair in the sense that the payoffs for all agents choosing mixed strategies are the same. However, the payoffs of all agents in this mixed situation is less than that for the case in which all agents use pure strategies. We thus observe that the conditions of equilibrium and equity contradict with the condition of efficiency.

In general, coordination failure is attributed to certain features of payoff functions that induce competition among agents attempting to maximize their own payoff. We will show that coordination success or failure depends heavily on the structure of the payoff functions.

<Payoff Scheme I> Let us consider the following payoff functions of a social dispersion game. The payoff of an agent choosing $S_1(e_1)$ is given as a linearly decreasing function of p, the ratio of agents who choose S_1. The payoff when she chooses $S_2(e_2)$ is given as a linearly increasing function of p, as shown in Figure 3.4,

$$U(e_1, p) = a(1 - p),$$

$$U(e_2, p) = bp. \tag{3.45}$$

Each agent non-cooperatively seeks to maximize her payoff, and a Nash equilibrium is achieved when each agent chooses the strategy that is the best to her. Specifically, an agent-optimized Nash equilibrium is reached when no agent may improve her payoff through unilateral change. Such a Nash equilibrium is achieved at the intersection, at which the ratio of agents choosing S_1 is $p=a/(a+b)$. Collective efficiency, at which the summation of the payoffs of all agents is maximized, is obtained as follows. The average payoff per agent is

$$E(p, p) = pU(e_1, p) + (1 - p)U(e_2, p)$$

$$= (a + b)p(1 - p) \tag{3.46}$$

The above average payoff is maximized at $p=0.5$ and does not depend on the payoff parameters a and b. Therefore, under the payoff functions given in Figure 3.4, the Nash equilibrium and collective efficiency become the same if we have $a=b$. On the other hand, if $a \neq b$ they are different.

<Payoff Scheme II> We define the payoff function to an agent choosing from $S_1(e_1)$ or $S_2(e_2)$ as follows:

$$U(e_1, p) = 1 - p.$$

$$U(e_2, p) = 1 - \theta. \tag{3.47}$$

The above payoff functions are depicted in Figure 3.11, and they have the same payoff structure as the functions in Figure 3.5. The two payoff functions intersect at $p=\theta$, which is a Nash equilibrium (the filled dot).

The average payoff per agent is obtained as

$$E(p,p) = pU(e_1,p) + (1-p)U(e_2,p)$$
$$= -p^2 + p\theta + 1 - \theta \qquad (3.48)$$

Therefore, collective efficiency is achieved at $p=\theta/2$ (the open dot) which is half of the Nash equilibrium.

The dispersion games with the payoff functions in Figure 3.11 can be decomposed into a pair-wise 2x2 game with the payoff matrix in Table 3.7, which has two pure Nash equilibria at (S_1, S_2) and (S_2, S_1), and one mixed Nash equilibrium. A geometric interpretation of the Nash equilibria is shown in Figure 3.12.

If both agents choose S_1 with a probability of θ and S_2 with a probability of $1-\theta$, they realize a mixed Nash equilibrium. At the two pure Nash equilibria (S_1, S_2) and (S_2, S_1), they receive different payoffs, 1 and $1-\theta$, respectively. However, at a Nash equilibrium involving mixed strategies, they receive the same payoff $1-\theta$. Therefore, this mixed equilibrium situation seems fairer than the two asymmetric equilibria.

However, the payoff to each agent is less than those of the two asymmetric equilibria of pure strategies. The sum of the payoffs at one of the pure equilibria is $2+\theta$, and that of at the fair mixed equilibrium is $2(1-\theta)$.

Table 3.7 Decomposition into a 2x2 game

Collective choice / Own choice	S_1		S_2	
S_1		0		$1-\theta$
	0		1	
S_2		1		$1-\theta$
	$1-\theta$		$1-\theta$	

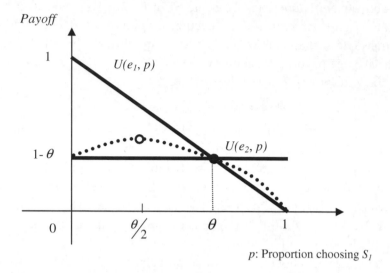

Figure 3.11 Payoff Scheme II: The function $U(S_1, p)$ shows the payoff to an agent choosing S_1, and the function $U(S_2, p)$ shows the payoff to an agent choosing S_2 when the proportion of agents who choose S_1 is p. Nash equilibrium is achieved at $p = \theta$ and collective efficiency is achieved at $p = \theta/2$

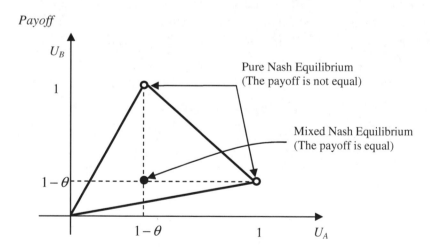

Figure 3.12 Geometric interpretation of the payoff matrix in Table 3.7. The filled dot represents a mixed Nash equilibrium and the empty dots represent pure Nash equilibria

We observe that the criterion for an efficient outcome contradicts that of equity. Consider two agents who face the 2x2 game with the payoff matrix in Table 3.7. If the first agent chooses S_1 and the second agent chooses S_2, and in the next turn, they change roles and the first agent chooses S_2 and the second agent chooses S_1, then they can sustain an equitable situation. However, this type of dynamic coordination by taking turns has not been studied within the framework of conventional game theory (Browning, 2004, Hanaki, 2005). We will discuss this issue in Chapter 8.

<Payoff Scheme III> We can modify the payoff functions in (3.45) if we assume that each agent can receive an extra payoff from the outside. Let us consider the following payoff functions:

$$U(e_1, p) = 1 - p + \theta p,$$

$$U(e_2, p) = 1 - \theta + \theta p. \tag{3.49}$$

A Nash equilibrium is achieved at the intersection in Figure 3.13 when the ratio of agents choosing S_1 is $p = \theta$, which is the same as Payoff Scheme II.

We now obtain collective efficiency, at which the average payoff per agent is maximized. Since the average payoff per agent is obtained as

$$E(p, p) = pU(e_1, p) + (1 - p)U(e_2, p)$$

$$= -p^2 + 2\theta p + 1 - \theta \tag{3.50}$$

collective efficiency is achieved at the Nash equilibrium $p = \theta$.

The equilibrium situation at which each agent uses a mixed strategy appears to be fair because the expected payoffs to all agents are the same. However, the sum of the payoffs of all agents under the mixed strategies is less than that in the case in which all agents use pure strategies. We thus observe that the combination of equilibrium and equity contradicts the combination of equilibrium and efficiency.

A Nash equilibrium (x, y) is symmetric if $x = y$, that is, if both agents use the same mixed or pure strategy. All three Nash equilibria of coordination games are symmetric. However, only the mixed equilibrium is symmetric for dispersion games, and the mixed Nash strategy is not efficient, except in a symmetric dispersion game.

We have observed that the criteria for a Nash equilibrium contradict the criteria for equity in asymmetric dispersion games. Collective efficiency of compound dispersion games will be affected by the normalization of the underlying payoff matrix. This property implies that by modifying asymmetric payoffs, the conflict between collective efficiency and equity is solved.

Table 3.8 Decomposition of the payoff functions in Figure 3.6 into a 2x2 game

Own choice \ Choice of other agents	S_1		S_2	
S_1	0	0	θ	$1-\theta$
S_2	$1-\theta$	θ	0	0

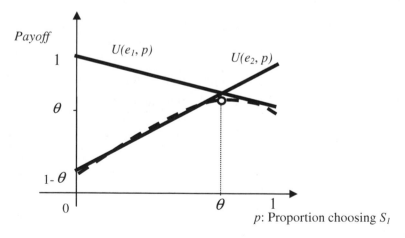

Figure 3.13 Payoff Scheme III: $U(S_1,p)$ and $U(S_2,p)$ show the payoffs to an agent choosing S_1 or S_2. Nash equilibrium and collective efficiency is achieved at the intersection (the open dot)

Chapter 4

Micro-Macro Dynamics

In examining collective systems, we draw heavily on deliberate individual decisions by applying rational procedures. In this chapter, we characterize the collective adaptive dynamics of heterogeneous agents, in which each agent adapts to every other agent. We obtain and analyze the micro-macro dynamics that characterizes the relation between an agent's micro-motivated behavior and the macroscopic behavior.

4.1 A Threshold Model for Dealing with Heterogeneity in Agents

We can observe many situations in which agents' microscopic behaviors, reflecting their micro-motives, combined with the behaviors of others produce unanticipated outcomes. These situations, in which an agent's decision depends on the decisions of other agents, usually do not permit any simple summation or extrapolation to the aggregates.

On the other hand, interacting agents sometimes produce coherent collective phenomena. Collective phenomena appear in the emergence of macro-structure from the bottom up and are driven by simple behavioral rules that outwardly appear quite different from the phenomena that they generate collectively (Gilbert and Troitzsch, 1999). Large-scale effects of interacting agents are called *emergent properties*. Emergent properties are often surprising because it can be hard to anticipate the full consequences of even simple forms of interactions. Therefore, we aim at discovering fundamental local or micro mechanisms that are sufficient to generate the macroscopic behavior of interest (Axelrod and Cohen, 2001).

Much literature on macroscopic behavior has contrasted the older notion that irrationality at the individual level is the key to explanation in generating unanticipated collective outcomes. Granovetter (1978) and Schelling (1978) are among the first to propose models that capture such a process that deviates from a rational choice model to describe an individual behavior. In their models, agents impinge on other agents and adapt to each other. The actions of each agent affects the actions of the other agents, and how well agents accomplish what they want to accomplish also depends on what other agents are doing. All of these models have common features in which an agent's behavior is influenced by other agents' behaviors and vice versa.

Heterogeneity turns up repeatedly as a crucial factor in explaining collective behavior. But the situation is not always as simple as saying that heterogeneity is desirable and homogeneity is not good. Then, the basic question is as follows. What is the right balance between heterogeneity and homogeneity? When heterogeneity is significant, we also need to investigate the gains from heterogeneity. However, the analysis of a collective of heterogeneous agents becomes difficult, and it is often intractable (Kirman and Zimmermann, 2001).

The approaches by Granovetter and Schelling are characterized as the threshold model, since their models use agent-specific *thresholds*. The threshold model is important for dealing with heterogeneity in agents. A threshold model is often used to explain collective phenomena in a society. For instance, a social network plays a fundamental role as a medium for the spread of information, ideas, and influence among its members. An idea or innovation that appears can either die out quickly or make significant inroads into a society. If we want to understand the extent to which such ideas are adopted, it is important to understand how the dynamics of adoption are likely to unfold within the underlying social network. The extent to which people are likely to be affected by the decisions of their friends and colleagues, or by the extent to which word-of-mouth effects will take hold.

Such social network diffusion processes have a long history of study using a threshold model in the following framework (Watts, 2002). In considering operational models for the spread of an idea or innovation through a social network, represented by a directed graph, we will speak of each individual node (agent) as being either *active* (an adopter of the innovation) or *inactive*. Then, we usually focus on the motivation, in which each agent's tendency to become active increases monotonically as more of her neighbors become active.

In the framework of a threshold model, an agent is influenced by her neighbor, which is represented by some weight. The dynamics of the process then proceed as follows. Each agent chooses a threshold θ uniformly at random from the interval $[0, 1]$, and this represents the weighted fraction of an agent's neighbors that must become active in order for that agent to become active. Given a random choice of thresholds, and an initial set of active agents, the diffusion process unfolds deterministically in discrete steps. In some step, agents that were active in the previous step remain active, and we activate any agent for which the total weight of her active neighbors reaches her threshold.

The threshold model represents the different latent tendencies of agents to adopt activation when their neighbors do. However, the resulting collective behavior may or may not maximize an agent's payoff or utility. From the threshold distribution alone, nothing can be said about this. A threshold model alone does not give information about the payoff to an individual at each possible equilibrium outcome.

4.2 A Micro-Macro Loop

If the system consists of many interacting components, which we call agents, then the system performance should be described on two different levels: the microscopic level, on which the decisions of the individual agents occur, and the macroscopic level, on which collective behavior can be observed. To make this connection we usually have to look at the system of interactions between individuals.

The greatest promise for determining how the heterogeneous micro-worlds of individuals generate macroscopic orders of interest or unanticipated outcomes lies in the analysis of linking microscopic behavior and macroscopic behavior. However, to understand the role of the link between these two levels remains a challenge (Schweitzer, 2002).

Therefore, we aim at discovering the fundamental role of the micro-macro link that is essential to study on collective systems.

For modeling purposes, we consider a collection of interacting heterogeneous agents who make decisions in the following stylized terms. Each agent continuously adapts to other agents in order to improve her payoff or fitness. The question of how does a collective of agents develop a macro-behavior of interest depends on how they interact as well as how they adapt their behavior to each other. We obtain the micro-macro dynamics that relates each individual's adaptive behavior by assuming that each agent myopically adapts her self-interested behavior by observing the aggregate information of the collective.

We consider a collective of heterogeneous agents $G = \{i : 1 \leq i \leq N\}$, each of which faces a binary choice problem with the two alternatives, S_1 and S_2. In the simplest form of our model, agents are born with their own idiosyncratic preference or interest. We also assume rationality based on their endogenous preference in choosing the alternatives. On the other hand, their decision is also contingent in the sense that their rational choice depends on how other agents make decisions. Although an agent's decision depends on how all other agents make decisions, they are not assumed to be knowledgeable enough to correctly anticipate all other agents' decisions. While no agent can directly observe all other agents' decisions, instead, she can obtain aggregated information. That is, each agent is assumed to be knowledgeable of the *strategy population* in the past. That is, at any given moment, each agent has the opportunity to observe the proportions of agents having chosen two strategies.

We model the individual binary decision problem as follows: the cost and benefit of each strategy also depend on how many other agents choose the same strategy. The repeated strategy choices by a large number of agents can be treated as a repeated two-person game. That is, each agent has the idiosyncratic payoff matrix in Table 4.1 and plays against all the other agents, who are assumed to play collectively.

We denote the proportion of agents having chosen S_1 at time t by $p(t)$ $(0 \leq p(t) \leq 1)$. We impose a weak monotonic condition reflecting the inertia and myopia hypotheses on the collective adaptive dynamics, which describe the temporal changes in the strategy population. At any given moment, each agent has the opportunity to observe the strategy

Table 4.1 The payoff matrix of agent i

Agent i ＼ Collectives	S_1 ($p(t)$)	S_2 ($1-p(t)$)
S_1	a_i	b_i
S_2	c_i	d_i

population, $p(t)=\{p(t), 1-p(t)\}$. Agents are assumed to be rational in the sense that they make their choice to maximize their expected payoff based on the observation of the strategy population, $p(t)$.

The expected payoffs to agent i received by choosing S_1 or S_2, conditional on everyone else continuing with their previous choices, are as follows:

$$U_i(S_1) = a_i p(t) + b_i(1-p(t)),$$
$$U_i(S_2) = c_i p(t) + d_i(1-p(t)).$$

(4.1)

Then, agent i chooses S_1 if

$$a_i p(t) + b_i(1-p(t)) > c_i p(t) + d_i(1-p(t)),$$

(4.2)

or S_2 if

$$a_i p(t) + b_i(1-p(t)) < c_i p(t) + d_i(1-p(t)).$$

(4.3)

We assume that the payoff values of Table 4.1 satisfy the condition $a_i + d_i - b_i - c_i \neq 0$. Then, the best-response strategy of agent i is obtained as follows:

Case 1: $a_i + d_i - b_i - c_i > 0$

(i) If $p(t) > (d_i - b_i)/(a_i + d_i - b_i - c_i) \equiv \theta_i$: then S_1

(ii) If $p(t) < (d_i - b_i)/(a_i + d_i - b_i - c_i) \equiv \theta_i$: then S_2

(4.4)

Case 2: $a_i + d_i - b_i - c_i < 0$

(i) If $p(t) < \theta_i$: then S_1,

(ii) If $p(t) > \theta_i$: then S_2. $\hspace{2cm}$ (4.5)

The payoff matrix in Table 4.1, one for each agent, can be replaced by one-dimensional threshold θ_i defined in (4.4). The crucial point in dealing with heterogeneity in payoffs is the associated threshold, one for each agent. This aggregation makes it easy to describe variations in heterogeneous agents. A threshold model makes this possible because a large number of payoff matrices, one for each agent, can be replaced by the distribution of a one-dimensional threshold. This allows enormous simplification in the ensuing analysis of heterogeneity in agents, which game theory handles only with difficulty.

Equations (4.4) and (4.5) also describe the relations between an agent's rational decision (microscopic behavior) and the collective decision (macroscopic behavior). We can explore the relation between the behavioral characteristics of the individuals who comprise the collective system and the aggregate behavioral characteristics of the collective system using these equations. We define the dynamics described by these equations as the *micro-macro dynamics*.

As we discussed in the previous section, the earliest and simplest *micro-macro link* was introduced by Schelling and was further discussed by Granovetter. They considered the following situation. A group of people faces a collective action problem such that an individual wants to participate only if many others join, and exactly how many total participants must join is given by her threshold. Each person in a group wants to participate only if the total number participating reaches her threshold. Only people with low thresholds participate, but their participation makes people with slightly higher thresholds want to participate. As the number participating grows, people join successively, and this is known as the *snowball* or *bandwagon effect*. This kind of effect is caused by a *micro-macro loop* between individuals and the collective.

Their threshold models can predict how and among whom collective action emerges and grows, as people learn more about each other over time. However, their models are not clear regarding some basic questions, such as where an agent's threshold comes from and how a threshold is related to a payoff maximizing behavior.

On the other hand, the payoff matrix of game theory allows us to investigate, for any particular agent, which outcome maximizes her utility, or whether an outcome is Pareto optimal. The conventional threshold model, however, does not permit this. When an individual is activated because her threshold is exceeded, she acts so as to maximize her utility under existing conditions. The resulting equilibrium may or may not maximize the overall utility of the collective. From the distribution of threshold alone, nothing can be said about this.

4.3 Two Facets of an Individual's Decision: Purposive and Contingent Decisions

An agent's decision is said to be *purposive*, if it is based on the notion of pursuing her own goal or maximizing preference. However, the behavior of an agent often relates directly to those of other agents, and it is constrained by other agents who are also pursuing their own goals or interests. We distinguish this aspect of the individual decision by referring it as *contingent* decision, since it depends on what other agents are doing.

As a specific example to illustrate both purposive and contingent aspects, we consider the situation in which each agent faces the following binary choice problem with two alternatives:

$$S_1: \text{votes } for, \qquad S_2: \text{votes } against.$$

One's decision to vote for a particular alternative may also heavily depend on what others decide to do, partly because of social influence, partly because one does not want to waste her own vote. In this particular example, the payoff values of agent i, $1 \leq i \leq N$, in Table 4.1 are given as

$$a_i = \alpha_i + \beta_i, \ b_i = \alpha_i, \ c_i = 0, \ d_i = \beta_i \ (-1 \leq \alpha_i \leq 1, \ 0 \leq \beta_i \leq 1) \quad (4.6)$$

If $\alpha_i > 0$, agent i personally prefers to vote *for*, and if $\alpha_i < 0$, she prefers to vote *against*. The absolute value $|\alpha_i|$ measures the preference strength. The value β_i measures the utility from the conformity with what the majority does. If $\beta_i > 0$, agent i prefers to choose the same choice as the majority. This type of an agent is defined as a "*conformist*".

In this section, we characterize a rational decision of a conformist. The threshold defined in (4.4) of a conformist is obtained as

$$\theta_i = (\beta_i - \alpha_i)/(\alpha_i + \beta_i + \alpha_i - \beta_i) = (1 - \alpha_i / \beta_i)/2 \qquad (4.7)$$

Since the payoff parameters in (4.6) of a conformist satisfies the condition $a_i + d_i - b_i - c_i > 0$. From (4.4), the best-response strategy of a conformist is obtained as follows:

<Best-response of a conformist: majority rule>

(i) If $p(t) > \theta_i$: then S_1 (votes *for*),

(ii) If $p(t) < \theta_i$: then S_2 (votes *against*). $\qquad (4.8)$

The strategy population at t, $\boldsymbol{p(t)}$, has a significant effect on an individual decision in the next time period. Since a conformist aims to choose the same strategy as the majority, we define the choice rule of the best-response strategy in (4.8) as the *majority rule*.

As an example, we consider Agent A and Agent B with different thresholds θ_A and θ_B, as shown in Figure 4.1. The vertical-axis represents $p(t)$, and the solid line represents the threshold as a function of α_i / β_i. Since α_A is negative, Agent A personally prefers to vote *against*. On the other hand, α_B is positive. Therefore, Agent B prefers to vote *for*. Suppose $p(t)$, the proportion of agents who vote *for* at time t, is given at $p(t)=p_1$. Since θ_A is greater than p_1, based on the majority rule in (4.8), Agent A decides to vote *against* at time $t+1$. However, if $p(t)$ goes up to p_2, then she changes her mind and decides to vote *for*. Similarly, at $p(t) = p_1$, Agent B decides to vote *for*. However, if $p(t)$ goes down to p_3, she changes her minds and decides to vote *against*.

We now consider another type of agent whose payoff values in Table 4.1 are given as

$$a_i = \alpha_i , \ b_i = \alpha_i + \beta_i , \ c_i = \beta_i , \ d_i = 0 \ (-1 \le \alpha_i \le 1, 0 \le \beta_i \le 1) \qquad (4.9)$$

This type of agent prefers the opposite choice of the majority. Therefore, we call this type of agent a *"nonconformist"*. The threshold of a nonconformist is given as

$$\theta_i = -(\alpha_i + \beta_i)/(\alpha_i - \alpha_i - \beta_i - \beta_i) = (1 + \alpha_i / \beta_i)/2 \qquad (4.10)$$

Since the payoff parameters of a nonconformist satisfies the condition $a_i + d_i - b_i - c_i < 0$, the best-response strategy of a nonconformist is obtained from (4.5) as follows:

<Best-response of a non-conformist: minority rule>

   (i) If $p(t) < \theta_i$: then S_1 (votes *for*),
   (ii) If $p(t) > \theta_i$: then S_2 (votes *against*).   (4.11)

Since a nonconformist aims to choose a different strategy from the majority, we define the choice rule of the best-response strategy in (4.11) as the *minority rule*.

As an example, we also consider two agents, *A* and *B*, with different thresholds θ_A and θ_B, as shown in Figure 4.2. If α_A is negative, then Agent *A* prefers to vote *against*. On the other hand, α_B is positive then, Agent *B* prefers to vote *for*. Suppose $p(t)$ is given at p_1. In this case θ_A is greater than p_1, Agent *A* will decide to vote *against*, according to the minority rule in (4.11). However, if $p(t)$ goes up to p_2, she changes her minds and decides to vote *for*. Similarly, at $p(t) = p_1$, Agent *B* will decide to vote *for*. However, if $p(t)$ goes down to p_3, she will change her minds and decide to vote *against*.

The payoff matrices of both a conformist and a non-conformist can be represented as the payoff matrix in Table 4.2. If $\beta_i > 0$, agent *i* is a conformist, and if $\beta_i < 0$, she is a nonconformist. Based the choice rules of the best-response strategy in (4.8) and (4.11), agents are classified into the four types:

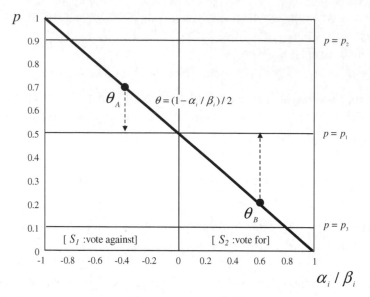

Figure 4.1 Best-response strategy of a conformist ($\beta_i > 0$) as a function of $p(t)$ and α_i / β_i

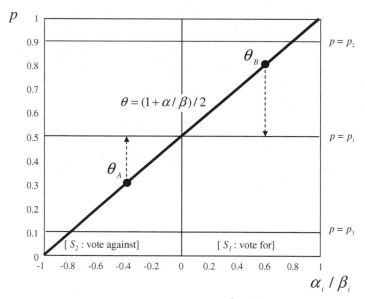

Figure 4.2 Best-response strategy of a nonconformist ($\beta_i < 0$) as a function of $p(t)$ and α_i / β_i

<Type 1: *Hardcore S_1 chooser>* If agent i is a conformist and her payoff values satisfy the relation $0 \leq \beta_i \leq \alpha_i$, or if she is a nonconformist and her payoff values satisfy $-\alpha_i \leq \beta_i \leq 0$, she always chooses S_1 without regard to the others' decisions. In this case, S_1 becomes a dominant strategy, and we define this type of agent as a *hardcore S_1* chooser.

<Type 2: *Hardcore S_2 chooser>* If agent i's payoff values satisfy the relation $0 < \beta_i < -\alpha_i$ and she is a conformist, or if her payoff values satisfy $\alpha_i < \beta_i < 0$ and she is a nonconformist, then she always chooses S_2 without regarding others' decisions. In this case, S_2 is a dominant strategy, and this type of an agent is defined as a hardcore S_2 chooser.

<Type 3: *Opportunist conformist>* If agent i is a conformist ($\beta_i > 0$), and her payoff values satisfy the relation $|\alpha_i| < \beta_i$, her best-response strategy depends on the others' choices. This type of a conformist is defined as an opportunist.

<Type 4: *Opportunist nonconformist>* If agent i is a nonconformist ($\beta_i < 0$), and her payoff values satisfy the relation $|\alpha_i| < -\beta_i$, her best-response strategy depends on the others' choices. This type of a nonconformist is also defined as an opportunist.

A *type* is a category of agents within the larger collective who share some characteristics. We can distinguish types by some aspects of agents' unobservable internal models that characterize their observable behaviors. The notion of type facilitates the analysis of heterogeneity. Heterogeneous agents can be classified into the above four types, as shown in Figure 4.3. In this figure, the horizontal-axis represents the parameter α_i, each agent's preference level over two choices (purposive behavior), and the vertical-axis represents the parameter β_i, which measures the comfort gained from the consistency of choice with the majority or minority (contingent behavior).

Table 4.2 Payoff matrix of a conformist ($\beta_i > 0$) and a nonconformist ($\beta_i < 0$)

Collectives Agent i	S_1 ($p(t)$)	S_2 ($1 - p(t)$)
S_1	$\alpha_i + \beta_i$	α_i
S_2	0	β_i

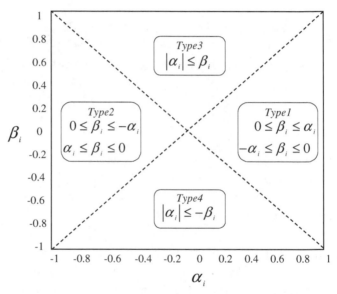

Figure 4.3 Classification of agent types from their idiosyncratic payoff values (α_i, β_i)

4.4 Micro-Macro Dynamics within a Collective

It is interesting to consider how a collective of interacting agents gropes its way towards equilibrium in an imperfect world in which agents adapt their strategy over time. Previous works have focused particularly on the relation between the microscopic and macroscopic behavior. The standard assumption, however, is that agents are endowed with similar behavioral rules (Kaniovski, 2000).

In this chapter, we departed from this assumption by considering the heterogeneity in agents with respect to their preferences as well as their behavioral rules. In particular, infinitely different types of agents could be classified into four types: hardcore S_1 or S_2 choosers, conformists who follow the majority does, and nonconformists who counter the majority.

In this section, we investigate the micro-macro dynamics that relate an agent's microscopic adaptation and the macroscopic behavior. We are especially interested in the long-run properties of collective adaptive dynamics in which agents adapt to each other over time. The dynamic adaptive process as a whole is guided by self-interest seeking behaviors of agents. This type of collective dynamics is similar to self-organizing processes observed in many natural systems (Camazine, 2001).

The collective decision starts from a set of unstructured local decisions, however, they are allowed to self-organize by establishing some orders or regularities. We investigate how agents' microscopic decisions combined with the others' decisions produce regularities and unanticipated outcomes of interest at the aggregate level.

Equilibrium collective behavior of interacting agents is characterized by the *threshold distribution* over the population. We denote the *cumulative distribution function* of the threshold, which is defined over the density function as

$$F(\theta) = \int_0^\theta f(\lambda)d\lambda \tag{4.13}$$

At first, we consider a collective of conformists. We denote the number of conformists ($\beta_i > 0$) who have the same threshold θ_i by $n_1(\theta_i)$. The proportion of conformists whose thresholds are less than θ is denoted as

$$H_1(\theta) = \sum_{\theta_i \leq \theta} n_1(\theta_i)/N_1 \tag{4.14}$$

where N_1 is the number of conformists in the collective.

We approximate the probability distribution $n_1(\theta_i)$ by the continuous function $f_1(\theta)$, which is defined as the *density function* of the threshold.

The heterogeneity in agents is characterized by this threshold density function.

We denote the proportion of agents to vote for (S_l) at time t by $p(t)$. We assume the following inertia and myopia on prediction of the collective behavior at the next time. The agents make decision conditional on everyone else continuing with their previous choices, which is given by $F_1(p(t))$. Therefore, $p(t+1)$, the proportion of agents who vote at $t+1$ is given as

$$p(t+1) = F_1(p(t)) \tag{4.15}$$

Since the above dynamics relate agents' micro-motives with the collective behavior, such dynamics is defined as *micro-macro dynamics* of conformists.

We can predict the ultimate proportion of the choice of each strategy. Given the threshold density, the question is one of finding the equilibrium of the micro-macro dynamics, which is obtained by the fixed point of (4.15), satisfying

$$p^* = F_1(p^*) \tag{4.16}$$

As an example, we consider a collective of conformists with the threshold density in Figure 4.4(a). In this case, most agents are *opportunists* and care about how other agents behave, rather than what they actually want to do. The cumulative distribution function is shown in Figure 4.5(a). The phase portrait in Figure 4.5(a) shows the convergence of the dynamics. There are two stable equilibria E_1 at the right-extremity and E_3 at the left-extremity, and one an unstable equilibrium E_2 in the middle.

In this case, two nearly identical initial conditions result in totally opposite outcomes. Suppose the initial proportion of agents who vote at the beginning is given, which is slightly less than the proportion at E_2, the collective decision converges to E_1, where all agents vote *for* or *against*. On the other hand, if the initial proportion to vote *for* is slightly higher than E_2, the collective decision converges to E_3, and in this case everybody votes *for*.

Similarly, we consider the density function in Figure 4.4(b). With this density function, some fractions of the agents ($\theta_i \cong 0$) are hardcore S_1

choosers, and they vote *for* independent of how many other agents vote *for*. On the other hand, some other fraction of the agents ($\theta_i \cong 1$) consists of hardcore S_2 choosers, and they also decide to vote *against* independent of how many other agents vote *against*. These agents care only about what they actually want to do personally.

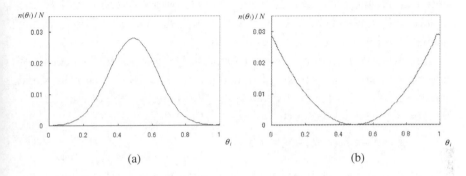

(a)   (b)

Figure 4.4 Density of the threshold over the collective captures the variability of individual characteristics. The vertical axis represents the ratio of agents of having a particular threshold. (a) The majority of the collective has intermediate thresholds. (b) The collective splits into two groups having extreme thresholds, which are close to $\theta=0$ and $\theta=1$

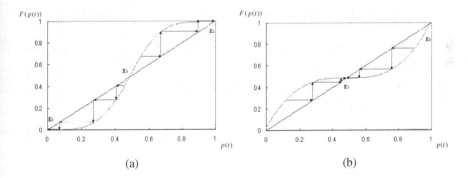

(a)   (b)

Figure 4.5 These graphs show the accumulative distributions of thresholds, $F(\theta)$, and the convergences of the collective decision of the collectives of conformists with the density functions of thresholds in Figure 4.4(a) and (b)

The cumulative distribution of the threshold is given in Figure 4.5(b). The fixed point of $F_1(p)$ is obtained as the point where it intersects with the line at a 45-degree angle. In this case, there are two equilibria: E_1 in the middle and E_2 at the right-extremity, in which E_1 is stable and E_2 is unstable. The phase portrait in Figure 4.5(b) also illustrates the convergence of the collective adaptive dynamics. Starting from any initial point, the collective decision converges to E_1, where half of the agents vote *for* and the rest of the agents vote *against*. Therefore, the agents split into two groups.

Similarly, we formulate the micro-macro dynamics of the collective of nonconformists. The number of nonconformists ($\beta_i < 0$) with the same threshold θ_i is denoted by $n_2(\theta_i)$. We denote the proportion of nonconformists whose thresholds are less than θ as

$$H_2(\theta) = \sum_{\theta_i \le \theta} n_2(\theta_i) / N_2 \qquad (4.17)$$

where N_2 is the number of nonconformists. We approximate the probability distribution $n_2(\theta_i)$ by the continuous density function $f_2(\theta)$. The cumulative distribution of the threshold density, which is defined in (4.13), is denoted by $F_2(\theta)$.

The micro-macro dynamics of nonconformists are described as follows: the proportion of agents who vote *for* at time t is given as $p(t)$. By the definitions of the cumulative distribution $F_2(\theta)$ and the rational decision rule of a nonconformist in (4.11), the proportion of nonconformists who vote *for* at $t+1$ is given as $1 - F_2(p(t))$. Therefore, we have the following dynamic equation, which is defined using the complimentary cumulative distribution of $F_2(\theta)$:

$$p(t+1) = 1 - F_2(p(t)) \qquad (4.18)$$

The fixed point of the above adaptive dynamics is obtained by solving the equation

$$p^* = 1 - F_2(p^*) \qquad (4.19)$$

We assume that the threshold density of nonconformists is given in Figure 4.4(a). The dynamics describing the collective adaptive behavior of nonconformists associated with this threshold density is shown in

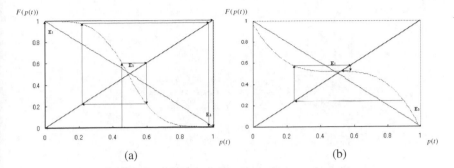

Figure 4.6 The graphs show the complimentary cumulative distribution functions of thresholds, $1-F(\theta)$ and the convergences of the collective decision of the collectives of non-conformists with the density functions of thresholds in Figure 4.4(a) and (b)

Figure 4.6(a). There is no stable equilibrium, and it produces cyclic behavior, which alternates between $p=0$ and $p=1$.

We consider the threshold density in Figure 4.4(b). The micro-macro dynamics is shown in Figure 4.6(b). In this case, there is the unique stable equilibrium at the middle point $p=0.5$, and starting from any initial point, the micro-macro dynamics converges to $p=0.5$.

We now consider a mixed collective consisting of both conformists and nonconformists. The proportion of conformists ($\beta_i > 0$) is $k = N_1 / N$ ($0 < k < 1$), and that of nonconformists ($\beta_i < 0$) is $1 - k = N_2 / N$, where $N = N_1 + N_2$ is the total number of agents in the mixed collective. Using Equations (4.16) and (4.18), the micro-macro dynamics of the mixed collective is given as

$$p(t+1) = kF_1(p(t)) + (1-k)(1 - F_2(p(t)))$$
(4.20)

where $p(t)$ is the proportion of agents who vote for at t. We characterize the micro-macro dynamics of the mixed collective by changing the value of k.

Let us suppose the threshold densities of both conformists and nonconformists are given in Figure 4.4(a). In Figure 4.7, we show the collective behavior in (4.20) when we set k as: (a) $k=0.3$, (b) $k=0.5$, (c) $k=0.8$. The vertical axis represents $p(t)$, the proportion of agents who vote for (S_1) and the horizontal axis represents the time t. When we start

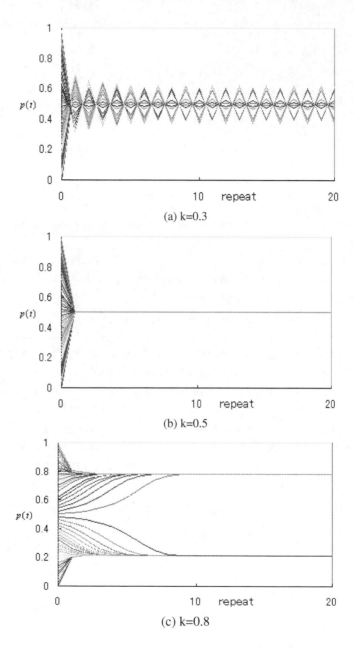

Figure 4.7 Convergence of collective decisions governed by (4.20) with different values of k, the proportion of conformists in the collective

from arbitrary initial conditions. The collective decision oscillates between 0.4 and 0.6 when we set $k=0.3$ (Figure 4.7(a)). However, when we set $k=0.5$ (Figure 4.7(b)), it converges to 0.5, starting from any initial condition. When we set $k=0.8$ (Figure 4.7(c)), it converges to either 0.2 or 0.8, depending on the initial condition.

We have addressed the question of how the heterogeneous micro-worlds of individuals generate the global macroscopic orders. We have also examined fundamental local or micro mechanisms that are sufficient to generate macroscopic structures of interest.

Interacting situations in which an agent's behavior depends on those of other agents usually do not permit any simple summation or extrapolation to the aggregates. We cannot simply jump to a conclusion about aggregate behavior from what one knows or can guess about individual preferences. To make that connection, we have to look at the micro-macro dynamics that between the micro-motives of agents and the aggregated behavior.

Knowing the preferences, motives, or beliefs of agents can only provide a necessary but not a sufficient condition for the explanation of the aggregated outcome. The purposes, as well as contingent behaviors, of individual agents produce coherent collective behavior, and sometimes cyclic behavior. The resulting micro-macro dynamics can be quite complex. The surprise lies in the emergence of macrostructure from the bottom up, which occurs from local adaptive decisions that outwardly appear quite remote from the collective outcomes they generate. In short, it is not the emergent macroscopic object per se that is surprising, but the accumulative effect of the local adaptive decisions that generate complex behaviors at the macroscopic level.

4.5 Micro-Macro Loop between Two Collectives

In this section, we extend our analysis of a single collective to multiple collectives. With this extension, an agent adapts her rational decision to the aggregated information of the other collective, and therefore, the micro-macro loop is formed between multiple collectives.

Table 4.3 Payoff matrix of agent A in G_A and agent B in G_B

Agent A \ Agent B	S_1	S_2
S_1	a_B a_A	c_B b_A
S_2	b_B c_A	d_B d_A

We consider pair-wise interactions between two collectives, G_A and G_B. A pair consisting of Agent A and Agent B, who are randomly chosen from each collective plays the underlying 2 x 2 game in Table 4.3. Each agent in each collective has the idiosyncratic payoff matrix.

The proportion of agents in G_A having chosen S_1 at time t is denoted by $x(t)$, and that of agents in G_B is $y(t)$. The strategy population of G_A at t is denoted as $x(t)=\{x(t),1-x(t)\}$, and that of G_B is $y(t)=\{y(t), 1-y(t)\}$. At any given moment, the agents have the opportunity to observe the strategy distribution of the other collective. All agents are assumed to share the aggregated information, and they are assumed to adapt to it with the best-response strategy.

We can reduce the four payoff parameters in Table 4.2 into two parameters by summarizing as follows:

$$\alpha_i = a_i - b_i, \quad \beta_i = d_i - c_i, \quad i = A, B . \tag{4.21}$$

In this section, we characterize a rational decision of an agent depending on the type of underlying game between two collectives.

<Case 1> *Coordination game*: $(\alpha_i > 0, \beta_i > 0, i = A, B)$
If both parameter values α_i, β_i, $i = A, B$, are positive, the underlying pair-wise interaction becomes a coordination game. In this case, if both agents choose the same strategy, they can receive a positive payoff, otherwise they receive nothing. The threshold of each agent is

$$\theta_i = \beta_i / (\alpha_i + \beta_i), \quad i = A, B . \tag{4.22}$$

The best-response strategies of Agent A and Agent B are determined from their threshold and the strategy distribution of the other collective as follows:

(a) Agent A in G_A,

  (i) If $y(t) > \theta_A$: S_1,

  (ii) If $y(t) < \theta_A$: S_2.   (4.23)

(b) Agent B in G_B,

  (i) If $x(t) < \theta_B$: S_1,

  (ii) If $x(t) > \theta_B$: S_2.   (4.24)

\<Case 2\> *Dispersion game:* $(\alpha_i < 0,\ \beta_i < 0,\ i = A, B)$

If both parameter values are negative, the underlying pair-wise interaction becomes a dispersion game. In this case, the best-response strategies of both agents are:

(a) Agent A in G_A,

  (i)   If $y(t) > \theta_A$: S_1,

  (ii)   If $y(t) < \theta_A$: S_2.   (4.25)

(b) Agent B in G_B,

  (i)   If $x(t) < \theta_B$: S_1,

  (ii)   If $x(t) > \theta_B$: S_2.   (4.26)

\<Case 3\> *Vicious-circle game*

We consider the following conflict situation, in which the parameter values of two agents have the opposite signs,

$$\alpha_A, \beta_A > 0, \text{ and } \alpha_B, \beta_B < 0. \qquad\qquad (4.27)$$

In this case, the underlying pair-wise interaction is defined as a *vicious-circle game*. The best-response strategies of Agent A and Agent B are

(a) Agent A in G_A,

      (i)   If $y(t) > \theta_A : S_1$,

      (ii)   If $y(t) < \theta_A : S_2$.   (4.28)

(b) Agent B in G_B,

      (i)   If $x(t) < \theta_B : S_1$,

      (ii)   If $x(t) > \theta_B : S_2$.   (4.29)

4.6 Micro-Macro Dynamics between Two Collectives

In this section, we investigate the micro-macro dynamics of the two collectives when the micro-macro loop is formed between two collectives. An agent interacts with an agent who is randomly chosen from the other collective. The micro-macro dynamics can be analyzed depending the type of the underlying game.

<Case 1> The underlying pair-wise interaction is a coordination game

The proportion of agents who have the same threshold θ_i in collective G_i are denoted by $n_i(\theta) / N$, $i = A, B$. We approximate the discrete function $n_i(\theta)/N$ by the continuous density function $f_i(\theta)$, $i = A, B$. The proportion of agents in collective G_i, $i = A, B$, whose threshold is less than θ is given by

$$F_i(\theta) = \int_0^\theta f_i(\lambda)d\lambda, \quad i = A, B. \tag{4.30}$$

The above functions are defined as the cumulative threshold distributions of collective G_i, $i = A, B$.

We denote the proportion of agents who choose S_1 at time t in G_B by $y(t)$. Agents in the collective G_B choose their best-response strategy by assuming that the same proportion of agents in G_A may choose S_1 at $t+1$. From the rule of choosing the best-response strategy in (4.23), the proportion of agents in G_A to choose S_1 at $t+1$ is given by $F_A(y(t))$. Therefore, the change of $x(t)$ is governed by the following dynamics:

$$x(t+1) = F_A(y(t)).$$

(4.31)

Similarly, the dynamics of $y(t)$, the proportion of agents who choose S_1 in G_B, is governed by the following dynamics:

$$y(t+1) = F_B(x(t)).$$

(4.32)

The pair of dynamic equations in (4.31) and (4.32) is defined as *the micro-macro dynamics between two collectives*. Our aim is to predict, starting from any initial value of $x(0)$ or $y(0)$, the ultimate strategy populations of both collectives. The collective behaviors at equilibrium are obtained as the fixed point satisfying

$$x^* = F_A(y^*),$$
$$y^* = F_B(x^*)$$

(4.33)

As an example, we consider the density functions of the two collectives given in Figure 4.8. This is the case in which a pair of agents randomly chosen from each collective play the *asymmetric coordination game*, which is also known as the *battle of sexes game*. In this asymmetric situation, their preferred choices are different. Agents in G_A prefer S_1 and agents in G_B prefer S_2.

We show the dynamics of $x(t)$ and $y(t)$ in Figure 4.9 by changing the initial ratio incrementally between 0 and 1. The horizontal axis represents the adaptation time, and the vertical axis represents the proportion of agents who choose S_1 at each time period. If the initial ratios of both collectives are relatively low (less than 0.35), then $(x(t), y(t))$ converges to (0,0). That is, all agents in both collectives finally come to choose S_2. If the initial ratios are high (greater than 0.65), then they converge to (1,1), and all agents come to choose S_1. If the initial ratios are between 0.35 and 0.65, then they produce cyclic behavior between at *p=0* and *p=1*. With this cyclic behavior, if all agents choose

S_1 at some time t, then at the next time $t+1$, all agents change to S_2, and this miscoordination is repeated endlessly.

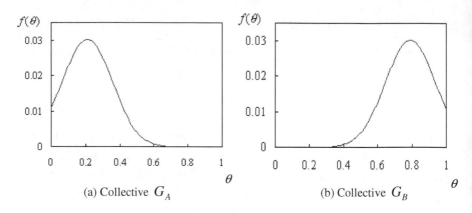

(a) Collective G_A (b) Collective G_B

Figure 4.8   The density functions of threshold of two collectives: (a) The majority of collective G_A has thresholds close to $\theta=0$. (b) The majority of collective G_B has thresholds close to $\theta=1$

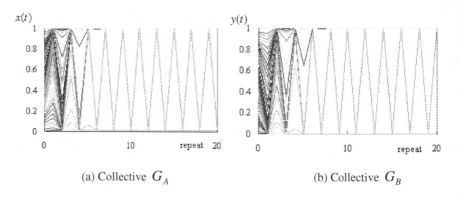

(a) Collective G_A (b) Collective G_B

Figure 4.9   The proportions of agents having chosen S_1 in G_A and G_B are different. An agent chosen from collective G_A is more likely to prefer S_1 to S_2, and an agent chosen from collective G_B is more likely to prefer S_2 to S_1

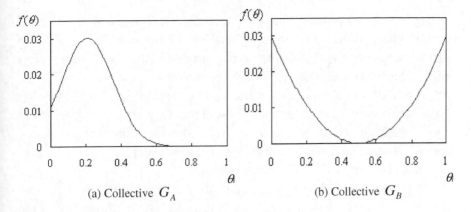

(a) Collective G_A (b) Collective G_B

Figure 4.10 The density functions of two collectives: (a) The majority of collective G_A has thresholds close to $\theta=0$. (b) The collective splits into two groups having extreme thresholds, which are close to $\theta=0$ and $\theta=1$

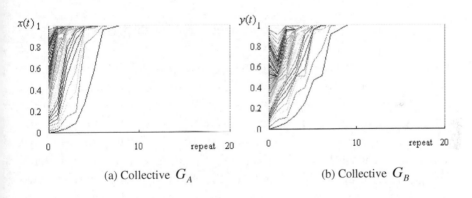

(a) Collective G_A (b) Collective G_B

Figure 4.11 The proportions of agents having chosen S_1 in G_A and G_B. Starting from any initial value, they converge to $x=1$ and $y=1$

Playing the same coordination game repeatedly in a population of agents who play based on their rational calculations of the payoff on a particular strategy with different expectations for the other strategy can easily lead to coordination failures (Fudenberg and Levine, 1998). The heterogeneity in payoffs poses more complex phenomena by producing both stable behaviors and cyclic oscillations. These examples have considerable intuitive appeal since they display situations in which agents' rational actions, in pursuit of well-defined preferences, lead to outcomes that are undesirable to all agents.

We now consider the pair of the density functions in Figure 4.10. The density function of collective G_A is as shown in Figure 4.8, and all of the agents in G_A are more likely to prefer S_1 to S_2 On the other hand, the collective G_B consists of two types of agents, one type is more likely to prefer S_1 to S_2, and the other type to prefer S_2 to S_1. The portrait of the micro-macro dynamics is shown in Figure 4.11. In this case, starting from any initial ratio, they converge to $x=1$ and $y=1$, and both collectives finally come to choose S_1, and therefore perfect coordination is achieved.

<Case 2> The underlying pair-wise interaction is a dispersion game

We now characterize the micro-macro dynamics when the underlying pair-wise interaction is formulated as a dispersion game. By the definition of the cumulative function $F_i(\theta)$ ($i = A, B$) in (4.30), and the rules t for choosing the best-response strategy in (4.25) and (4.26), the micro-macro dynamics are obtained as follows. The proportions of agents who choose S_1 at t+1 in G_A and G_B are given as $1 - F_A(y(t))$ and $1 - F_B(x(t))$, respectively. Therefore, the micro-dynamics between two collectives is described using the complimentary cumulative distribution functions as:

$$x(t+1) = 1 - F_A(y(t)),$$
$$y(t+1) = 1 - F_B(x(t)). \tag{4.34}$$

The above micro-macro dynamics is characterized at equilibrium by obtaining a fixed point satisfying:

$$x^* = 1 - F_A(y^*),$$
$$y^* = 1 - F_B(x^*). \tag{4.35}$$

We consider the pair of density functions $f_i(\theta)$, $i = A, B$, in Figure 4.12. Agents in G_A are more likely to prefer S_2 to S_1. On the other hand, the collective of G_B consists of two different types of agents, one type is more likely to prefer S_1 to S_2, and the other type is more likely to prefer S_2 to S_1.

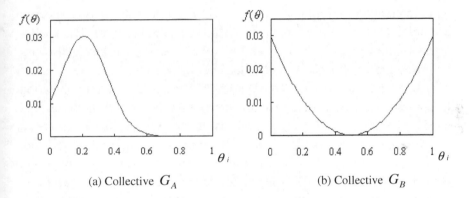

(a) Collective G_A (b) Collective G_B

Figure 4.12 The density functions of two collectives. (a) The majority of collective G_A has thresholds close to $\theta=0$. (b) The collective splits into two groups having extreme thresholds that are close to $\theta=0$ and $\theta=1$

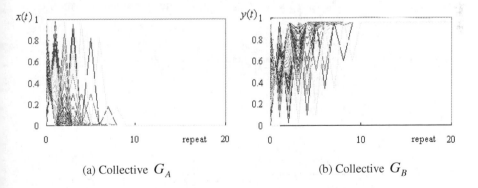

(a) Collective G_A (b) Collective G_B

Figure 4.13 The proportions of agents having chosen S_1 in G_A and G_B. Starting from any initial value, they converge to $x=0$ and $y=1$

The micro-macro dynamics is shown in Figure 4.13. Starting from any initial value, $x(t)$ converges to $x=0$, and all agents in G_A choose S_2. On the other hand, $y(t)$) converges to $y=1$, implying that all agents in G_B come to choose S_1. In this case, perfect coordination is realized between the two collectives.

<Case 3)> The underlying pair-wise interaction is a vicious-circle game

We now obtain the micro-macro dynamics when the underlying pair-wise interaction is formulated as a vicious-circle game. As a specific example, we consider two populations of sellers and buyers. Each seller has two strategies, S_1 (honest) and S_2 (cheat), and each buyer also has two strategies, S_1 (inspect) and S_2 (does not inspect).

A seller and a buyer who are randomly chosen from each population face a trading game with the payoff matrix in Table 4.4. If the seller A is honest and the buyer B inspects, that is, at (S_1, S_1), the seller receives a positive payoff, $\alpha_A > 0$. Or, if the seller cheats and the buyer does not inspect, that is, at (S_2, S_2), the seller also receives a positive payoff $\beta_A > 0$, then cheating is better than being honest if the buyer does not inspect.

In this case, however, the buyer receives nothing. On the other hand, if the seller is honest and the buyer does not inspect, then at (S_1, S_2), the buyer receives a positive payoff, $\beta_B > 0$ (because of the inspection cost and defective production). Or, if the seller cheats and the buyer inspects, then at (S_2, S_1), the buyer receive $\alpha_B > 0$. In the latter two cases, the buyer

Table 4.4 Payoff matrix of a buyer and a seller ($\alpha_i, \beta_i > 0$, $i = A, B$.)

Seller A \ Buyer B	S_1 (inspect)	S_2 (no inspect)
S_1 (honest)	α_A 0	0 β_B
S_2 (cheat)	0 α_B	β_A 0

receives nothing. In this trading game, there is no pure strategy Nash equilibrium, and only a mixed-strategy equilibrium is possible.

From (4.28) and (4.29), we can obtain the micro-macro dynamics. The proportion of agents who choose S_I in G_A at $t+1$ is given by the cumulative function $F_A(y(t))$, and that in G_B is given by the complementary function $1 - F_B(x(t))$. Then, the micro-macro dynamics are obtained as:

$$
\begin{aligned}
x(t+1) &= F_A(y(t)) \\
y(t+1) &= 1 - F_B(x(t))
\end{aligned}
\tag{4.36}
$$

The micro-macro dynamics at equilibrium is characterized by the fixed point satisfying

$$
\begin{aligned}
x^* &= F_A(y^*) \\
y^* &= 1 - F_B(x^*)
\end{aligned}
\tag{4.37}
$$

We consider the pair of density functions $f_i(\theta)$, $i = A, B$, in Figure 4.14. The micro-macro dynamics are shown in Figure 4.15. Starting from any initial value, both $x(t)$ and $y(t)$ converge to 0.5. In this case, both collectives split into two groups, and half of the agents of both collectives come to choose S_1, and the rest choose S_2.

All of these examples have considerable intuitive appeal, since they display situations in which agents' rational decisions, in pursuit of well-defined preferences, sometimes lead to surprising outcomes. One may also wonder why there are no situations in which the behavior of agents cannot usefully be summed and predicted by the initial proportions of agents who engage in one of two possible strategies. At each time period, agents decide which strategy to choose given the information of the aggregate of the other collective. They adapt rationally, knowing that everyone else is also making a rational choice. As time progress, and agents come to know more about the strategy population of the other collective, a specific strategy may become more likely to be chosen. However, correct predictions do not happen because of heterogeneity in agents.

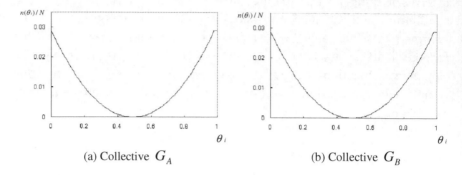

(a) Collective G_A (b) Collective G_B

Figure 4.14 The density function of two collectives. Both collectives split into two groups having extreme thresholds that are close to $\theta=0$ and $\theta=1$

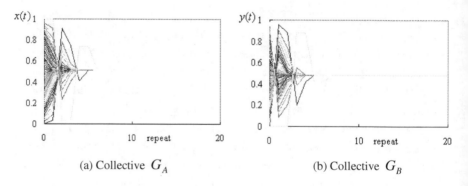

(a) Collective G_A (b) Collective G_B

Figure 4.15 The proportions of agents having chosen S_1 in G_A and G_B. Starting from any initial value, they converge to $x=0.5$ and $y=0.5$

Chapter 5

Knowledge Transaction Games

In this chapter, we formulate knowledge transaction games. We consider a collective of agents who trade their private knowledge with each other. The dynamic knowledge trading process can be formulated as the micro-macro dynamics discussed in the previous chapter. Agents trade their private knowledge with other members, and the disclosed knowledge is shared as common knowledge. Shared knowledge also causes agents to accumulate their private knowledge at an individual level at an accelerated rate. The main concern is then under what circumstances a collective of self-interested agents can accelerate knowledge accumulation at both the individual level and the collective level.

5.1 Merit of Knowledge Sharing

In modern societies, knowledge is not only closely connected to innovation and technological advances, it also becomes an economic commodity in its own right. The creation and distribution of knowledge becomes a central part of the analysis and discussion because we live in the age of the information economy.

Defining knowledge is a first essential step for considering knowledge intensive activities. However, there are many definitions of knowledge. To some, knowledge concerns wisdom, the result of learning and experience, to others knowledge is only learning or only experience, whereas others believe knowledge involves information or data (Fischer and Frohlich, 2001).

In their book "*The Knowledge-Creating Companies*", Nonaka and Takeuchi (1995) distinguish two types of knowledge, *tacit knowledge* and *explicit knowledge*. Tacit knowledge is knowledge that is hard to articulate with formal language. It is personal knowledge embedded in individual experience and personal belief. In other words, it is part of what we know that we can explain. The other type of knowledge is explicit knowledge, which can be articulated in formal language including grammatical statements, mathematical expressions, specifications, manuals, and so forth. Knowledge transformation is thought of as a spiral construction, where transformation of tacit knowledge into explicit knowledge leads to the diffusion of knowledge, which can then be built on and incorporated back into the tacit knowledge of the members of the same organization or group.

Organization cannot create knowledge on its own without the initiatives of individuals and the interactions that takes place within the organization. Individual knowledge is transformed into organizational knowledge. However, it is difficult to promote this transference in an environment in which attendants have conflicts of interest. Transferring from the individual level to an organization level requires costs time and money, and requires a great deal of effort.

The goal of this chapter is to model the knowledge accumulation process by formulating knowledge transference as a knowledge transaction game. We classify knowledge into two types. One is shared knowledge, which is common to all members of the same organization or group. This type of knowledge can be transmitted across agents explicitly. The other type of knowledge is private knowledge, which is personal knowledge that is embedded in individual experience or individually created.

When agents have the chance to trade their knowledge, they try to trade their private knowledge with others so that their utility or payoff from a transaction is improved. Factors such as the value of acquiring new knowledge from trading partners and the cost of disclosing their private knowledge to others should be considered.

If agents trade their private knowledge, then disclosed knowledge becomes common knowledge. If many agents are willing to trade their knowledge, they can share common knowledge at a higher level. Transacted knowledge comes to be shared and common knowledge also causes agents to accelerate their creation of new private knowledge. That is, shared knowledge has positive feedback with respect to knowledge creation at an individual level. The micro-macro link between individual knowledge and shared knowledge is conceptually depicted in Figure 5.1.

Agents may recognize that sharing knowledge with each other is important for achieving joint works effectively. On the other hand, they may sometimes try to hide their private knowledge from disclosure if they behave selfishly. In this case, they cannot share common knowledge at a higher level. Then, the main concern is under what circumstances can knowledge sharing be accelerated.

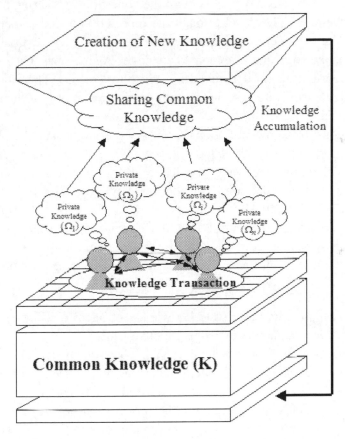

Figure 5.1 Knowledge sharing and creation through knowledge trading

5.2   A Formulation of Knowledge Transaction Games

Agents can acquire new knowledge only through knowledge trading, and trading can integrate transacted knowledge with one's own private knowledge to create new knowledge. However, knowledge trading has some unique property, which is not found in the trading of economic goods. That is, if knowledge is diffused, it is beneficial to any agent who is at least partly capable of understanding it.

In this section, we formulate knowledge transaction between two agents as a 2x2 game. We also obtain the condition for sharing common knowledge at a higher level through the repeated knowledge transaction games. We consider two agents who have both types of knowledge, private knowledge and common knowledge. Agents may benefit from knowledge transaction if their utility will be increased. Therefore, they will trade their private knowledge with another agent only if their utility is improved.

We consider knowledge transaction between agent A, who has the collection of private knowledge $\Omega_A = \{x_j;\ 1 \le j \le N_A\}$, and agent B, who has the collection of private knowledge $\Omega_B = \{y_j;\ 1 \le j \le N_B\}$. Each agent makes a rational decision considering both the benefit and cost associated with each trade. Factors such as the value of knowledge possessed by the other agent and the loss associated with sharing her own knowledge should be considered before transaction.

We assume a semi-linear function of each agent in the form of

$$U_i(\Omega_i, K) = \Omega_i + v_i(K), \qquad i = A, B.\qquad (5.1)$$

where Ω_i represents the private knowledge of agent i, $i = A, B$, and K represents the common knowledge of both agents.

Let us assume agent i, where $i = A, B$, has knowledge of the value X. The difference $X - v_i(X)$ represents the relative value of agent i when she keeps it as private knowledge. When the condition $X - v_i(X) > 0$ holds, she places a higher priority on having X as private knowledge. On the other hand if the condition $v_i(X) - X > 0$ holds, she places a higher priority on having it as common knowledge.

We define the following three types of value function:

Definition 5.1 *For a knowledge pair X and Y, $(X \neq Y)$*

(1) *If $v_i(X+Y) = v_i(X) + v_i(Y)$, then the value function $v_i(X)$ is linear.*

(2) *If $v_i(X+Y) > v_i(X) + v_i(Y)$, then the value function $v_i(X)$ is super-additive.*

(3) *If $v_i(X+Y) < v_i(X) + v_i(Y)$, then the value function $v_i(X)$ is semi-additive.*

If the value function $v_i(X)$ is super-additive, then the knowledge accumulation process satisfies the property of *increasing-returns to scales*. In this case, the sharing of common knowledge with the other agent brings additional value. If this property holds, then increasing the level of common knowledge implies sharing more experiences with each other for effective joint works. In this case, agents may achieve greater collective understanding for achieving common tasks. On the other hand, if the value function is semi-additive, sharing more knowledge has the property of *decreasing-return to scales*.

We formulate knowledge transaction between two agents as a 2x2 game. Each agent i, $i = A,B$, has two strategies:

S_1 : Trades a piece of private knowledge in Ω_i, $i = A,B$.
S_2 : Does not trade
(5.2)

Let us consider the knowledge transaction between agent A with knowledge X and agent B with knowledge Y, as shown in Figure 5.2. The payoffs to both agents when they choose each strategy are given as the payoff matrix in Table 5.1. The payoffs to agent A in Table 5.1 are

$$U_A(S_1,S_1) = \Omega_A - X + v_A(X+Y) \equiv a_A,$$
$$U_A(S_1,S_2) = \Omega_A - X + v_A(X) \equiv b_A,$$
$$U_A(S_2,S_1) = \Omega_A + v_A(Y) \equiv c_A,$$
$$U_A(S_2,S_2) = \Omega_A \equiv d_A.$$
(5.3)

The payoffs to agent B are

$$U_B(S_1,S_1) = \Omega_B - Y + v_B(X+Y) \equiv a_B,$$
$$U_B(S_2,S_1) = \Omega_B - Y + v_B(Y) \equiv b_B,$$
$$U_B(S_2,S_1) = \Omega_B + v_B(X) \equiv c_B,$$
$$U_B(S_2,S_2) = \Omega_B \equiv d_B.$$

$$(5.4)$$

When both agents decide to trade their private knowledge, the payoffs are defined as the value from common knowledge minus the value of private knowledge. On the other hand, if one agent does not trade while her partner does trade, she receives some gain by knowing the new knowledge held by the other agent. If an agent trades her private knowledge and her partner does not trade, then her traded knowledge becomes common knowledge, and some of the value of the knowledge is lost. If both agents are not involved in the transaction, they receive nothing. Therefore, agents may not lose all of the value of their knowledge, and they also receive some gain even if the agent does not trade while the other agent does. This is a unique feature of knowledge transaction that is not found in the trading of economic commodities.

We define the following payoff parameters:

$$\alpha_A \equiv a_A - c_A = -X + v_A(X+Y) - v_A(Y),$$
$$\beta_A \equiv d_A - b_A = X - v_A(X),$$
$$\alpha_B \equiv a_B - c_B = -Y + v_B(X+Y) - v_A(X),$$
$$\beta_B \equiv d_B - b_B = Y - v_B(Y).$$

$$(5.5)$$

From the above, we have the following relation:

$$\alpha_i + \beta_i = v_i(X+Y) - v_i(X) - v_i(Y), \quad i = A, B. \qquad (5.6)$$

We also define the following thresholds for both agents.

$$\theta_A \equiv \beta_A /(\alpha_A + \beta_A) = \{X - v_A(X)\}/\{v_A(X+Y) - v_A(X) - v_A(Y)\},$$
$$\theta_B \equiv \beta_B /(\alpha_B + \beta_B) = \{Y - v_B(Y)\}/\{v_B(X+Y) - v_B(X) - v_B(Y)\}.$$

$$(5.7)$$

The denominators in (5.7) represent the multiplier effects of sharing knowledge, and the numerators represent the costs associated with transaction.

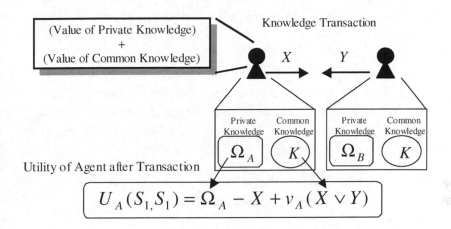

Figure 5.2 Knowledge trading between two agents

Table 5.1 Payoff matrix of knowledge trading games

Agent A \ Agent B	S_1 (trade)	S_2 (not trade)
S_1 (trade)	a_B a_A	c_B b_A
S_2 (not trade)	b_B c_A	d_B d_A

5.3 Characteristics of Knowledge Transaction

The threshold associated with each piece of knowledge to be traded reflects an agent's value judgments on knowledge transaction. Each agent reasons the value of knowledge held by other agents. The value of knowledge of each agent is also reflected in her threshold defined in (5.7).

<Case 1> $v_i(X)$ is super-additive

We denote the probability of her partner choosing S_1 (trade) by p. If the value function agent i is super-additive, then the payoff parameters in (5.5) satisfy the relations $\alpha_i > 0$ and $\beta_i > 0$. The best-response strategy of agent i is obtained from (4.8) as:

$$
\begin{aligned}
&\text{(i) If } p \geq \theta_i, \quad S_1 \text{ (Trades)} \\
&\text{(ii) If } p < \theta_i, \quad S_2 \text{ (Does not trade)}
\end{aligned}
\tag{5.8}
$$

We can classify agents who have super-additive value functions into three types, depending on threshold value of θ defined in (5.7).

(a) $\theta_i \approx 0$ $(\alpha_i \ggg \beta_i)$: Hard-core contributor

From the best-response strategy in (5.8), an agent whose threshold is close to zero has S_1 as a dominant strategy. Since she is willing to disclose her private knowledge without regard for the other agent's strategy, an agent with a lower threshold is defined as a hard-core contributor.

(b) $\theta_i \approx 1$ $(\beta_i \ggg \alpha_i)$: Free rider

An agent whose threshold is close to one has S_2 as a dominant strategy. She does not trade her knowledge without regard for the choice of the other agent. We define such an agent as a free rider.

(c) $0 < \theta_i < 1$: Opportunist

In this case, the best-response strategy of agent i depends on her partner's strategy. We define this type of agent as an opportunist.

\<Case 2\> $v_i(X)$ is semi-additive

If the value function of agent i is semi-additive, the payoff parameters satisfy the relations $\alpha_i < 0$ and $\beta_i < 0$. Therefore, the best-response strategy of agent i is obtained from (4.11) as

$$
\begin{aligned}
&\text{(i) If } p \le \theta_i,\ S_1 \text{ (Trades)},\\
&\text{(ii) If } p > \theta_i,\ S_2 \text{ (Does not trade)}.
\end{aligned}
\tag{5.9}
$$

Agents with semi-additive value functions are also classified into the three types depending on their threshold value, as defined in (5.7).

(a) $\theta_i \approx 0$ ($\beta_i \ggg \alpha_i$): Free rider

From (5.13), an agent with a lower threshold has S_2 as a dominant strategy. She does not trade her knowledge without regard for the choice of the other agent. We define such an agent as a free rider.

(b) $\theta_i \approx 1$ ($\alpha_i \ggg \beta_i$): Hard-core contributor

An agent with a high threshold has S_1 as a dominant strategy. She is willing to trade her knowledge without regard for the other agent's choice. Such an agent is defined as a hard-core contributor.

(c) $0 < \theta_i < 1$: Opportunist

In this case, the best-response strategy of agent i depends on her partner's strategy. We define such an agent as an opportunist.

As an example, we consider knowledge transaction between two agents A and B, each of which has the super-additive value function $v_i(K)$, $i = A, B$. Each agent reasons the value of knowledge held by the other agent in terms of her own private knowledge. That is, the value of knowledge held by her partner can be estimated as a function of the value of her own knowledge. An agent with knowledge of the value X reasons the value of the other agent's knowledge Y as:

$$Y = \alpha X \quad (\alpha > 0).$$ (5.10)

If $0 < \alpha < 1$, an agent believes her partner has knowledge of lower value, and if $\alpha > 1$, her partner is believed to have knowledge of higher value.

We also assume that the super-additive value functions of both agents have the following specific form:

$$v_i(X) = kX \ln(X), \quad i = A, B.$$ (5.11)

In Figure 5.3, we depict the function in (5.11) with $k = 0.5$. The horizontal axis represents the value of private knowledge X, and the vertical axis represents the value of $v_i(X)$, which corresponds to the value of X when it becomes common knowledge to both agents. When the value function $v_i(X)$ is super-additive, the denominator and numerator of the threshold in (5.7) can be approximated as:

$$v_i(X + \alpha X) - v_i(X) - v_i(\alpha X) = kX(\ln(1 + \alpha) + \alpha \ln(1 + 1 / \alpha))$$
$$X - v_i(X) = X(1 - k \ln X)$$ (5.12)

Therefore, the threshold in (5.7) represents the function of the value of knowledge X and α as

$$\theta(X, \alpha) \cong \frac{1 / k - \ln X}{\ln(1 + \alpha) + \alpha \ln(1 + 1 / \alpha)}$$ (5.13)

In Figure 5.4, we depict the value of the threshold in (5.13) as a function of X and α. The horizontal axis represents the value of knowledge X, and the vertical axis represents the threshold in (5.13). From this figure, if the value of knowledge X increases, its associated threshold decreases sharply. The threshold also decreases as α increases. Therefore, if an agent estimates that her partner has more valuable knowledge, her threshold will decrease. Therefore, in this case an agent is more likely to trade her knowledge.

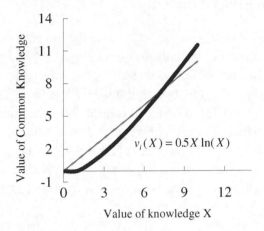

Figure 5.3 Super-additive value function in (5.11) ($k = 0.5$)

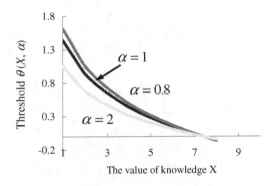

Figure 5.4 Threshold $\theta(X, \alpha)$ as a function of α and X

5.4 Repeated Knowledge Transaction

In this section, we consider repeated knowledge transaction between agent A with a collection of knowledge $\Omega'_A = \{X_j : 1 \le j \le N_A\}$ and agent B with a collection of knowledge $\Omega'_B = \{Y_j : 1 \le j \le N_B\}$. Each agent makes a rational decision as to whether to trade each piece of knowledge.

The rational decision for knowledge transaction is characterized by the threshold associated with each knowledge transaction, as defined in (5.13). We denote the proportion of knowledge of agent i that is characterized by the same threshold θ by $n_i(\theta)/N$, $i = A, B$. We approximate these discrete functions by the continuous function $f_i(\theta)$, $i = A, B$, as shown in Figure 5.5.

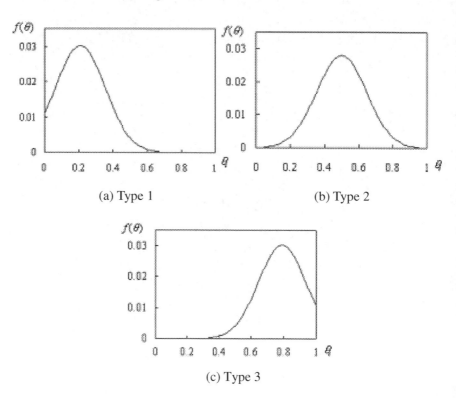

(a) Type 1   (b) Type 2

(c) Type 3

Figure 5.5 Characterization of private knowledge in terms of a threshold. (1) Type 1: An agent with high-value knowledge, (2) Type 2: An agent with intermediate-value knowledge, (3) Type 3: An agent with low-value knowledge

An agent having the density function illustrated in Figure 5.5(a) (Type 1) is characterized as having knowledge of high value, since the associated threshold function takes low values. An agent having the density function shown in Figure 5.5(b) (Type 2) is characterized as having knowledge of intermediate value. An agent having the density function shown in Figure 5.5(c) (Type 3) is characterized as having knowledge of low value, since the associate threshold function takes high values.

We denote the proportion of knowledge for which the threshold is less than θ in a collection of knowledge Ω_i held by agent i by

$$F_i(\theta) = \int_{\lambda \leq \theta} f_i(\lambda)d\lambda \qquad i = A, B. \tag{5.14}$$

We also denote the ratio of successful transaction of agent A and agent B by the *t-th* transaction as $x(t)$ and $y(t)$, respectively. From the rational transaction rule in (5.9), agent A will trade her knowledge if its associated threshold satisfies $y(t) \geq \theta_A$. Similarly agent B will trade her knowledge if its associated threshold satisfies $x(t) \geq \theta_B$. The proportion of knowledge to be traded at the next time period $t+1$ is given by $F_A(y(t))$ for agent A and $F_B(x(t))$ for agent B. Therefore, the dynamics of knowledge transaction is described as:

$$\begin{aligned} x(t+1) &= F_A(y(t)) \\ y(t+1) &= F_B(x(t)) \, . \end{aligned} \tag{5.15}$$

The above dynamics may reach equilibrium at the fixed point satisfying

$$\begin{aligned} x^* &= F_A(y^*) \\ y^* &= F_B(x^*) \, . \end{aligned} \tag{5.16}$$

We consider repeated knowledge transaction in the following three cases:

<Case 1> Agent A: intermediate-value knowledge (Type 2). Agent B: high-value knowledge (Type 1) as shown in Figure 5.6.

Figure 5.7 illustrates the dynamics of repeated knowledge transaction. The horizontal axis represents the ratio of successful trading of agent A ($x(t)$), and the vertical axis represents the ratio of successful trading of agent B ($y(t)$). The dynamics in (5.15) have two stable equilibria at left-extremity E_0 and at right-extremity E_3. At the lowest equilibrium at E_0, where $(x, y) = (0,0)$, neither agent trade knowledge. On the other hand, at the highest equilibrium E_3, $(x, y) = (1,1)$, both agents trade all of their knowledge. If the pair of initial ratios $(x(0), y(0))$ is in Region I in Figure 5.7, then the dynamics converges to E_0, and if the pair is in Region IV, then the dynamics converges to E_3. If the initial values are in either Region II or Region III, the dynamics will cycle between $(x, y) = (1,0)$ and $(x, y) = (0,1)$.

<Case 2> Agent A: intermediate-value knowledge (Type 2), Agent B: low-value knowledge (Type 3) as shown in Figure 5.8.

In this case, agent A is Type 2, as in Case 1. On the other hand, agent B is Type 3 in Figure 5.8. The dynamics is shown in Figure 5.9. By comparison with Case 1 in Figure 5.9, Region I, in which the dynamics converges to $(x, y) = (0,0)$ becomes larger, and Region IV, in which the dynamics converges to $(x, y) = (1,1)$ becomes smaller.

<Case 3> Agent A: high-value knowledge (Type 1), Agent B: low-value knowledge (Type 3) as shown in Figure 5.10.

We now consider the completely asymmetric case in which agent A has high-value knowledge and agent B has low-value knowledge. Their threshold densities are as illustrated in Figure 5.10. The dynamic process is shown in Figure 5.11, and both agents mostly repeat miss-coordination, since Region II and Region III, in which the cyclic behavior between $(x, y) = (1,0)$ and $(x, y) = (0,1)$ occurs, become larger.

In Case 1, knowledge sharing is promoted because both agents have incentive for sharing knowledge through transaction. On the other hand, in Case 2, knowledge sharing is relatively discouraged. An agent is rational and trades only if her utility can be improved. She fears a loss in disclosing her knowledge, because she estimates that the trading partner does not have valuable knowledge. In Case 3, they encounter another problem of miss-coordination. Consider the situation in which one agent discloses her knowledge and the other agent does not, and in the next period the previously non-disclosing agent discloses her knowledge but the previously disclosing agent does not disclose. Assuming that this miss-coordination continues, we found that the relative knowledge level of both agents plays a significant role in controlling knowledge transaction. Knowledge transaction between two agents having different values of private knowledge becomes difficult.

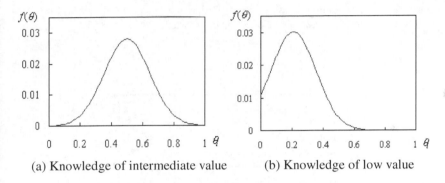

(a) Knowledge of intermediate value   (b) Knowledge of low value

Figure 5.6 Characterization of values of knowledge in terms of threshold: (a) Collection of knowledge of agent A: Ω_A (b) Agent B: Ω_B

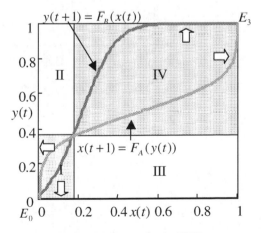

Figure 5.7 Dynamics in (5.15)

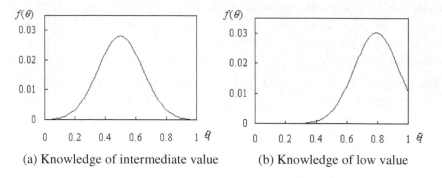

(a) Knowledge of intermediate value   (b) Knowledge of low value

Figure 5.8 Characterization of values of knowledge in terms of threshold: (a) Collection of knowledge of agent A: Ω_A , (b) Collection of knowledge of agent B: Ω_B

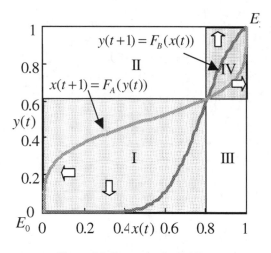

Figure 5.9 Dynamics in (5.15)

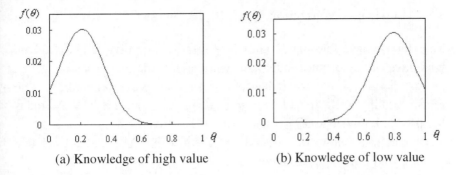

(a) Knowledge of high value   (b) Knowledge of low value

Figure 5.10 Characterization of values of knowledge in terms of threshold: (a) Collection of knowledge of agent A: Ω_A, (b) Collection of knowledge of agent B: Ω_B

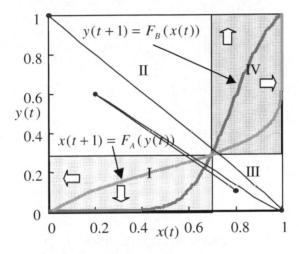

Figure 5.11 Dynamics in (5.15)

5.5 Knowledge Transaction by Multiple Agents

Thus far we have formulated knowledge transaction between two agents who have plenty of knowledge and who have made numerous decisions as to whether of not to trade. In this section, we extend knowledge transaction in a collective of agents, $G = \{i : 1 \leq i \leq N\}$. Each agent trades her private knowledge only if her utility is improved.

We denote knowledge traded by agent i by X_i, and knowledge traded by all other agents except agent i by

$$X(i) = (X_1, X_2, ..., X_{i-1}, X_{i+1}, ..., X_N).$$

By treating all other agents except agent i by one representative agent with the two strategies, S_1: trades knowledge $X(i)$, and S_2: does not trade, we can obtain the payoff matrix of agent i in Table 5.2. The payoff parameters in Table 5.2 are

$$
\begin{aligned}
a_i &= \Omega_i - X_i + v_i(K + X_i + X(i)) \\
b_i &= \Omega_i - X_i + v_i(K + X_i) \\
c_i &= \Omega_i + v_i(K + X(i)) \\
d_i &= \Omega_i + v_i(K)
\end{aligned}
\tag{5.17}
$$

where Ω_i represents the private knowledge of agent i, and K represents the common knowledge shared with all other agents.

The threshold of agent i with the payoff matrix in Table 5.2 is defined as

$$\theta_i = (d_i - b_i)/(a_i + d_i - b_i - c_i). \tag{5.18}$$

Substituting (5.17), the above threshold has the form of

Table 5.2 Payoff matrix of agent i

agent i \ Other agents	S_1 (trade $X(i)$)	S_2 (not trade)
S_1 (trade X_i)	a_i	b_i
S_2 (not trade)	c_i	d_i

$$\theta_i = \frac{X_i + v_i(K) - v_i(K + X_i)}{v_i(K + X_i + X(i)) - v_i(K + X_i) - v_i(K + X(i)) + v_i(K)} \qquad (5.19)$$

The denominator in (5.19) represents the multiplier effect of sharing knowledge, and the numerator represents the disclosure cost for of private knowledge.

Next, we consider repeated knowledge trading in the group and observe how both private knowledge and common knowledge is accumulated through knowledge transaction. We assume that the value functions $v_i(K)$, $i=1,2,...,N$, are super-additive in the form of

$$v_i(X) = kX \ln(X) \qquad (1 \le i \le N). \qquad (5.20)$$

In the above equations, the parameter value k is set as $k = 0.2$. In Figure 5.12, we describe the numerator of the threshold in (5.19) as a function of X, when we set $K = 40$. From this figure, if $X > 30$, the value of β_i becomes negative.

We now investigate the dynamic knowledge accumulation process starting with the different values of private and common knowledge as shown in Table 5.3. We consider two groups, and each group consists of 50 agents.

Group G_A : The private knowledge of all members is high.

Group G_B : Half of the group has high-value private knowledge and the rest has low-value private knowledge.

Table 5.3 Initial private and common knowledge levels

	Low	High
Common Knowledge (K)	10	40
Private Knowledge (Ω)	10-80	10-300

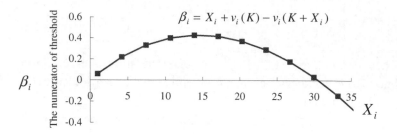

Figure 5.12 Value of the numerator in (5.19) ($K = 40$)

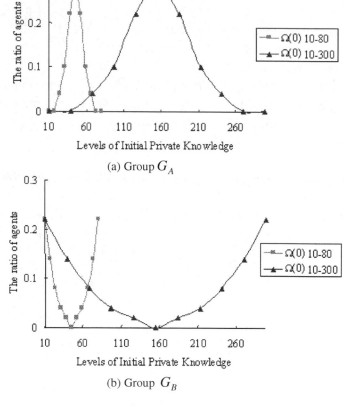

Figure 5.13 Ratio of agents having knowledge of the same value

The value distribution of private knowledge of each group is shown in Figure 5.13, where the vertical axis represents the ratio of agents who have the same value of private knowledge. Heterogeneity in the private knowledge of each group in Figure 5.13 can be interpreted in terms of the threshold densities, as shown in Figure 5.14. From this figure, we can induce two important points. First, if knowledge is valuable, its associated threshold becomes low. Second, the threshold density is ranged within a relatively small area.

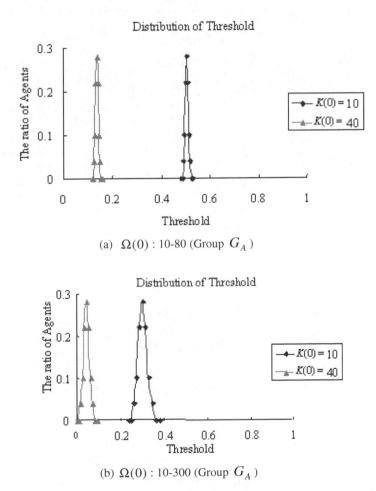

(a) $\Omega(0)$: 10-80 (Group G_A)

(b) $\Omega(0)$: 10-300 (Group G_A)

Figure 5.14 Ratio of agents having the same threshold

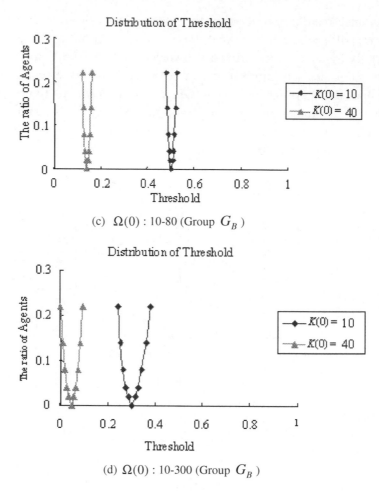

(c) $\Omega(0)$: 10-80 (Group G_B)

(d) $\Omega(0)$: 10-300 (Group G_B)

Figure 5.14 (*Continued*)

5.6 The Knowledge Accumulation Process as a Micro-Macro Loop

In this section, we investigate the knowledge accumulation process by specifying the micro-macro loop between individuals and the collective. The accumulation process of common knowledge is described as shown in Figure 5.1, and knowledge transaction at the microscopic level plays a key role in fruitful knowledge accumulation.

The micro-macro link is also interpreted as the process of knowledge re-combination of agents. Once common knowledge is accumulated, agents may absorb it and they can create new knowledge. The absorption ability of common knowledge of individuals can be interpreted as the strength of the micro-macro link. Knowledge sharing is an important value-adding component of knowledge management initiatives in organizations. We also investigate how the re-combination ability of knowledge at the micro level affects knowledge accumulation at the macro level.

We formulate the repeated knowledge transaction by multiple agents. The levels of both private and common knowledge may change over time through knowledge transaction. We denote the level of private knowledge of agent i as $\Omega_i(t)$ and the level of common knowledge by $K(t)$ at the t-th transaction period. We define the following production function of private knowledge:

$$\Omega_i(t+1) = (1 - \delta_i)\Omega_i(t) - X_i + \gamma_i K(t) \qquad (5.21)$$

where δ_i represents the depreciation rate of private knowledge and γ_i represents the re-combination ability of agent i. The re-combination ability becomes important in creating new knowledge by combining existing knowledge.

Similarly, we introduce the following production function for common knowledge:

$$K(t+1) = (1 - \kappa)K(t) + \sum_{i=1}^{N} X_i(t) \qquad (5.22)$$

where κ represents the depreciation rate of common knowledge. We assume that the knowledge to be trade by each agent is in proportion to the level of her private knowledge. Then, we assume that agent i trades knowledge given by

$$X_i = x_i \Omega_i(t) . \qquad (5.23)$$

We also focus on the effect of the re-combination ability in knowledge accumulation. We consider the following two cases:

<Case 1> Fifty agents have different re-combination ability γ, which ranges from 0.02 to 0.1 with an increment of 0.02.

<Case 2> All agents have low re-combination ability of $\gamma = 0.02$. The other parameter values are set as follows:

$$\delta_i = 0.1, \quad \kappa = 0.1, \quad x_i = 0.1 \tag{5.24}$$

In Figure 5.15, we show the case in which the initial levels of private knowledge of all agents are set to be low ($\Omega(0) = 10-80$), and the re-combination ability γ is uniformly distributed in [0.02, 0.1] (Case 1). The proportion of trading agents is shown in Figure 5.15(a) for two groups with the different initial common knowledge $K(0) = 10$ and $K(0) = 40$, respectively. The initial ratio of trading agents is set to 0.3.

In the group with the high initial common knowledge ($K(0) = 40$), all agents eventually come to be traded. On the other hand, for the group with low initial common knowledge ($K(0) = 10$), no agent trades. The accumulated private and common knowledge of both groups are shown in Figure 5.15(b)(c). Despite the large difference in the trading patterns at the individual level, however, there is little difference in accumulated knowledge.

In Figure 5.16, we show the simulation result when all agents have the low re-combination capability of $\gamma = 0.02$. One group starts with low common knowledge $K(0) = 10$, and the other group starts with high common knowledge $K(0) = 40$. The transaction process shown in Figure 5.16(a) is the same as that shown in Figure 5.16(a). However, even if the group has high common knowledge initially, they cannot accumulate private and common knowledge at higher levels, as shown in Figure 5.16(b)(c).

We now consider the group of agents in which each agent has a different value of private knowledge ranging from $\Omega(0) = 10$ to $\Omega(0) = 300$. In Figure 5.17, we show the case in which the re-combination ability is distributed uniformly over [0.02, 0.1]. We also consider two groups with initial common knowledge $K(0) = 10$ and $K(0) = 40$, respectively. The proportions of agents that trade their knowledge are shown in Figure 5.17(a). Even if the initial common knowledge is low, all agents eventually trade their knowledge. The accumulated private knowledge and common knowledge of both groups are shown in Figure 5.17(b)(c). They succeed in accumulating both private and common knowledge at higher levels.

In Figure 5.18, we show the simulation result when all agents have the low re-combination capability of $\gamma = 0.02$. One group starts with a low level of common knowledge $K(0) = 10$, and the other group starts with a high level of common knowledge $K(0) = 40$. The transaction processes of both groups are shown in Figure 5.18 (a), and all agents in both groups eventually trade their knowledge. The accumulated private knowledge and common knowledge are shown in Figure 5.18 (b)(c). It is shown that both groups fail to accumulate knowledge at both the private and common levels even if all agents trade their knowledge.

From these simulation results, we conclude the following. If some agents in a group have more valuable knowledge, all agents come to trade their knowledge and succeed in accumulating common knowledge at a higher level, even if the initial level of common knowledge is low. However, if the re-combination abilities of agents are low, they cannot accumulate knowledge at a higher level. They fail to create new knowledge even if they frequently trade their knowledge. Therefore, the re-combination ability of knowledge is important for accumulating knowledge on both the individual and collective levels.

Knowledge sharing is an important value-adding component of knowledge management initiatives. However, it is not clear that it has the effect of knowledge creation. It may be simply diffused among agents without creating new knowledge. The model in this chapter explicitly includes the accumulation processes of both private and common knowledge. Knowledge sharing becomes one of the important issues for many activities in an organization. The above simulation results imply that the re-combination ability has a great influence on knowledge accumulation. Even if most agents trade their private knowledge, they may fail to accumulate knowledge at a sufficient level if the re-combination ability of common knowledge and private knowledge of each agent is low.

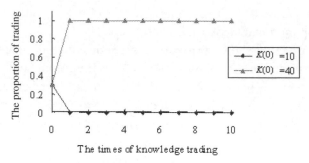

(a) Proportion of agents who trade

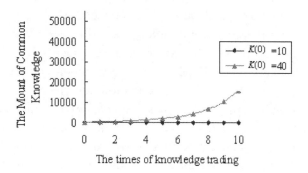

(b) Accumulation of common knowledge

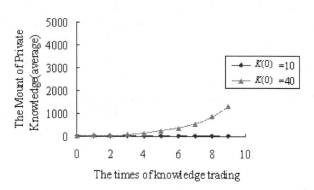

(c) Accumulation of private knowledge

Figure 5.15 Knowledge trading and accumulation of knowledge
($\Omega(0):10-80$, $\gamma_i:0.02$-0.10)

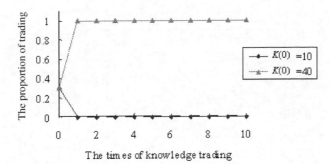

(a) Proportion of agents who trade

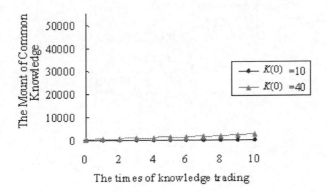

(b) Accumulation of common knowledge

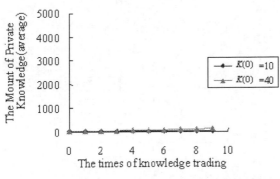

(c) Accumulation of private knowledge

Figure 5.16 Knowledge trading and accumulation of knowledge
($\Omega(0):10-80$, $\gamma_i:0.02$)

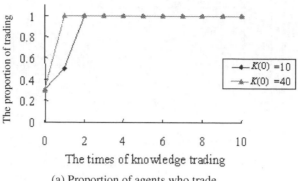

(a) Proportion of agents who trade

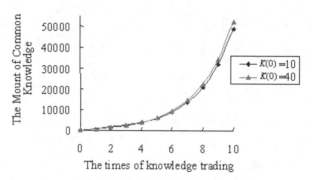

(b) Accumulated common knowledge

(c) Accumulation of private knowledge

Figure 5.17 Knowledge trading and accumulation of knowledge
($\Omega(0) : 10 - 300$), $\gamma_i : 0.02\text{-}0.10$)

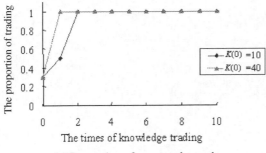

(a) Proportion of agents who trade

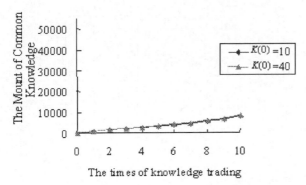

(b) Accumulation of common knowledge

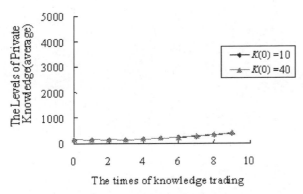

(c) Accumulation of private knowledge

Figure 5.18 Knowledge trading and accumulation of knowledge
$((\Omega(0):10-300),\ \gamma_i : 0.02)$

Chapter 6

Gains from Diversity

This chapter investigates the gains from diversity through heterogeneous interactions. We conduct a comparative study of the collectives of interacting agents, one in a global environment, and the other in a spatial environment. Each agent repeatedly plays either a coordination game or a dispersion game by adapting her best-response strategy to the global strategy population in a global environment, and to the local strategy population in a local environment. The performances of the global and local collective adaptive dynamics are evaluated in terms of stability, efficiency, and equity. The spatial environment is shown to encourage higher performance compared to the global environment.

6.1 Identity and Diversity

Many physical systems consist of an identical or lower number of different types of interacting particles. As a consequence, the widely studied physical systems assume that all particles follow identical laws of motion. Many economists also try to explain human behavior on the assumption of identical agents with the same personality or preference. However, recent literature has found that individuals' personalities vary widely. Thus, when individuals differ in personalities or preferences, they will behave differently, even when they face the same problem with an identical environment.

In many economic and social contexts, the diversity of individual interests should be a central consideration. However, the issue of diversity in agents does not arise in many practical problems. In fact, many disciplines tend to make the assumption of a *representative agent*.

That is, the macroscopic behavior arising from interactions of many agents can be modeled as if it were the behavior of a single agent. One way this might happen is if all agents are identical, however, to retain the possibilities of extending our understanding of collective phenomena of interest, we must relax the condition that all agents are identical or that they adapt to the same aggregate information.

The economic approach to human behavior has traditionally emphasized the role of individual preferences in explaining social phenomena. On the other hand, the sociological approach essentially focuses on heterogeneity in individuals as the determining factor in explaining social phenomena.

An emerging body of research on social interactions has attempted to breach the gap between these two approaches. Recent research on social interaction models has pointed out two key crucial aspects in explaining collective behavior: *heterogeneity* in individual preferences and *interactions* among individuals. These models also take into account the fact that the preferences of individuals with respect to actions can depend on the actions of other individuals. The emphasis is also put on the interplay between the heterogeneity of individual preferences and interactions in a collective of agents.

Heterogeneity in individual preferences is treated via the random utility approach (McFadden, 1975). Suppose each agent in a collective of N agents faces a binary choice problem with the two options, S_1 and S_2. The payoff difference of the two choices takes the form

$$U_1 - U_2 + \varepsilon \qquad (6.1)$$

where U_i, $i=1,2$ are the payoffs associated with the choice of S_i, $i=1,2$. These payoffs are the same for all agents representing representative preference. Heterogeneity of individual preferences is modeled via the random term ε that varies randomly across the agents.

We assume the rational-choice model, which is the option with the larger utility, is selected. Here, we also assume that an agent's choice is characterized by some *threshold value,* and each agent selects S_1 if her payoff difference in (6.1) is greater than or equal to her specific threshold θ. Therefore, an agent's specific choice depends on the payoff difference, the heterogeneity term ε and the threshold θ.

Then the proportion of agents who choose S_1 is obtained as the probability satisfying

$$Pr(S_1) = Pr(U_1 - U_2 > \theta - \varepsilon) \qquad (6.2)$$

The cumulative of the *Gumbel density* function takes the form

$$F(x) = \exp\{-\exp(-\kappa x)\} \qquad (6.3)$$

where κ is a diversity parameter. Large κ indicates that agents share similar individual preferences or thresholds, and small κ indicates a large heterogeneity of preferences or thresholds.

If we assume that θ and ε are independently drawn from the above Gumbel function, then $x = \theta - \varepsilon$ is logistically distributed with the cumulative function

$$F(x) = 1/\{1 + \exp(-\kappa x)\} \qquad (6.4)$$

By retranslating this into the original variables in (6.2), we obtain

$$Pr(S_1) = 1/[1 + \exp\{-\kappa(U_1 - U_2)\}] \qquad (6.5)$$

The diversity parameter κ determines the shape of the logistic distribution. Depending on the value of κ, the logistic probability function in (6.5) has the following characteristics. (1) If κ takes a larger value, the function is close to the step function. In this case, if the utility U_1 associated with S_1 becomes larger than U_2 associated with S_2, all agents choose S_1. In contrast, if the utility U_2 becomes larger than U_1, then all agents choose S_2. (2) If κ takes a small value, then the function takes a value close to 0.5. Therefore, the collective outcome is separated between two choices. In this case, each agent behaves randomly and her choice does not depend on the associated utility. (3) If κ takes an intermediate value, then the ratio of agents who choose S_1 will increase if its associated utility U_1 is higher than U_2. However, even if U_1 is larger than U_2, both agents who choose S_1 and agents who choose S_2 coexist.

More precisely, the above results mean that when individual tastes are sufficiently heterogeneous with a large value of κ, the distribution of choices is similar to the case with the collective of identical preference. On the other hand, small diversity means small κ, and the collective choice comes to be more random. There is a threshold value of κ_1, above which social interactions dominate individual heterogeneity to the point of altering the collective outcome. There is another threshold value of κ_2, below which social interactions also dominate individual heterogeneity to the point of causing the collective outcome to be random. This abrupt change in collective behavior is usually called a *phase transition* and is observed in many models of social interactions with externalities.

If the value of κ is between these two thresholds, then the collective behavior depends on heterogeneity in individuals. If the utility associated with S_1 becomes larger, more agents come to choose S_1. However, the difference becomes small, and the collective outcome becomes separated between two choices. Normally, the ratio of agents who choose S_1 will increase if its associated utility U_1 is higher than U_2, the utility of S_2. However, there is some probability that the option S_2 will be chosen.

Let consider a single agent referred as a representative agent with a utility function that takes the form

$$F(U) = 1/\{1 + \exp(-\kappa U)\} \tag{6.6}$$

Since (6.5) and (6.6) take the same form, the collective decisions of many heterogeneous agents can be treated as the decision of this representative agent. This relation simplifies the analysis of a collective of heterogeneous agents. However, this simplification depends on the assumption that two parameters θ and ε representing heterogeneity in preferences and thresholds, obey the Gumbel function and are statistically independent.

The underlying logic of social interaction models with individuality and heterogeneity of agents is to understand the collective behavior rather than that of a single agent. The main focus of the analysis is on the role of externalities across the agents in determining the collective behavior. In examining the collective behavior, the social interaction approach treats collective behavior as a regularity of the collection of individual decisions as they are determined through the interactions and idiosyncratic characteristics of the agents. Individual choice is guided by payoffs as well as social influences on individual preferences. The main point for the analysis is then the assumption that agents are influenced by the choices of others. The resulting collective systems with a micro-macro loop are the object of study.

6.2 Integration and Segregation

Evolution is responsible for a lot of sorting and separating, and the coexistence of various creatures. Individuals become mixed or separated in accordance with many factors. However, we have little knowledge regarding why and how heterogeneous individuals come to aggregate, in that individuals neither intend nor need to be aware of it.

To understand what kinds of segregation or integration may result from individual behavior, we have to look at the processes by which various mixtures and separations are brought about. Schelling (1978) investigated the problem of segregation that can result from individual discriminate behavior. He examined that some individual perceptions of differences, such as color, can lead to segregation. He also examined the extent to which inferences can be drawn from actual segregation with respect to the preferences of individuals.

Social interaction models focus on the role of externalities across the agents in determining aggregate behavior. The main point for the analysis is the assumption that agents are influenced by the choices of others. Young (1993) investigated dynamic processes in which the adoption of a specific behavior from two alternatives becomes more likely than its adoption by one's neighbor. He examined a conformist adaptive dynamics in which agents change their behaviors to comport with the choices of neighbors. He interprets this type of positive reinforcement as a *conformity effect*, since each agent obtains positive reinforcement from conforming with her neighbors.

Although the specific motivations for conforming differ across agents, the dynamic process exhibits quite complex behavior in the aggregate. The obvious equilibrium is for everyone to adopt the same alternative. There exist other equilibrium states in which some agents are coordinated on one alternative while others are coordinated on the other alternative. An outcome is defined as completely integrated if all agents adopt the same alternative, or is completely segregated if agents adopting one alternative continuously form one group and all other agents adopting the other alternative form another group. Young shows that many intermediate patterns that are partly integrated and partly segregated are observed when the agents adapt their choices to neighbors.

This result is also evidence of the collective system in which adaptation at the individual level can lead to a sub-optimal outcome.

In this chapter, we investigate whether it is possible to form desirable integrated or segregated patterns from the bottom-up that may satisfy everybody? It is important to consider with whom individual agents interact, and how they adapt or learn from others.

We attempt to gain a deeper understanding of this issue by specifying the way of adaptation at the individual level. To do this, we consider two fundamental models, global and local adaptation. A comparison is made between collective behavior evolved in the global interaction model and that evolved in the local interaction model.

Our work extends the analogy by acknowledging that social interactions are modeled in the framework of coordination or dispersion games. We consider a collective of heterogeneous agents located in a two-dimensional space, and they play either a coordination game or a dispersion game. We especially investigate the gains from diversity through the comparative simulation study of two adapting collectives: one in a global environment and the other in a local environment. We then clarify the most crucial factor that considerably improves the performance of the collective of adaptive agents. In order to do so, we also need to specify the configurations of heterogeneous agents.

The study takes is conducted in distinct two stages. We first consider the case in which each agent adapts her strategy to all other agents. Following the global adaptation model, we consider the case in which each agent adapts to only her neighbors. Instead of having agents interacting on a macro scale, we look at the introduction of locality and of neighborhood relationships. The selection pressure in a local arrangement may be lower, if agents are only assessed on a local level, and not in a global fashion. This allows for agents who may have been eliminated if assessed against all agents to survive in a local space by forming a niche.

6.3 Global and Local Adaptation Models

As we discussed in Chapter 4, in the global adaptation model, agents adapt to aggregate information about how all other agents behave, as shown in Figure 6.1. An important assumption of the global adaptation model is that each agent has knowledge of the aggregate of interactions. An agent compares her payoffs associated with possible alternatives and chooses her best response strategy to this aggregate information.

Instead of the local adaptation model, each agent adapts to her neighbors. Local adaptation may be a more realistic model since interactions in real life rarely happen on a macro scale and are generally confined to their neighbors. Implementation of spatial interaction is achieved through the use of a two-dimensional (2D) lattice with each agent inhabiting a cell on the grid, and interaction between agents is restricted to neighboring cells, as shown in Figure 6.2. The hypothesis of the local adaptation model also reflects the limited ability of agents to receive, decide, or act based upon information they receive in the course of interactions.

We consider a collective of N agents, each faces binary decision problems with the payoff matrix in Table 6.1 or Table 6.2. The crucial factor for describing heterogeneity in agents is the payoff parameter (or threshold), θ, and each agent takes a different value.

An agent who plays the coordination game in Table 6.1 receives a higher payoff if more agents choose the same strategy. Therefore, an agent who plays a coordination game is characterized as a conformist, since her adaptive behavior is based on the majority rule. On the other hand, an agent who plays the dispersion game in Table 6.2 receives a higher payoff if she chooses a distinct strategy from the majority. Therefore, an agent who plays a dispersion game is characterized as a nonconformist, since her adaptive behavior is based on minority rule.

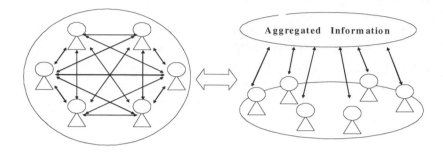

Figure 6.1 Global interaction. Each agent interacts with all other agents. Equivalently, each agent adapts to the aggregated information of the collective

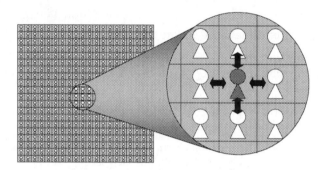

Figure 6.2 Local interaction. Agents located in the 2D lattice interact with their nearest neighbors

\<Conformist Adaptive Dynamics\>

We consider conformist adaptive dynamics, in which an agent interacts with the payoff matrix in Table 6.1. Suppose the proportion of agents who choose S_1 at time t is $p(t)$. The expected payoffs to an agent i (conformist) choosing from S_1 or S_2, conditional on everyone else continuing with their previous choices are

$$U_i(S_1) = p(t)(1-\theta), \qquad U_i(S_2) = (1-p(t))\theta. \qquad (6.7)$$

By comparing the expected payoffs to S_1 and S_2., the best-response strategy of agent i who interacts globally with the payoff matrix in Table 6.1 is obtained as:

<Global majority rule>

(i)   If $p(t) > \theta$, then S_1,

(ii)   If $p(t) < \theta$, then S_2..   (6.8)

(If $p(t) = \theta$, S_1 or S_2 is chosen randomly).

Each agent observes the global information on $p(t)$ and adapts as follows. If at least a threshold fraction θ of the collective chooses S_1, then she chooses S_1, else she chooses S_2. Since an agent adapts to the direction of the majority, we define the adaptation rule in (6.8) as the *global majority rule*.

We now obtain the best-response strategy when each agent adapts to her neighbors. We denote the proportion of the neighbors of agent i to choose S_1 at time t by $p_i(t)$. The expected payoffs of agent i to choosing form S_1 or S_2 are

$$U_i(S_1) = p_i(1-\theta_i), \qquad U_i(S_2) = (1 - p_i(t))\theta_i.$$ (6.9)

By comparing the expected payoffs to S_1 and S_2., the best response-strategy of agent i who interacts locally with the payoff matrix in Table 6.1 is obtained as:

Table 6.1 Payoff matrix of agent i (conformist) $(0 \le \theta \le 1)$

Agent i \ Other agents	S_1 (p)		S_2. (1-p)	
S_1	$1-\theta$	$1-\theta$		0
S_2.	0		θ	θ

<Local majority rule>

   (i)   If $p_i(t) > \theta$, then S_1,

   (ii)   If $p_i(t) < \theta$, then S_2.   (6.10)

(If $p_i(t) = \theta$, S_1.or S_2. is chosen randomly).

Each agent observes the local information $p_i(t)$ of her nearest neighbors and adapts by choosing S_1 if at least the fraction θ of her neighbors choose S_1, else she adapts by choosing S_2. Since an agent adapts to the direction of the majority of the neighbors, we define the adaptation rule in (6.10) as the *local majority rule*.

<Nonconformist Adaptive Dynamics>

We next consider a collective of N agents, each of which faces a binary decision with the payoff matrix in Table 6.2. In this situation, she receives a positive payoff if she chooses the strategy that is distinct from the majority, and we characterize this type an agent as a nonconformist.

   Suppose the proportion of agents who choose S_1 at time t is $p(t)$. The expected payoffs of agent i choosing from S_1 or S_2, conditional upon everyone else continuing with their previous choices are as follows:

$$U_i(S_1) = (1 - p(t))\theta, \quad U_i(S_1) = p(t)(1 - \theta).$$ (6.11)

Then the best-response strategy of agent i who adapts to the aggregate information is obtained as

Table 6.2 Payoff matrix of agent i (nonconformist) $(0 \le \theta \le 1)$

Agent i \ Other agents	S_1 (p)	S_2 (1-p)
S_1	0 0	$1-\theta$ θ
S_2	$1-\theta$ $1-\theta$	0 0

<Global minority rule>

    (i)   If $p(t) < \theta$, then S_1,

    (ii)   If $p(t) > \theta$, then S_2.   (6.12)

Since an agent adapts to the direction of the minority, we define the adaptation rule of a nonconformist in (6.12) as the *global minority rule*.

    Similarly, we can obtain the best-response strategy when each agent adapts to her neighbors. The proportion of the neighbors of agents i choosing S_1 at time t is denoted by $p_i(t)$. The expected payoffs of agent i choosing from S_1 or S_2 are

$$U_i(S_1) = p_i(t)(1 - \theta), \qquad U_i(S_2) = (1 - p_i(t))\theta \qquad (6.13)$$

The best-response strategy of agent i who adapts to her neighbors is obtained as

<Local minority rule>

    (i)   If $p_i(t) < \theta$, then S_1,

    (ii)   If $p_i(t) > \theta$, then S_2.   (6.14)

We define the adaptation rule of a nonconformist in (6.14) as the *local minority rule*.

6.4 Threshold Distributions and Locating Heterogeneous Agents

To account for variations in preferences, each agent is assumed to be idiosyncratic with respect to the payoff parameter θ in Tables 6.1 or 6.2. This critical number, the individual's threshold, is distributed across the population according to some probability distribution. We denote the number of agents with the same threshold θ in the population of N agents by $n(\theta)$. The discrete distribution $n(\theta)/N$ is approximated by the continuous function $f(\theta)$. This *threshold density* characterizes heterogeneity in agents.

    Each agent is assigned threshold θ drawn at random from the density function $f(\theta)$ distributed over the unit interval [0, 1]. Here, we assume the following two basic conditions. The first condition is that the threshold density is symmetric and satisfies

$$f(\theta) = f(1 - \theta).$$ (6.15)

The second condition is that the threshold density has the same average of 0.5, i.e.,

$$\int_0^1 \theta f(\theta) d\theta = 0.5.$$ (6.16)

We set up the five different threshold densities shown in Figure 6.3. The density function of Case 1 (unit density) represents the collective of identical agents with the same threshold $\theta=0.5$. The rest of the density functions represent collectives of heterogeneous agents. The collective with the threshold density of Case 2 is divided into two extreme groups: half of the agents have the threshold $\theta=0$, and the other half of the agents have the threshold $\theta=1$. In Case 3, the threshold density is normally distributed with the peak at $\theta=0.5$. In Case 4, the threshold density is uniformly distributed between 0 and 1. In Case 5, the threshold density has two peaks at $\theta=0$ and $\theta=1$.

When the collective is characterized with the density function of Case 3 (normal density), all agents consider the decisions of other agents before they make their own decisions. However, in the collective with the density function of Case 2 (density with two peaks), Case 4 (uniform density), or Case 5 (polarized density), some fraction of the agents are hardcore agents who choose S_1 (agents with $\theta=0$) and will choose S_1 independently of what the other agents decide. There also exist some hardcore agents who choose S_2 (agents with $\theta=1$) and they choose S_2 without regarding the decisions of other agents. These hardcore agents care only about what they actually want to do personally and do not consider the decisions of the other agents.

When heterogeneous agents interact locally, the agents with which they interact becomes important. Spatial interaction is achieved through the use of a 2D grid in Figure 6.2. Each agent chooses a best-response strategy based on local information about what her nearest neighbors have chosen in the previous period. Therefore, in the local adaptation model, we need to consider the location configuration of heterogeneous agents of different thresholds.

In the collective with the threshold density in Figure 6.3, their preferred choices differ depending on their thresholds. However, we classify heterogeneous agents into the following two types:

<Type 1> Agent with the threshold satisfying $\theta < 0.5$

<Type 2> Agent with the threshold satisfying $\theta > 0.5$

If an agent plays a coordination game with the payoff matrix in Table 6.1, and she is Type 1 with $\theta \leq 0.5$, she prefers S_1 to S_2, or if an agent is Type 2 with $\theta > 0.5$, she prefers S_2 to S_1. On the other hand, if an agent plays a dispersion game with the payoff matrix in Table 6.2, and she is Type 1 with $\theta \leq 0.5$, she prefers S_2 to S_1, or if she is Type 2 with $\theta > 0.5$, she prefers S_1 to S_2.

Each agent is assigned a threshold drawn at random from one of the threshold densities in Figure 6.3. Therefore, infinitely many location configurations may be possible. Here, we consider the following three basic assignments.

(1) *Random assignment*: Agents are randomly located on the lattice, and each type of agent has a chance to interact with agents of any type.

(2) *Well-mixed assignment*: Agents are located structurally so that they interact only with agents of the opposite type.

(3) *Sorted assignment*: Agents are located structurally so that they interact only with agents of the same type.

The above three basic assignments are illustrated in Figure 6.4.

Let us consider the case in which two agents (conformists) play a coordination game with the payoff matrix in Table 6.1. In this case, each agent is better off if she interacts with an agent of the same type. For example, if agent A with $\theta_A = 0.2$ (Type 1) interacts with agent B of the same type with $\theta_B = 0.3$ (Type 1), the payoff matrix is given in Table 6.3. In this case, their preferred strategies are the same, and the payoff matrix becomes symmetric. In this symmetric situation, both agents can easily establish the Pareto-optimal outcome by choosing S_1. On the other hand,

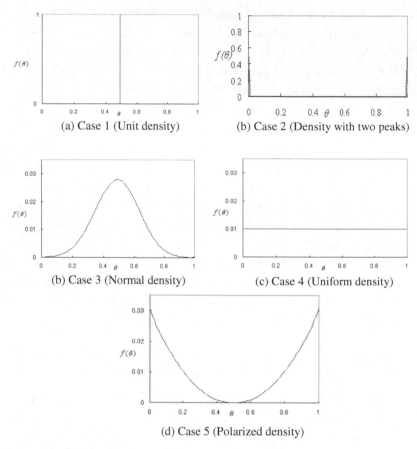

(a) Case 1 (Unit density)   (b) Case 2 (Density with two peaks)

(b) Case 3 (Normal density)   (c) Case 4 (Uniform density)

(d) Case 5 (Polarized density)

Figure 6.3   Density functions of the payoff parameter θ. Case 1: unit density and all agents have the same threshold $\theta=0.5$. Cases 2: density with two peaks at $\theta=0$ and $\theta=1$. Case 3: normal density. Case 4: uniform density. Case 5: polarized density at $\theta=0$ and $\theta=1$

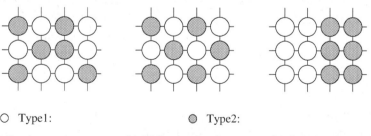

○ Type1:   ◉ Type2:

(a) Random assignment   (b) Well-mixed assignment   (c) Sorted assignment
Figure 6.4   Locating heterogeneous agents

On the other hand, if agent *A* interacts with agent *B* of a different type with $\theta_B = 0.7$ (Type 2), the payoff matrix is given in Table 6.4. In this case their preferred strategies are different and the payoff matrix becomes asymmetric. In this asymmetric situation, a coordination failure may occur because the agents have distinct preferred strategies.

We now consider the case in which two agents (nonconformists) play a dispersion game with the payoff matrix in Table 6.2. In this case, an agent is better off if she interacts with an agent of a different type. For instance, if agent *A* with $\theta_A = 0.8$ (Type 2) interacts with agent *B* with $\theta_B = 0.3$ (Type 1), their payoff matrix is given in Table 6.5. In this case, both agents can easily achieve a Pareto-efficient outcome by choosing distinct strategies. However, if agent *A* interacts with agent *B* of the same type with $\theta_B = 0.7$ (Type 2), the payoff matrix is given in Table 6.5. In this situation, in which their preferred strategies are the same, a coordination failure may occur by choosing the same strategy.

Table 6.3 Payoff matrix when the same types of agents interact

Agent A \ Agent B	S_1	S_2
S_1	0.7 / 0.8	0 / 0
S_2	0 / 0	0.3 / 0.2

Table 6.4 Payoff matrix when different types of agents interact

Agent A \ Agent B	S_1	S_2
S_1	0.3 / 0.8	0 / 0
S_2	0 / 0	0.7 / 0.2

Table 6.5 Payoff matrix when the same types of agents interact

Agent A \\ Agent B	S_1	S_2
S_1	0 0	0.7 0.8
S_2	0.3 0.2	0 0

Table 6.6 Payoff matrix when different types of agents interact

Agent A \\ Agent B	S_1	S_2
S_1	0 0	0.3 0.8
S_2	0.7 0.2	0 0

6.5 Performance Measures

In this section, we introduce *stability*, *efficiency* and *equity* as measures for evaluating the performance of collective systems. The priority for a desirable collective outcome is stability, which is crudely modeled using the idea of equilibrium of an underlying game. Why should we care about equilibrium? If a game has a rational solution that is common knowledge among agents, it must be equilibrium. If not, then some agents would have to believe that it is rational for them not to select the best-response to what they know agents are going to do. But it cannot be rational not to choose their best-response strategy.

However, the condition of stability is not sufficient, and we need the efficiency and equity criteria. Efficiency means that nothing gets wasted. In economics, the Pareto-optimality is followed in taking the absence of waste to be equivalent to the requirement that nobody can be made better off without someone else being made worse off. Efficiency stands for the measurement of the desirability of a collective outcome at the macro level. On the other hand, equity stands for the measurement of the desirability at the micro level.

In the beginning, agents choose their strategies randomly, and adapt them to the whole strategy population or their neighbors based on the rules obtained in Section 6.3. We evaluate collectives at equilibrium when the strategy population converges to a particular state. In our simulations, we change the initial conditions, i.e., the proportion of agents to each strategy, and observe the process of convergence of the strategy population.

<Stability> We obtain the proportion of agents who choose each strategy starting from arbitrary initial conditions and observe how the collective behavior converges to a particular outcome after repeated adaptations by all agents. The stability is also concerned with the path-dependency of the collective adaptive system.

<Efficiency> Efficiency is evaluated by obtaining the average payoff per agent. Efficiency stands for the measure used to evaluate the desirability of collective behavior at the macro level. The average payoff per agent U is defined as

$$U = \int_0^1 ug(u)du \qquad (6.17)$$

where u is the payoff to each agent, and $g(u)$ is the payoff distribution of the collective.

<Equity> Equity is also measured by obtaining the payoff distribution $g(u)$ of the collective. The *Lorenz curve L(x)* is often used to measure the extent of the payoff distribution. The Gini ratio is used to measure inequality, which is obtained from the Lorenz curve. It is defined as the area surrounded by the Lorenz curve $L(x)$ in Figure 6.5. The horizontal axis represents the cumulative proportion of agents, and the vertical axis represents the cumulative proportion of the total payoff $L(x)$, which is cumulated to the proportion at the level x starting with the poorest agents. The *Gini ratio φ* is defined as

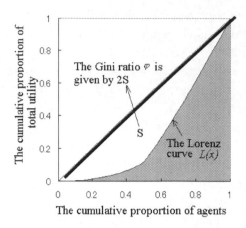

Figure 6.5 The Lorenz curve and the Gini ratio

$$\varphi = 2S \tag{6.18}$$

where S is the area between the 45-degree line and the Lorentz curve $L(x)$. In the most equitable case, $L(x)$ becomes the 45-degree line. The equity measure E is then defined as

$$E = 2\int_0^1 L(x)dx \tag{6.19}$$

which is obtained as twice the gray area in Figure 6.5.

The Lorenz curve $L(x)$ is defined using the payoff distribution function $g(u)$ of the collective as

$$L(x) = \int_0^x \tau g(\tau)d\tau / \int_0^1 \tau g(\tau)d\tau \tag{6.20}$$

where w is the value satisfying the following relationship:

$$x = \int_0^w g(\tau)d\tau \tag{6.21}$$

The denominator of (6.20) is the aggregated payoff of the collective and the numerator is the sum of the payoff to the $100x\%$ of agents starting with the poorest agent.

We can theoretically obtain efficiency and equity of the collective systems with the density functions of some simple forms.

<Case 1> *Conformist adaptive dynamics: The underlying game has the payoff matrix in Table 6.1*

When each agent in the collective plays a coordination game with the payoff matrix in Table 6.1, she adapts with the majority rule in (6.7). Let us suppose the proportion of agents who choose S_1 converges to p^*.

<Efficiency> The average payoff at equilibrium is obtained as follows. An agent, with a threshold θ less than or equal to p^* chooses S_1, and receives the payoff

$$u = p^*(1-\theta) \quad (0 \le \theta \le p^*).\tag{6.22}$$

On the other hand, an agent, with the threshold θ greater than p^* will choose S_2, and receives the payoff

$$u = (1-p^*)\theta \quad (p^* < \theta \le 1).\tag{6.23}$$

Then, the average payoff U of the collective is obtained as

$$U = \int_0^{p^*} (1-\theta)p^* f(\theta)\,d\theta + \int_{p^*}^1 (1-\theta)p^* f(\theta)\,d\theta\tag{6.24}$$

Therefore, the average payoff per agent (efficiency) is obtained as the function of the equilibrium p^* and the threshold density $f(\theta)$ of the collective.

As examples, we consider the following two extreme cases:

(i) all agents choose the same strategy: S_1 ($p^* = 1$) or S_2 ($p^* = 0$),

(ii) half of the agents choose S_1 and the other half choose S_2. (i.e., $p^* = 0.5$).

The average payoffs per agent for each case is obtained as follows:

(i) $p^* = 1$ (or $p^* = 0$): $U = 0.5$,

(ii) $p^* = 0.5$: $\qquad\qquad U = 0.5 - \int_0^{0.5} \theta\, p^* f(\theta)d\theta.\tag{6.25}$

<Equity > The proportion of agents who gain payoff u by choosing S_1 is $f(1-\theta)$. Therefore, the payoff distribution of agents who choose S_1 is given as

$$g_1(u) = f(1-\theta) = f(u/p^*) \quad (0 \leq \theta \leq p^*, p^* \neq 0). \tag{6.26}$$

Similarly, the proportion of agents who gain the payoff u by choosing S_2 is $f(\theta)$, and the payoff distribution of agents who choose S_2 is

$$g_2(u) = f(\theta) = f(u/(1-p^*)) \quad (p^* < \theta_i \leq 1, p^* \neq 1) \tag{6.27}$$

Then, the payoff distribution of the collective is obtained as the sum of the above two distributions as

$$g(u) = g_1(u) + g_2(u). \tag{6.28}$$

The payoff distributions when the strategy distribution converges to one of these two cases are obtained as follows:

(i) $p^* = 1$ (or $p^* = 0$): $g(u) = f(u) \quad (0 \leq u \leq 1)$

(ii) $p^* = 0.5$: $g(u) = 2f(2u) \quad (0.25 \leq u \leq 0.5) \tag{6.29}$

<Case 2> *Nonconformist adaptive dynamics: The underlying game has the payoff matrix is Table 6.2*

When an agent plays a dispersion game with the payoff matrix in Table 6.2, she adapts with the minority rule in (6.9). Then, an agent with the threshold θ less than or equal to p^* will choose S_1 and will receive the payoff

$$u = (1-p^*)\theta \quad (p^* \leq \theta \leq 1) \tag{6.30}$$

An agent with the threshold θ greater than p^* chooses S_2, and receives the following payoff:

$$u = p^*(1-\theta) \quad (0 < \theta \leq p^*). \tag{6.31}$$

Therefore, the average payoff per agent (efficiency) and the equity of the collective system are obtained to be the same as in Case 1.

6.6 Evaluation of Collective Adaptive Dynamics

In this section, we present comparative simulation results of two adapting collectives, one in a global environment and the other in a local environment. The underlying social interaction between agents is modeled either a coordination game or a dispersion game.

The strategy population is evolved when each agent adapts her best-response strategy. We are interested in the long-run collective behavior when each agent adapts to the rest of the all agents or her nearest neighbors over time. We investigate which model, global adaptation or local adaptation, encourages the emergence of high performance. We impose only a weak monotonic condition reflecting the inertia and myopia hypotheses on the collective dynamics, which describe the changes in the number of agents playing each strategy.

<Case 1> *Conformist adaptive dynamics: The underlying game has the payoff matrix in Table 6.1*

We consider the global adaptation model of a collective of conformists. The collective dynamics, in which each agent (conformist) adapts to the aggregate information with the majority rule in (6.7), is shown in Figure 6.6. In this figure, the horizontal axis represents the initial proportion of agents who choose S_1, and the vertical axis represents the proportion of agents p^* having chosen S_1 at the end.

The collective behavior of identical agents (density of the threshold is Case 1 in Figure 6.3) is simple. It only depends on the initial value of $p(0)$, the proportion of agents who choose S_1 at the beginning. When $p(0) > 0.5$, it converges to $p^* = 1$, where all agents choose S_1, and if $p(0) < 0.5$, it converges to $p^* = 0$, where all agents choose S_2.

We show the collective dynamics with the threshold densities in Cases 2, 3, 4, and 5 in Figure 6.6. The collective behavior of heterogeneous agents with the polarized threshold density (Case 2 in Figure 6.6) is also simple and remains at $p(t) = 0.5$ starting from any initial value of $p(0)$.

The performance of the collective system with the density of Case 3 is the same as the collective system of the identical agents in Case 1. When $p(0) > 0.5$, it converges to $p* = 1$, where all agents choose S_1, and if

$p(0) < 0.5$, it converges to $p* = 0$, where all agents choose S_2. More precisely, the above result means that only the initial ratio $p(0)$ that divides the collective most evenly will play a role in determining the long-run equilibrium.

There is a *critical* value of the initial condition, below which every agent chooses S_1 and above which every agent chooses S_2. Therefore, social interactions dominate individual heterogeneity to the point of altering the nature of equilibria. This abrupt change in the collective outcome is usually called a *phase transition* and is observed in many social interaction models with positive externalities. The collective adaptive system under the threshold density of Case 4 remains as the same as the initial value. On the other hand, the collective system with the density in Case 5 converges to $p* = 0.5$, starting from any initial value, which is the same as Case 2 of the polarized threshold density.

The equity (E) and the average payoff per agent U (efficiency) of the collective system having each threshold density in Figure 6.3 are

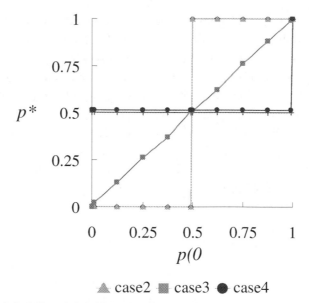

Figure 6.6 Stability of global adaptive dynamics with the density functions in Figure 6.3. Each agent globally adapts to the majority rule. The horizontal axis is the initial ratio of choosing S_1 ($p(0)$), and the vertical axis is the ratio $p*$ for choosing S_1 at equilibrium

obtained as follows:

Case 1: $(E,U) = (1.0, 0.5)$, Case 2: $(E,U) = (0.99, 0.5)$,
Case 3: $(E,U) = (0.84, 0.5)$, Case 4: $(E,U) = (0.89, 0.38)$, and
Case 5: $(E,U) = (0.94, 0.44)$.

The above pairs of equity and efficiency are shown in Figure 6.7, where the horizontal axis denotes equity (E) and the vertical axis denotes the average payoff (U). The equity is high for each case. Essentially, there is little difference in the performances, regardless of the heterogeneity. The exception to this is that a slightly higher equity and efficiency is achieved if the agents are identical.

We now evaluate the local adaptive dynamics, in which each agent adapts locally, and compare the results of the global adaptive dynamics. The collective behavior of local adaptive dynamics when heterogeneous agents are randomly located is shown in Figure 6.8. The collective system associated with the polarized threshold density (Case 2 in Figure 6.4) remains constant at $p(t) = 0.5$ for any initial value of $p(0)$. In all other cases, agents who choose S_1 and agents who choose S_2 coexist,

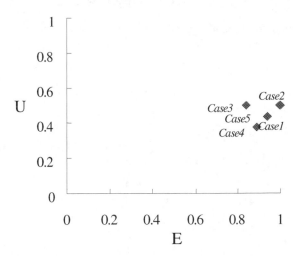

Figure 6.7 Plot of equity and average payoff per agent of the collective system having each threshold density in Figure 6.3. The horizontal axis is equity (E), and the vertical axis is the average payoff (U) when agents adapt with the majority rule of global adaptation

and this is a significant difference from the result of the global adaptive dynamics shown in Figure 6.6. The efficiency and equity under the random assignment are obtained as follows:

Case 1: (E,U) = (0.38,0.2), Case 2: (E,U) = (0.72,0.5), Case 3: (E,U) = (0.57,0.38), Case 4: (E,U) = (0.65, 0.42), Case 5: (E,U) = (0.7, 0.5).

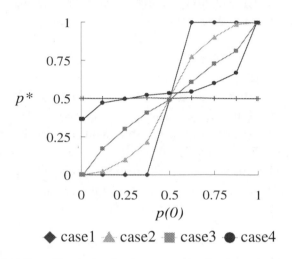

Figure 6.8 Stability of local adaptive dynamics of collectives with the density functions in Figure 6.3 under random assignment

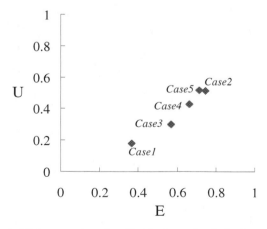

Figure 6.9 Plot of efficiency and equity. The horizontal axis is the equity (*E*), and the vertical axis is the average payoff (*U*) when agents adapt with the majority rule of local adaptation under random assignment

Figure 6.9 shows the pairs of equity and efficiency. Efficiency and equity become worse in all cases compared with the global adaptation model. We especially notice that the disparity between rich and poor agents becomes extreme under the local adaptation model.

We now evaluate the local adaptive dynamics in the structured environment in which heterogeneous agents are sorted so that they can interact only with agents of the same type, as shown in Figure 6.4(c). The simulation results are shown in Figure 6.10. The results for Case 1 are the same with random assignment. This is not necessarily surprising since all agents adapt to the same direction and receive almost the same payoff in the non-spatial environment. The collective dynamics with the threshold densities of Case 3, Case 4, or Case 5, become almost the same as that for polarized density in Case 2. The collective behavior converges and remains constant at $p(t) = 0.5$, starting from any initial value of $p(0)$.

The equity and efficiency of the local adaptation model under the sorted assignment are obtained as follows:
Case 1: $(E,U) = (0.85, 0.4)$, Case 2: $(E,U) = (0.95, 0.95)$, Case 3: $(E,U) = (0.89, 0.6)$, Case 4: $(E,U) = (0.83, 0.7)$, Case 5: $(E,U) = (0.85, 0.83)$. These results are depicted in Figure 6.11.

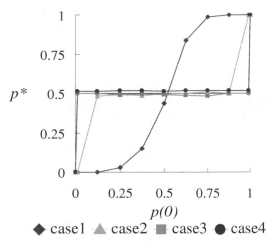

Figure 6.10 Stability of local adaptive dynamics with the density functions in Figure 6.3 for local adaptation under sorted assignment

In short, efficiency and equity are high under the well-mixed assignment, where agents interact with agents of the opposite type, but they are low under the random assignment, where they have chance to interact with any type of agent. Essentially, there are big improvements in the performance of the collective system compared with the system under random assignment. For a collective of identical agents (Case 1), all agents have the same threshold. Therefore, the equity is the highest. However, the efficiency is low and becomes equal to that of the random assignment model. If each agent adapts globally in a diverse collective, efficiency is moderate and equity is high. In local adaptation with random assignment, both efficiency and equity are low. Therefore, the diversity tightens the gap between efficiency and equity. However, in local adaptation with sorted assignment, both efficiency and equity become high.

Figure 6.11 summarizes the experimental results under the spatial framework. There are a couple of important differences from the results obtained using the non-structured environment shown in Figure 6.9.

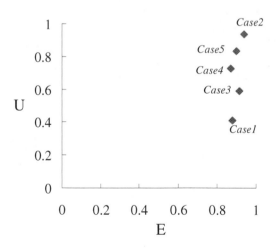

Figure 6.11 Experimental results under the spatial framework. The horizontal axis is the equity (E), and the vertical axis is the average payoff (U) when agents adapt with the majority rule for local adaptation under the sorted assignment

Figure 6.11 shows that it is actually *easier* to achieve both high efficiency and high equity in a spatial and structured environment where heterogeneous agents are located such that they only interact with agents of the same type. This important result occurs due to the individuals in the spatial framework being restricted to interact with neighbors having similar preferences.

\<Case 2\> *Nonconformist adaptive dynamics: The underlying game has the payoff matrix in Table 6.2*

Here, we consider the global adaptation model in which each agent (nonconformist) plays a dispersion game in Table 6.2 and adapts to the aggregate information with the minority rule in (6.12).

The equity E and efficiency U (average payoff) of the collective with each threshold density in Figure 6.1 are obtained as follows:
   Case 1: $(E,U) = (0.9, 0.4)$, Case 2: $(E,U) = (0.4\ 0.25)$,
   Case 3: $(E,U) = (0.7, 0.3)$, Case 4: $(E,U) = (0.94, 0.44)$,
   Case 5: $(E,U) = (0.6\ 0.25)$.
In Figure 6.12, we summarize these results.

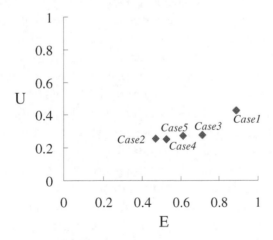

Figure 6.12 Plot of equity and efficiency (average payoff) of the collective with each threshold density in Figure 6.1. The horizontal axis is equity (E), and the vertical axis is the average payoff (U) when agents adapt with the minority rule for global adaptation

The resulting volatile collective behavior in each case is often far from efficient and equitable. The reason for the low efficiency is that the collective dynamics behaves cyclically, alternating between the two extremes, $p=0$ and $p=1$. Under this cyclic collective behavior, almost all agents choose the same strategy, and that results in lowering the average payoff.

In local adaptation with random assignment, we have the following results:

Case 1: $(E,U) = (1.0, 0.5)$, Case 2: $(E,U) = (0.85, 0.45)$,
Case 3: $(E,U) = (0.6, 0.38)$, Case 4: $(E,U) = (0.63, 0.4)$,
Case 5: $(E,U) = (0.82, 0.45)$.

In Figure 6.13, we summarize these results.

However, in local adaptation with well-mixed assignment, we have the following results:

Case 1: $(E,U) = (0.85, 0.4)$, Case 2: $(E,U) = (0.95, 0.95)$,
Case 3: $(E,U) = (0.89, 0.58)$, Case 4: $(E,U) = (0.89, 0.75)$,
Case 5: $(E,U) = (0.89, 0.83)$.

In Figure 6.14, we summarize these results. In short, efficiency and equity are high under the well-mixed assignment, in which agents interact with agents of the opposite type, but they are low under the random assignment, in which they interact with agents of any type.

Under the well-mixed assignment model, in which heterogeneous agents are located such that they only interact with neighbors of the opposite type, the efficiency comes to depend on the diversity of the collective. Moreover, among the five threshold densities, Case 2 achieves the highest efficiency and Case 1 achieves the lowest efficiency. So, we can conclude that a collective of agents with very diverse preferences generates the most efficient and equitable outcome.

Meanwhile, performances also depend on the diversity of the collective when agents are located randomly. That is, equity depends on the diversity of the collective but efficiency does not, which is very different from the situation of the global interaction model. Moreover, Case 1 has the highest equity, so that adaptation induces an equitable outcome in the collective of identical agents with the same preference. Conversely, the collective with the density of Case 2 has the highest efficiency and equity. Thus, we can conclude that the local adaptation model under the structured assignment produces an efficient and equitable outcome, especially in collective system with very diverse preferences.

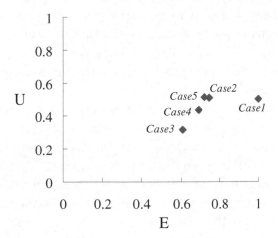

Figure 6.13 Results for local adaptation with random assignment. The horizontal axis is equity (*E*), and the vertical axis is the average payoff (*U*) when agents adapt with the minority rule

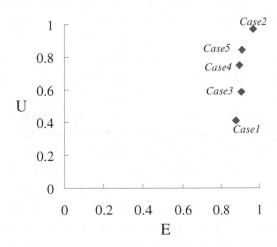

Figure 6.14 Results for local adaptation with well-mixed assignment. The horizontal axis is equity (*E*), and the vertical axis is the average payoff (*U*) when agents adapt with the minority rule

We also investigated whether a collective of heterogeneous agents that are locally connected without a central authority can produce better performance. We investigated the crucial factors that considerably improve the performance. The aggregate information in the global adaptation model is shown to be inefficient. The performance of the collective adaptive system depends on with whom interaction occurs, rather than how the agents adapt to each other. Therefore, assigning heterogeneous agents on the space where interactions occur outperforms adaptation at the individual level.

Comparison of the collective behavior evolved in spatial and non-spatial environments also yielded some other interesting results. It has been demonstrated that interaction on a spatial framework encourages and promotes efficiency and equity to a greater extent than when interaction is performed on a global level. When interaction occurs in a global, macro way, our results show that the environment produces no gain from diversity of the collective.

In summary, it is clear that a spatial environment results in a collective that is more efficient and equitable than collective adaptation in a global environment. However, in a spatial environment, while advantageous, the collective may have no gain and little impact on the performance of individuals if heterogeneous agents are randomly assigned and have no chance to interact with the appropriate neighbors.

The lesson here is that the collective dynamics of heterogeneous agents can be very sensitive to the composition of micro-motives of agents. The critical number, the individual's threshold, is assumed to be distributed across the collective according to some probability distribution. The collective outcomes depend on how the heterogeneous agents with different thresholds are located in the two-dimensional lattice.

Diversity plays a more important role when a spatial structure is used. If the locations of heterogeneous agents are well set, spatially interacting agents generate a more desirable collective outcome, compared with the global interaction model. The reason for this needs to be explored further and will form the basis for further study. This issue will be discussed in Chapter 7.

Chapter 7

Selective Interaction and Reinforcement of Preference

In this chapter, we examine the effect of the combined models of partner choice and preference reinforcement in social interaction. Agents choose which partners to interact with and then decide on a mode of behavior for the interaction. After successful interactions, they increase the payoff parameter of fitter strategies. We show that a collective of identical agents with the same preference in the beginning evolves into heterogeneous agents with diverse preferences by achieving the most efficient and equitable collective outcome.

7.1 Selective Interaction in Games

A different kind of collective behavior arises when agents change those with whom they interact before they make up their mind how to behave. In this chapter, we study a model in which agents can select partners with whom to interact. An agent may need to select her neighbors to interact with while considering a tradeoff between joining a neighborhood in which most agents share the same preference or another neighborhood in which they have different preferences. Agents also move because they prefer the neighborhood they are moving into compared with the neighbors they are moving away from. Therefore, we assume that agents are assumed to have the ability to move and interact selectively with other agents while making interaction mandatory for other agents.

For instance, consider dilemma games in which agents are endowed with the ability to interact selectively with other agents. The idea of selective interaction in dilemma games is as follows. Agents are assumed to have the ability to avoid bad matches, and they want to interact with other agents who cooperate and not with those who defect. This is obvious for agents who benefit from the cooperative outcome, but it is also true for agents who want to exploit other agents. Exploitative agents do well when they find other agents who cooperate and do not do well when they interact with other agents who also defect. So exploitative agents also benefit from selective interaction only with those agents who cooperate and avoid interaction with those agents who defect.

Selective interaction in dilemma games was introduced in previous studies (Tesfatsion, (1996), Axelrod, (1997)). When agents interact with other agents, they begin to develop a history of play. They keep track of how many times the other agent defects. If the other agent defects more than a certain number of times in previous interactions, then the agent will avoid interaction with that agent again.

Another crucial effect of selective interaction is that it allows agents to group together. An agent can avoid interaction with other agents if she receives a payoff that is lower than some threshold and moves to another site in order to have a chance to interact with different agents. Because of the gain from cooperation, cooperators that are surrounded by other cooperators can earn higher payoffs than defectors who are primarily surrounded by other defectors. Thus, endowing agents with the capability of selective interaction substantially increases the chances that cooperative agents will survive and that cooperative behavior will evolve.

The work by Schelling (1978) and Young (1998) introduced briefly in the previous chapter also triggered a lot of interest with respect to the question of the selection of neighbors. The aims of their models are to explain how social integration or segregation may occur spontaneously, even if people do not intend for them to occur. Individuals interact locally, having preference over their neighborhood. Taking the color of an individual (for instance white or black) as the criteria for discrimination, the problem faced by each individual is to choose a location given an individual threshold of acceptance for the proportion of individuals of different color in their neighborhood. They showed that a different kind of social norm arises when people change those with whom they associate, instead of changing how they behave given their associates. In other words, they choose their neighbors instead of conforming to their neighbors. This is called a *sorting process*.

In their models, agents behave based on the following simple rule. An agent agrees to stay in a neighborhood with agents that are mainly of the same color. More specifically, the following behavioral rule is used. An agent with one or two neighbors will try to move if there is not at least one neighbor of the same color. Under the assumption of a local behavioral rule for each agent, a fully integrated structure is observed at equilibrium, where no agent wants to move. However, they show that a slight perturbation is sufficient to induce a chain reaction and the emergence of aggregate behavior of segregation. The agents move at random towards a new location in agreement with their own preferences. The mobility of agents generates new discontented agents through a chain reaction until a new equilibrium is reached, and finally spatial segregation between two groups of agents with different colors often emerges. Thus, they show that selective interactions are sufficient for the occurrence of complete segregation, while it is not an attribute of the individual agents.

In game theory, the problem of equilibrium selection is an important issue. Important research concerns the impact of different network structures on equilibrium selection when agents can choose their network of interactions. Ellison (1993) analyzed the role of local interaction networks for the spread of particular strategies when the underlying game is a coordination game. He showed that the collective outcome converges to the risk-dominant equilibrium of the underlying coordination game if agents are located on a circle and interact with their two nearest neighbors. Similarly, Blume (1993) and Kosfeld (2002) proved the convergence to the risk-dominant equilibrium in a population of agents who are located on a two-dimensional lattice.

In contrast, Ely (2002) and Bhaskar and Vega-Redondo (2002) showed that once agents are allowed to choose which partners to interact with, the situation is very different. They introduced a number of locations where agents can meet and play the coordination game with each other. Thus, at any time, agents choose both a location and a strategy. With the combination of the partner selection and the strategy choice, they showed that risk dominance looses its selection force and that the population of agents is most likely to coordinate to realize the Pareto-efficient equilibrium. The reason for this is intuitive. Since agents can freely choose their interaction partners, they are able to select neighbors who engage in the Pareto-efficient equilibrium strategy in order to gain higher payoff, and at the same time, they can avoid agents who choose the inefficient risk-dominant strategy to obtain a lower payoff.

7.2 Evolution of Preference

Economists typically object to preference-based explanations of human behavior because differences in preferences can explain everything, and therefore nothing. On the other hand, over the past decade, psychologists have produced a robust collection of stylized facts about human preferences. While preferences are empirically quite *stable*, they are far from *identical*. Then, one of the most challenging issues is to identify the mechanism of forming heterogeneous preferences among individuals. Another important issue is the relation between adaptation of behavior and evolution of preference.

Individualism assumes that agent preferences are endogenous and selfish and that they are not affected by outside factors. It is amazing how little we know about the effects of the environments on preferences. The primary effects appear to operate through motivational rewards and the evolution of norms through social interactions. However, we lack adequate conceptual tools and empirical information on the process of preference formation. Therefore, it may be useful to consider a formal model of the process of preference formation (Bowles, 2004).

Agents are generally heterogeneous with respect to certain attributes. When agents have some heterogeneity by themselves, without any interaction, this characteristic is referred as *idiosyncratic heterogeneity*. When agents interact with each other, with the combined model of adaptation or learning and the insertion of a specific interaction structure, the agents are generally driven toward heterogeneous individual preferences, even if they are initially identical. We refer to this characteristic as *interactive heterogeneity*.

In the previous chapter, we were concerned with the diversity effect of the idiosyncratic preferences of agents. In this chapter, we are mainly concerned with interactive heterogeneity, and we show how a collective of identical agents having the same preferences evolves into heterogeneous agents with diverse preferences.

In general, adaptation of the behavior of an agent based on endowed preference is much faster than evolution of preference. It is often argued that in order to understand how individuals adapt, it is sufficient to observe their preferences. However these situations, in which an agent's adaptation depends on other agents' adaptations, usually do not permit any simple induction or extrapolation as to preference. The greatest promise lies in further analysis of situations in which agents behave in ways contingent on one another, and these interactive situations are also central in the analysis of the linkage between adaptation in behavior and preference evolution.

Equilibrium and efficiency are defined over the set of preferences expressed in the form of payoff functions of the agents, and their preferences are usually fixed. Traditional models take the individual preferences as an exogenous data and do not consider their particular form as a relevant object of study. Moreover, there appears to be a consensus in the research field about which type of preferences to allow in models. The working assumption in this regard is that an individual's behavior is guided by the sole individual motive of the maximization of one's own preference. However, this assumption has recently come under criticism. In turn, this has led many researchers to consider alternatives to the rational-choice model based on preference, such as the *non-individualistic model* or the *social preference model* (Bowles, 2004).

Therefore, it appears that time has come to critically examine the validity of modeling agents with fixed preference, and to ask deeper questions about the basis and plausibility of changing the structure of individual preference. One natural approach to addressing this issue is to adopt an evolutionary perspective in preference developments.

There has been some research on the study of *preference evolution* in the following framework. A population of agents repeatedly plays the underlying game. The payoff represents the evolutionary fitness, and the question arises as to what type of preferences are evolutionarily stable, in the sense of inducing a payoff that is at least as high as any alternative mutant in any given environment. More specifically, the following viewpoints are described:

(1) Success means an increase of payoff.

(2) Individual preferences of more fit agents are inherited by the genetic operation.

The above evolutionary explanation of the preference structures may be conceived to be identical to that of natural selection, in the sense that more evolutionarily fit agents can survive. However, it would be a mistake to conclude that evolution favors unequivocally agents that have preferences that are more evolutionarily fit. We may need to know more about the structure of the interaction mechanism in order to identify the precise implications of evolutionary forces on the selection of preference.

Human behavior is mainly driven by a conscious choice rather than natural selection. Many economic models, for instance, describe how agents behave based on their preferences. Game theory is typically based on the assumption of the rational-choice model. In our view, the reason for the dominance of the rational-choice approach is not that scholars think it to be realistic. Nor is game theory used solely because it offers good advice to the decision maker, because its unrealistic assumptions undermine much of its value as a basis for advice. The real advantage of the rational-choice model is that it often allows reasonable deduction to explain why an agent chooses a specific choice.

While we usually study the collective behavior of agents with endowed preferences, it is worthwhile to try to explain where and how these preferences appear. Unlike their behavior, the preferences of agents are traits, some of which are determined by natural selection. Preference leading to reproductive success causes an agent to thrive at the expense of the other agents. The effects of preferences on reproductive fitness are also mediated through the choice of behavior.

One alternative to the above model of preference evolution is the model of preference reinforcement. The basic premise in reinforcement learning is that the possibility of taking a strategy at present increases with the payoff that resulted from taking that strategy in the past. For instance, agents may try any number of alternative strategies, and repeat those that led to high payoffs in the past. The propensity to try a strategy increases according to the associated payoff. Therefore, agents are assumed to tend to adopt strategies that yielded higher payoffs, and to avoid strategies that yielded low payoffs. Although payoff characterizes choice of behavior, it is an agent's own past payoffs that matter, not the payoffs of the other agents.

Agents may consequently engage in trial and error by changing their preferences as well as their interaction partners. Preferences determine an agent's behavior, which in turn determine her fitness. Because preference generates fitness in this way, in order to understand preference reinforcement, we also need to focus on the interaction mechanism. In particular, we focus on how a collective of identical agents with the same preference is formed and what characteristic of *interactive heterogeneity* is formed through selective interactions. In order to do so, we must concurrently describe how agents select interaction partners as well as how they reinforce their preferences.

7.3 Social Games with Neighbor Selection

In many social interactions, agents consider not only which actions to choose, but also with whom they should interact. Similarly, in some social contexts, dissatisfied agents seek to break up some partnerships or alliances and to form new ones. This ability to rematch has strong implications for behavior within social relationships. While this observation is a relatively obvious, we have no systematic method of modeling such choice behavior depending on an agent's ability to select partners in the framework of game theory. In this section, we introduce such a methodology and examine a new class of social games in which agents also decide with whom they will play the game.

In Section 7.1, we have observed that agents endowed with the ability to select interaction partners in dilemma games have a strong advantage. Furthermore, selective interaction is a more useful mechanism to realize a cooperative outcome in a society of selfish agents. In this section, we introduce the combined model of selective interaction with preference reinforcement combined in the context of social games with positive externalities and with negative externalities.

In our model, a collective of agents repeatedly plays the underlying 2x2 game, formulated as a coordination game or a dispersion game. The payoff to each agent represents the fitness in this case. While preference determines an agent's strategy, the success or failure of her strategy choice determines which strategy should be reinforced. The model of preference evolution consists of two aspects, one governing the strategy choice based on the current preference and the other describing the direction of preference reinforcement.

We shall see that the combined model of the partner choice and preference evolution requires special analysis techniques. In our model, agents repeatedly play the underlying game with the current neighbors and myopically adapt their strategies with regard to neighbors in order to maximize their payoffs. After a number of repetitions of the game, they evaluate their performance in terms of the average payoff (fitness), and the successful agents increase the payoff parameter associated with the current strategy, and decide to remain in the same game. On the other hand, dissatisfied or unsuccessful agents move to new games in order to change the partners and interact with new neighbors.

More specifically, an agent decides to stop interaction with her current neighbors if she receives a payoff that is below some threshold, and moves to another game in order to interact with other neighbors. On the other hand, if her gain by choosing some specific strategy exceeds a certain threshold, then she continues to interact with the same neighbors and the preference (associated payoff parameter) of that strategy increases. Preference evolution therefore leads us to consider dynamics that run at two different speeds at once.

Although we treat selective interaction and preference evolution of the individual as occurring simultaneously, the former may proceed much faster than the latter. Agents can quickly switch to their preferred strategies, but changes to preferences driven by successful strategy choices may occur later.

Behavior trajectories of the collective can look quite different when social interaction has positive externalities, in which case it is modeled as a coordination game, or when it has negative externalities, in which case it is modeled as a dispersion game. In social interaction with positive externalities, increasing the number of agents using the same strategy increases each agent's payoff. Therefore, preference reinforcement often forces collective behavior to adjust discontinuously. As an example, let us consider the case in which the agents play a coordination game with the payoff matrix in Table 7.1, in which the choice of S_1 or S_2 results in the same payoff for each agent. Suppose some agents gain more by choosing the same strategy S_1 as their neighbors than other agents, who take a distinct strategy S_2. In this case, reinforcement of preference causes S_1 to become preferred, and it becomes more prevalent in the population.

As preferences change, agents decide their behavior based on a new preference level that favors S_1 and makes S_2 less attractive relative to S_1. Thus, the secondary effect of the good performance of S_1 is that agents who have originally chosen S_2 will begin to choose S_1. This secondary effect inhibits the growth of S_2. The primary effect of this change in preferences is to increase the proportion of agents who choose S_1. With this distribution of preference changes, a moment is reached at which equilibrium play can only be maintained if a significant fraction of the agents simultaneously switch strategies. Thus, when a collective of agents benefits from acting in concert, we should expect sudden shifts in the way they behave.

On the other hand, in social interaction with negative externalities, increasing the number of agents who choose the same strategy lowers each agent's payoff. Let us assume the agents face a dispersion game with the payoff matrix in Table 7.2. Increasing the representation of S_1 makes this strategy less attractive. As biases prompting S_2 become more prevalent, many agents switch from S_2 to S_1, reinforcing the growth of S_1. Then, most agents choose S_1. Surprisingly, this effect also causes agents to switch to S_2 again. In this case, more complex phenomena will be observed, and cyclic behavior occurs between the extreme situations in which all agents choose S_1 or all agents choose S_2. In this case of causing cyclic behavior, no agent can gain a payoff and their preferences are not reinforced.

The payoff matrices in Table 7.1 and Table 7.2 have one payoff parameter (or threshold), which is θ. The crucial concept for describing heterogeneity of agents is their payoff parameter, and they take different values, one for each agent. The heterogeneity of a collective of agents is then characterized by the density function of θ, as shown in Figure 6.3.

In Chapter 6, we described a comparative study of global interaction and local interaction in a collective of heterogeneous agents. Heterogeneity in agents makes it possible to introduce another means of interaction, *selective interaction*. This is possible because agents have different preferences, represented by parameter values or thresholds, and they can include partners by focusing their heterogeneity in preferences.

In Chapter 6, we classify heterogeneous agents into the following two types, depending on their payoff parameter values:

<Type 1> An agent with the payoff parameter satisfying: $\theta < 0.5$.

<Type 2> An agent with the payoff parameter satisfying: $\theta > 0.5$.

Table 7.1 Payoff matrix for a coordination game

Choice of the other agent / Choice of agent i	S_1	S_2
S_1	$1-\theta$ / $1-\theta$	0 / 0
S_2	0 / 0	θ / θ

Table 7.2 Payoff matrix for a dispersion game

Choice of the other agent / Choice of agent i	S_1	S_2
S_1	0 / 0	$1-\theta$ / θ
S_2	θ / $1-\theta$	0 / 0

In Figure 7.1, we describe the partner selection process. Each agent interacts with her neighbors by choosing her preferred strategy. If she gains an average payoff per neighbor of more than 0.5, she remains at the same location, otherwise she moves to new location in order to interact with different neighbors.

We consider collectives of heterogeneous agents, with threshold densities as shown in Figure 6.3. We observe how heterogeneous agents located randomly in the beginning will self-organize their configurations through endogenous selection of partners.

We show the simulation results in Figure 7.2 for the case in which each agent with the payoff matrix in Table 7.1 plays a coordination game with her neighbors. As shown in Figure 7.2(a), in the beginning, we allocate 2,500 heterogeneous agents randomly in the lattice. After a few hundred repetitions of selective interaction, each of the collectives has a threshold density (case 1 through case 5) and moves toward a completely separated configuration, as shown in Figure 7.2(b), in which most agents come to interact with neighbors of the same type.

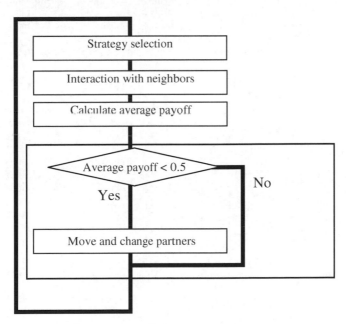

Figure 7.1 Process of selective interaction

We also show the simulation results in Figure 7.3, when each agent with the payoff matrix in Table 7.2 plays the dispersion game with her neighbors. After a few hundred repetitions of selective interaction, the collective of agents, each of which has a different threshold density (case 1 through case 5), moves toward to a completely mixed configuration, as shown in Figure 7.3, and in these cases, most agents finally select neighbors of the opposite type. That is, in this mixed situation, agents of Type 1 play with agents of Type 2, and vice versa.

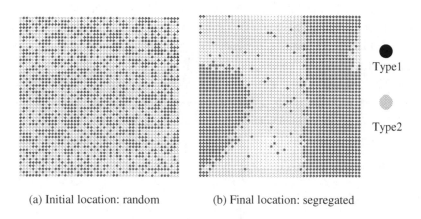

(a) Initial location: random   (b) Final location: segregated

Figure 7.2   Locations of agents after selective interaction. Each agent has the payoff matrix of a coordination game

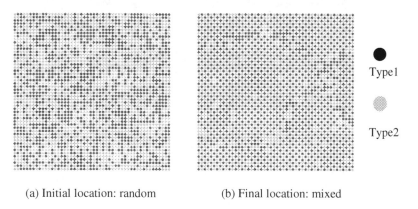

(a) Initial location: random   (b) Final location: mixed

Figure 7.3   Locations of agents after selective interaction. Each agent has the payoff matrix of a dispersion game

The pairs of efficiency (average payoff) and equity in the final configuration of each case are shown in Figure 7.4. When the underlying game is a coordination game, we have the results shown in Figure 7.4(a), which are almost the same as the results shown in Figure 6.11. When the underlying game is a dispersion game, we have the results in Figure 7.4(b), which are also almost the same results shown in Figure 6.14.

Therefore, a collective of heterogeneous agents initially located randomly could self-organize their locations through selective interactions and achieve the most efficient and equitable collective outcome. This desired collective outcome is achieved by self-organizing their location configuration so that they can interact with appropriate neighbors.

We found that through selective interaction, the most desirable conformal behavior emerged in social interactions with positive externalities, and the most desirable dispersed behavior emerged in social interactions with negative externalities, which made use of the diversity of a collective. This collective behavior has high efficiency and equity, so that it becomes desirable on both the micro and macro levels. The most crucial factor, which considerably improves the overall performance of the collective system, is the selection of the correct agents with whom to interact.

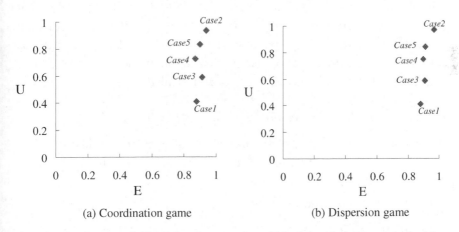

(a) Coordination game   (b) Dispersion game

Figure 7.4   Results obtained for the case in which the underlying game is (a) a coordination game or (b) a dispersion game. The horizontal axis shows the equity (E) and the vertical axis shows the average payoff (U)

7.4 Preference Reinforcement through Selective Interaction

In this section, we examine the effect of the combined model of selective interaction and preference reinforcement. As a specific model, we assume that agents reinforce their preferences over two possible strategies. Consider a collective of identical agents who have the same payoff parameter of $\theta = 0.5$ in the payoff matrices in Table 7.1 or Table 7.2 in the beginning. Agents myopically adapt their strategies to their neighbors in the direction that maximizes the expected payoff. After repeating the underlying game with the current neighbors, the agents gradually reinforce their preferences as well as select interaction partners based on the success of the repeated plays.

The basic premise in reinforcement learning is that the possibility of taking a strategy at present increases with the payoff that resulted from taking that strategy in the past. Agents try one of two strategies, and repeat the strategy that led to a high payoff in the past. This basic premise in reinforcement learning is modified as follows in our framework. The payoff parameter is increased according to the success of trying a strategy. Therefore, agents are more likely to adopt the strategy that yielded a higher payoff and to avoid the strategy that yielded a low payoff.

In Chapter 6, we classified heterogeneous agents into the following two types: conformists and nonconformists. Agents who play a coordination game with the payoff matrix in Table 7.1 are classified as conformists, and those who play a dispersion game with the payoff matrix in Table 7.2 are classified as nonconformists.

<An adaptation rule of a conformist: the local majority rule>

We denote the proportion of the neighbors of agent i who choose S_1 at time t as $p_i(t)$. The best-response strategy of agent i (conformist) is described as the local majority rule as

   (i) If $p_i(t) > \theta$, then S_1,

   (ii) If $p_i(t) < \theta$, then S_2.   (7.1)

(In the case $p_i(t) = \theta$, S_1 or S_2 is chosen randomly).

<An adaptation rule of a nonconformist: the local minority rule>

The best-response strategy of agent i (nonconformist) is described as the local minority rule as

(i) If $p_i(t) < \theta$, then S_1,

(ii) If $p_i(t) > \theta$, then S_2. (7.2)

In Chapter 6, we have observed that it is actually easier to achieve both high efficiency and equity in a spatial and structured environment. This important result occurs due to the fact that individuals in a spatial framework are restricted to interact with appropriate neighbors having similar preferences.

Among the several heterogeneities observed in the payoff parameter, the collective having the threshold density with two peaks, in which half of the agents have $\theta=0$ and the other half have $\theta=1$, achieved the greatest efficiency and equity. In the beginning, all of the agents are identical and have $\theta = 0.5$.

We now show how a collective of identical agents with the same preference evolves into heterogeneous agents so that they can achieve the collectively desirable outcome of the most efficiency and equity.

Figure 7.5 shows the collective preference reinforcement process. Each agent interacts with her neighbors by choosing her preferred strategy. If the average payoff per neighbor is more than 0.5, she reinforces the payoff parameter associated to her current choice. The reinforcement of the payoff matrix of a conformist is shown in Table 7.3, and that of a nonconformist is shown in Table 7.4

More specifically, each agent (conformist) repeatedly plays the underlying game with the nearest four neighbors. If the average payoff per neighbor is greater than 0.5 by choosing S_1, an agent increases the parameter value $1 - \theta$ associated with S_1 by $\Delta\theta = 0.01$ and decrease the parameter value θ associated with S_2 by $\Delta\theta = 0.01$. Similarly, an agent (nonconformist) who gains an average payoff per neighbor of more than 0.5 by choosing S_2 increases the parameter value θ associated with S_2 by $\Delta\theta = 0.01$ and decreases the parameter value $1 - \theta$ associated with S_1 by $\Delta\theta = 0.01$.

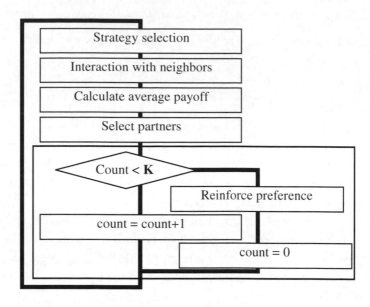

count: number of successful gains

Figure 7.5 Collective preference reinforcement process

Table 7.3 Reinforcement of the payoff-parameter for a conformist

Choice of the other agent / Choice of agent i	S_1	S_2
S_1	$1-\theta+\Delta\theta$ $1-\theta+\Delta\theta$	0 0
S_2	0 0	$\theta-\Delta\theta$ $\theta-\Delta\theta$

Table 7.4 Reinforcement of the payoff-parameter for a nonconformist

Choice of the other agent Choice of Agent i	S_1		S_2	
S_1		0	$\theta - \Delta\theta$	
	0			$\theta - \Delta\theta$
S_2		$1 - \theta + \Delta\theta$	0	
	$1 - \theta + \Delta\theta$			0

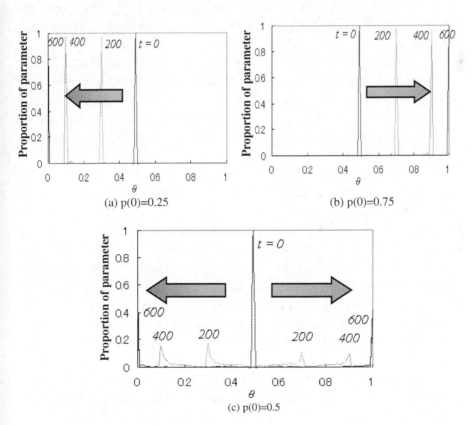

(a) p(0)=0.25

(b) p(0)=0.75

(c) p(0)=0.5

Figure 7.6 Transition of the density function of a collective of conformists. The underlying game is a coordination game

Figures 7.6(a) through 7.6(c) show the cases in which the initial value is set to $p(0) = 0.25$, $p(0) = 0.5$, and $p(0) = 0.75$, respectively. After $t=600$, half of the agents reinforce $\theta = 0$, and the rest of the agents reinforce $\theta = 1$. In these cases, a collective of identical agents succeeds in reinforcing their preference, so that the most efficient and equitable collective outcome is achieved. The performance of the collective reinforcement learning process depends on the initial condition of $p(0)$.

In Chapter 6, we analyzed the stability of collective adaptive dynamics and showed that the initial ratio $p(0)$ plays a role in determining the long-run equilibrium. The initial ratio of S_1 selection, $p(0) = 0.5$, eventually divides the collective outcome at equilibrium. Below this ratio, every agent chooses S_1, and above this ratio, every agent chooses S_2. This abrupt change in the collective outcome is usually called a *phase transition*.

The collective reinforcement learning process has the same property as collective adaptive dynamics. The initial ratio $p(0) = 0.5$ also becomes crucial in dividing the collective behavior. Below this ratio, every agent reinforces $\theta = 0$, so that S_1 becomes the dominant strategy, and above this ratio, every agent reinforces to $\theta = 1$, so that S_2 becomes the dominant strategy.

We show the simulation results of a collective of nonconformists in Figure 7.7. In this case, the underlying game is formulated as a dispersion game. The performance of collective reinforcement learning heavily depends on the initial conditions. In Figure 7.7(a), the initial proportion of agents who choose S_1 in the beginning is set to either $p(0) = 0.25$ or $p(0) = 0.75$. In these cases, the parameter values of $\theta=0.5$ remain, and therefore the agents do not reinforce their preferences.

In Figure 7.7(b), the initial proportion of agents who choose S_1 in the beginning is set to $p(0) = 0.5$. Agents with the same parameter value of $\theta = 0.5$ gradually self-reinforce, and after $t=600$, half of the agents reinforce to $\theta = 1$ and the rest of the agents reinforce to $\theta = 0$. This result implies that agents succeed in collectively reinforcing their preferences so that the most efficient and equitable collective behavior is achieved.

Therefore, except in the case in which the initial ratio is carefully chosen and set at $p(0) = 0.5$, the collective reinforcement learning fails in a collective of nonconformists who behave based on the minority rule.

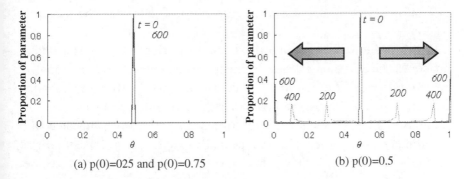

(a) p(0)=025 and p(0)=0.75   (b) p(0)=0.5

Figure 7.7 Transition of the density function of a collective of nonconformists. The underlying game is a dispersion game

7.5 Coexistence of Conformists and Nonconformists

In the previous section, we investigated the collective dynamics of selective interaction with reinforcement of endogenous preference. We have shown that the most crucial factor that considerably improves the performance of the collective system is the combination of the partner selection model with the process preference evolution.

In a collective of conformists, the underlying social interaction has the property of positive externalities, and their behavioral rule is characterized as the majority rule. In this case, the success of collective reinforcement learning does not depend on the initial conditions.

However, the initial ratio $p(0) = 0.5$ becomes a critical point that determines the direction in which the collective reinforcement process will evolve. If $p(0) > 0.5$, all agents reinforce to $\theta = 0$ and come to have S_1 as a dominant strategy. If $p(0) < 0.5$, all agents reinforce to $\theta = 1$ come to have S_2 as a dominant strategy. Therefore, such a phase transition occurs, and $p(0) = 0.5$ becomes a critical point. In a collective of nonconformists, the underlying social interaction has the property of negative externalities, and their behavioral rule is characterized as the minority rule. In this case, the success of collective reinforcement learning also crucially depends on the initial condition. In addition, except for the case in which the initial ratio $p(0)$ is set at 0.5, they fail to reinforce their preference in the direction of achieving the desirable outcome.

In this section, we examine the combined effect of conformists and nonconformists, which are heterogeneous at the meta-level with opposite behavioral rules. We consider a mixed collective in which half of the collective are conformists and the other half are nonconformists.

Initially, conformists and nonconformists are randomly allocated in a two-dimensional lattice. They repeatedly interact with their nearest neighbors for a time. If they gain a payoff above than a certain level (set to 0.4 in this case), they stay the same site and reinforce the payoff parameter associated with their current choice.

We show the simulation results in Figure 7.8 when the initial proportion of agents (including both conformists and nonconformists) who choose S_1 is set as $p(0) = 0.25$. A mixed collective of conformists and nonconformists with the same initial parameter value of $\theta = 0.5$ gradually self-reinforce their preferences, and after t=1,000 repetitions almost all of the conformists (49% of the collective, where 50% of the agents in the collective are conformists) reinforce to $\theta = 1$, and the remaining 1% of the conformists reinforce to $\theta = 0$. On the other hand, half of the nonconformists (25% of the collective) reinforce to $\theta = 1$, and the rest of the nonconformists (25% of the collective) reinforce to $\theta = 0$. Therefore, the percentage of agents who choose S_1 is 75%. Therefore, all conformists (50% of the total population) and half of the nonconformists (25% of the total population) choose S_1, and the other half of the nonconformists choose S_2.

In Figure 7.9, we show the results when the initial proportion is $p(0) = 0.75$. After t=1,000 repetitions, almost all of the conformists (49% of the collective, where 50% of the agents in the collective are conformists) reinforce to $\theta = 0$, and the remaining 1% of the conformists reinforce to $\theta = 1$. On the other hand, half of the nonconformists reinforce to $\theta = 1$, and the other half of the nonconformists reinforce to $\theta = 0$. The ratio of agents who choose S_1 is 25%. Therefore, all conformists choose S_2 and half of the nonconformists

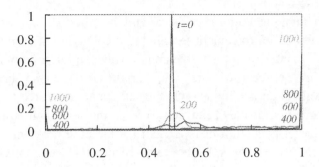

Figure 7.8 Transition of the density function of the payoff parameter θ: p(0)=0.25. The underlying games are a mix of coordination and dispersion games

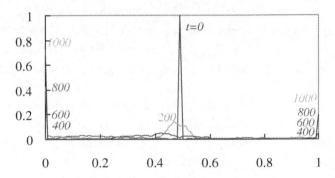

Figure 7.9 Transition of the density function of the payoff parameter θ: p(0)=0.75. The underlying games are a mix of coordination and dispersion games

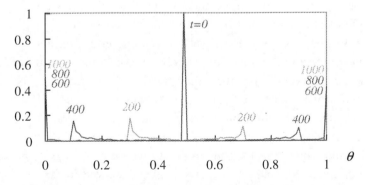

Figure 7.10 Transition of the density function of the payoff parameter θ. p(0)=0.5. The underlying games are a mix of coordination and dispersion games

(25% of the total population) choose S_2 and the other half choose S_1.

The success of reinforcement learning in a collective of conformists or a collective of nonconformists depends on the initial conditions. For a collective of conformists, the initial ratio $p(0) = 0.5$ becomes a *threshold* value that determines whether all agents reinforce to S_1 as the dominant strategy, or they reinforce to S_2 as the dominant strategy. For the collective of nonconformists, except for the case in which the initial ratio is set to $p(0) = 0.5$, collective reinforcement learning fails.

In Figure 7.10, we show the result when the initial proportion is set to $p(0) = 0.5$. In this case, after t=600 repetitions, half of the conformists (25% of the collective) and half of nonconformists (25% of the collective) reinforce to $\theta = 1$, and the remaining agents reinforce to $\theta = 0$. The ratio of agents who choose S_1 is 50%, and half of the conformists (25% of the total population) and half of the nonconformists (25% of the total population) choose S_1. The same is true for agents who choose S_2.

In this case, a collective of identical agents (both conformists and nonconformists) with the same parameter value of $\theta = 0.5$ in the beginning evolves into a collective of heterogeneous agents in which half of the agents have the parameter value of $\theta = 0$, and the remaining agents have the parameter value of $\theta = 1$. Therefore, the coexistence of conformists and nonconformists in the same collective promotes the achievement of the most desirable outcome. They collectively succeed in reinforcing their preferences and evolve into heterogeneous agents, so that the most efficient and equitable outcome is reached.

Conformists follow the majority, and nonconformist act in a manner that is contrary to the majority. Therefore, conformists tend to accelerate toward convergence. On the other hand, the convergence behavior of nonconformists tends to alternate between choices. By combining conformists and nonconformists, who have opposite behavioral characteristics, we observe the following interesting properties. Conformists have the lock-in property, whereby they always make the same choice. This lock-in property is also observed in the reinforcement of preference. Depending on the majority of the initial ratio, they reinforce their preference in the same direction. However, the vacillating property of nonconformists is modified. The coexistence of conformists and nonconformists, i.e., heterogeneity at the meta-level, prompts the success of collective reinforcement learning. In this mixed collective, without regarding the initial ratio, all conformists and nonconformists succeed in reinforcing their preferences so that the most efficient and equitable collective outcome is realized.

7.6 Development of Preference through Interaction

There are many social interactions with positive externalities in which the underlying game has multiple equilibria. A very simple example is games involving contributions to the public community. For an example, on Sunday morning we can choose to participate in volunteer work to clean up a public park or to stay at home. The underlying game becomes a coordination game that has three Nash equilibrium situations.

In the first round, we all choose the strategy of contributing the community. In the second round, we all choose to stay at home and nobody cleans up the public park. In the third round, we each toss a coin to decide whether to contribute. The third alternative may seem dubious, but if everybody else is randomizing her choice, tossing a coin to decide what to do is as good as any other method of selection. Therefore, we face an equilibrium selection problem, and the condition of efficiency takes us some way towards solving this equilibrium selection problem.

In Chapter 3, we observed that there is a conflict between Nash equilibrium and efficiency in social interaction with negative externalities. There is also an efficiency-equity tradeoff. An equilibrium situation is defined as a stable situation in which no agent changes her strategy. Since each agent seeks to optimize her payoff, an equilibrium situation is also defined as the situation in which no agent improves her payoff by unilateral changing her strategy, and the payoffs of all agents should be optimized simultaneously. However, it is observed that the conditions of equilibrium and efficiency contradict each other. It is obvious that some agents agree to choose their strategy and the other agents who benefit from a larger payoff reimburse them as a side-payment, whereby they may realize an efficient equilibrium. However, this type of subdivision of payoff is not studied in the framework of the theory of non-cooperative games. Rather, this type of problem is investigated in the theory of cooperative games.

Although the individual decision problem is important to understand, it is not sufficient to describe how a collection of agents arrives at specific desirable collective outcomes. Therefore, we aim to discover the fundamental micro-mechanisms that are sufficient to generate the desirable macroscopic structures of interest. This type of self-organization is referred as the emergence of desired orders from the bottom up.

The first priority for a desirable collective outcome is stability, which is crudely modeled using the idea of equilibrium of an underlying game. The next priority is efficiency, which is also defined as following Pareto optimality and is equivalent to the requirement that nobody can be made better off without someone else being made worse off. The third priority is equity.

The question of whether interacting agents self-organize desirable macroscopic behavior from bottom up depends on the type of social interaction as well as heterogeneity in agents. While agents may understand an outcome to be inefficient, by acting independently, they are powerless to manage the collective to overcome this inefficiency.

An agent's decision is *purposive* if she behaves to pursue her own goal to maximize her own payoff. However, the behavior of an agent often relates directly to those of other agents, and it is constrained by other agents who are also pursuing their own interests. Therefore, individual decisions are characterized as both purposive and contingent. In Chapter 4, we observed situations in which agents' microscopic behaviors reflecting their micro-motives combined with the behaviors of others often produce inefficient outcomes.

In the previous section, we introduced the combined model to examine the relationship between partner choice and evolution of preference. Agents choose which partners to interact with and decide on a mode of their preference, which influences their strategy choice. A collective of identical agents with the same preference in the beginning eventually evolves into a collective of heterogeneous agents with diverse preferences. The combined model of selective interaction and preference evolution formalizes the idea that agents facing decisions under interdependent environments may seek guidance from the way that other agents that they are familiar with have acted in similar situations. Implicit elements of this problem are a social structure indicating with whom an agent interacts and an inference process describing how an agent incorporates her observations in reinforcing her preference and choosing her optimal behavior.

In particular, we have considered a mixed collective of conformists who behave under the majority rule and nonconformists who behave under the minority rule. The coexistence of these heterogeneous agents at the meta-level is crucial for increasing the performance of the collective. The simulation results in the previous section suggest that diversity effects of the mixed collective have been observed in a few aspects. Initially conformists who share 50% of the collective and nonconformists who share the remaining 50% are randomly located in a two-dimensional lattice. They repeatedly interact with their nearest neighbors for a certain period. If they gain a payoff greater than a certain level, they remain at the same site and reinforce their payoff parameter as described in the previous section.

Heterogeneity across a collective of agents reflects a balance between purposive behavior and contingent behavior. In Chapter 4, we classify heterogeneous agents into basically two types: hardcore agents and opportunists. A hardcore agent has a dominant strategy and can make choices without regarding the others' decisions. On the other hand, the optimal choice of an opportunist depends on the choices of the others.

In the beginning, all conformists and nonconformists are identical and have the same parameter value of $\theta = 0.5$ and the threshold of the density is given in Figure 7.11(a). Therefore, they are all opportunists, since their best-response strategy heavily depends on the behavior of their neighbors. After collective reinforcement of preference, they evolve into heterogeneous agents with the density function in Figure 7.11(b), in which half of the agents, including both conformists and nonconformists, have the parameter value of $\theta = 0$, and the remaining agents have the parameter value of $\theta = 1$. The coexistence of conformists and nonconformist promotes the achievement of the most desirable outcome.

The mechanism behind the most efficient and equitable outcome achieved is that a collective of opportunists succeeds in reinforcing its preferences and evolves into a collective of hardcore agent. Therefore, they develop their preference so that they have their dominant strategies and can choose their preferred strategy without worrying about the others' choices.

Thus, the desirability of the collective reinforcement process is determined by the combination of conformists and nonconformists. Conformists do what the majority does and nonconformist do the opposite of what the majority does. Conformists have a feature whereby their collective action accelerates toward convergence. On the other hand, nonconformist has a feature whereby they alternate between choices. By combining conformists and nonconformists, the lock-in property of conformists and the property of alternating choices of nonconformists are merged, and they produce an efficient stable macro-behavior.

However, after a successful preference reinforcement process, conformists and nonconformists are segregated, so that conformists interact only with conformists, and nonconformists interact with nonconformists. In the niche of conformists, the conformists of the same type also form a sub-niche. Conformists who have S_1 as a dominant strategy by reinforcing the parameter value as $\theta = 0$ (Type 1) are located next to each other and they interact with agents of the same type. On the other hand, conformists who have S_2 as a dominant strategy by reinforcing the parameter value as $\theta = 1$ (Type 2) are located next to each other and interact with agents of the same type, as shown in Figure 7.12(a).

On the other hand, nonconformists do not form any sub-niche and are located so as to interact with agents of the opposite type. That is, nonconformists who have S_1 as a dominant strategy by reinforcing the parameter value as $\theta = 1$ (Type 1) are located so that they interact with nonconformists of Type 2 who have S_2 a dominant strategy by reinforcing the parameter as $\theta = 0$, as shown in Figure 7.12(b).

If there were only a single type of agent, then standard models of reinforcement learning would fit quite well. However, when agents have diverse preferences and different choices about with whom they interact, the analysis becomes more complex. The idea that a diversity of preferences can benefit a collective by discouraging it from swinging to extremes is not so surprising. There is a natural extension of this idea to learning, namely that neighborhoods including different types of agents are less susceptible to herding toward the wrong action. In strategic environments, if agents can evolve their preferences to the point that they can choose a dominant strategy, then they can choose their most preferred strategy without regarding the others' choices. With this property at the individual level, the resulting collective outcome becomes the most desirable outcome.

Most work on learning has focused on the inference process, taking the social structure to be exogenous. However, when agents differ in their preferences, the value of learning to an agent depends on choosing the correct agents with whom to interact. This chapter has looked at a model in which agents with diverse preferences must first choose neighbors and then choose an action based on their observations of how other agents in the neighborhood behave.

The reinforcement learning process is guided by the self-interest seeking of agents. The mechanism has a strong similarity to the nature of a self-organizing and growing process. The growth starts from the collective of identical agents. However, they are allowed to self-organize by establishing a desirable collective outcome. The resulting collective dynamics can be quite complex. The combined model of selective interaction and preference evolution makes it possible to focus on the positive effect by forming proper niches. Agents recognize that there is something inherently complex about decision-making and that this complexity has to do with its strategic nature.

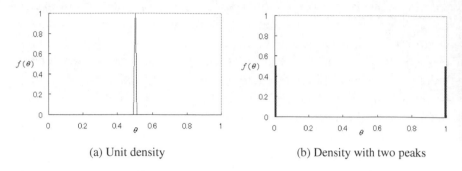

(a) Unit density   (b) Density with two peaks

Figure 7.11 Transition of the identical threshold into the most desirable diversity

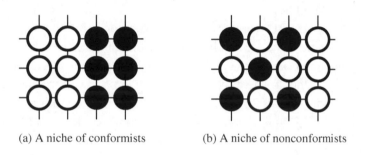

(a) A niche of conformists   (b) A niche of nonconformists

Figure 7.12   The final location of conformists and nonconformists The empty circle denotes an agent with $\theta = 0$, and the filled circle denotes an agent with $\theta = 1$

Chapter 8

Give-and-Take in Social Interaction

In our daily life, we face many congestion problems, and solving these problems has become an important issue. Congestion problems always arise when we need to utilize limited resources. The dispersion game provides a simple model for understanding the mechanisms behind many congestion situations. In this chapter, a simple behavioral rule that has an intriguing property for dealing with congestion problems is derived. We introduce a new behavioral rule of give-and-take, in which an agent changes her strategy in order to yield to others if she could gain a payoff. We show that a collective of agents, each acting with the principle of give-and-take, self-organizes to obtain the most desirable collective outcome.

8.1 Social Interaction with the Logic of the Minority

The term *emergent* is used to denote stable macroscopic patterns that arise from interactions of agents who behave with their idiosyncratic behavioral rules. *Emergent properties* are often surprising because it is hard to anticipate the full consequences of actions, even if the underlying behavioral rules are simple. However, there remain many issues as to how to derive a set of behavioral rules that induce a desirable collective outcome.

In this chapter, we consider strategic environments in which a large number of agents have to be dispersed. A rational approach to modeling individual learning may be useless in solving these dispersion problems. In particular, we address the following basic questions: (1) How does a collective of self-motivated agents self-organize collective behavior that satisfies the constraints without a central authority? (2) How does learning at individual levels lead to efficient collective behavior? (3) How does the principle of give-and-take in a collective of agents play the part of an invisible hand to promote self-organization of emerging desired collective behavior?

Coordination is necessary in social interactions to ensure that the individual actions of many agents are carried out with few conflicts. Coordination problems arise mainly because individuals do not consider the effects of their actions on others. The class of coordination problems that has been investigated has the property whereby increased effort by some agents leads the remaining agents to follow suit, which gives rise to *multiplier effects*.

Social interaction problems such as sharing or allocating limited resources in an efficient way result in different types of coordination among individuals. This complementary class of social interactions, in which agents gain payoffs only when they choose distinct action, as the majority does, has received relatively little attention. Examples of this type of social interaction include traffic or Internet congestion problems. This type of social interaction is also related to the problem of division of labor or dispersion of several agents in an efficient way.

Social interactions with positive or negative externalities are modeled in the following common framework. We assume that each agent has the same payoff function $u(x, X)$, where the agent's action x is taken in a set that is a subset of real numbers, and the second argument, X, is the average of the others' actions. In this case, the others may be a finite number or a continuum of agents. The second argument generates the payoff externality to each agent.

We distinguish *strategic compatibility* (or social interaction with *positive externality*) from *strategic complementarity* (or social interaction with *negative externality*). In the first case, a higher level of activity X by others increases the marginal payoff of each agent and stimulates the incentive to act in the same manner as the others. In this case, each agent behaves based on the *logic of majority*. In the second case, on the contrary, a higher level of activity X by others reduces the marginal payoff. For example, each person who travels on a congested highway or visits a popular restaurant increases the waiting time of other travelers.

In this case, an agent gains a payoff if she chooses the opposite route to what the majority does, and we define that an agent behaves based on the *logic of minority*.

Alpern (2001) introduced a *dispersion problem*, in which agents prefer to be more dispersed by illustrating the following typical examples:

(1) Location problems: Retailers simultaneously choose their positions within a common space so as to maximize the area in which they are the closest retailer.

(2) Habitat selection: Males of a species choose territories in which there are no other males. Animals choose feeding patches with low population density with respect to food supply.

(3) Congestion problems: Individuals seek facilities or locations of low population density.

(4) Network problems: Travelers choose routes with low congestion levels.

These dispersion problems, in which an agent behaves based on the logic of minority, arise in a large number of domains, including load balancing in computer science, niche selection in biology, and division of labor in economics. Social interaction with negative externalities poses many difficulties that are not found in social interactions with positive externalities. In particular, in situations in which self-motivated agents behave based on the logic of minority require better coordination to disperse them efficiently so as to produce equal benefits to each of them.

Effective solutions to social congestion problems or scarce resource allocation problems may require the invocation of an authority. The central authority may find the social optimum and impose the optimal behavior on all agents. Although such an optimal solution may be easy to find, the implementation becomes difficult to enforce in practical situations. For instance, to alleviate social congestion, the central authority often explicitly charges users in order to eliminate the socially inefficient congestion of a scarce resource. However, this approach often requires equilibrium solutions in which all agents are fully informed about the structure of the problem and the behaviors of all other agents. Consequently, the relationship between each agent's microscopic behavior and the congestion at the aggregate level they experience is easily discerned. However, the reliance on information-intensive equilibrium solutions limits the usefulness of the models in solving many congestion problems.

Most attractive in science is a brief story that can be easily told to people outside the specific scientific field, the core of which, however, constitutes a salient and deeper problem. The *El Farol bar problem*, introduced by Arthur (1994), is a thought-provoking model related to learning and bounded rationality that has received much attention as a paradigm to discuss many issues, including social inefficiency resulting from rational behavior.

There is an Irish bar named *"El Farol"* in downtown Santa Fe, New Mexico. The *El Farol* bar has live Irish music on every Thursday night. Each of the staff in the Santa Fe institute (referred to herein as "agents") are interested in going to the bar on Thursday night to enjoy the live music. All agents have identical preferences. They will enjoy the night at *El Farol* very much if the bar is not so crowded. However, each of them will suffer miserably if the bar is crowded. The bar has a maximum capacity. In Arthur's example, the total number of agents is $N=100$, and the capacity is set to $C=60$.

Arthur used this very simple yet interesting problem to illustrate the effective uses of inductive reasoning by agents. The only information available to agents is the number of visitors to the bar on previous Thursday nights. Agents make their choices by predicting whether the attendance on the current Thursday night will exceed capacity, and they then take the appropriate action. Arthur investigated the number of agents attending the bar over time by using a diverse collection of simple prediction rules that were followed by the agents. The agents make their choices by predicting whether the attendance on the current Thursday night will exceed the capacity and then take the appropriate action

What makes this problem particularly interesting is that it is impossible for each agent to be perfectly rational, in the sense of correctly predicting the attendance on any given night. This is because if most agents predict that the attendance to be low (and therefore decide to attend), the attendance will actually be high, whereas if they predict that the attendance will be high (and therefore decide not to attend), the attendance will be low.

One interesting result obtained by Arthur is that, over time, the average attendance of the bar is approximately equal to the maximum capacity. Arthur examined that the driving force behind the equilibrium situation around the capacity is realized. In Arthur's simulations, agents attempt to predict how many others will attend *El Farol* each time using a simple rule of inductive reasoning. If they predict attendance will be less than 60, then they go to the bar. If they predict attendance will be greater than 60, then they stay at home. Each agent uses a number of different "rules of thumb", such as simple averages, moving averages, and linear or nonlinear models to formulate predictions. They then act on the prediction that has been most frequently correct in the recent past.

The *El Farol bar problem* has received a fair amount of attention from computer scientists and physicists as well as from researchers in the area of complex systems. Casti (1996) uses the *El Farol bar problem* to frame his definition of a complex adaptive system as one with "a medium-sized number of intelligent, adaptive agents interacting on the basis of local information.

Challet and Zhang (1997) simplify the *El Farol bar problem* even further by considering a *minority game* in which agents choose one of two groups to join and receive positive payoffs only when they choose the smaller group and receive negative payoff as penalty if they choose the larger group.

We need to explore the mechanism in which interacting agents who are stuck at an inefficient equilibrium can move toward a better outcome. While agents understand that the outcome is inefficient, each agent acting independently may be unable to manage the collective activity concerning what to do and also how to decide. Self-enforcing solutions, in which agents achieve a desirable allocation of limited resources while pursing their self-interests without any explicit agreement with others, are of great practical importance.

8.2 Formalisms of Dispersion Games

In the examples of social interaction with negative externalities discussed in the previous section, agents want to disperse rather than meet. In this section, we formalize dispersion games as an integrated framework of the *El Farol* bar problem and its variant, the minority game. Dispersion games will display important and interesting properties in a number of different domains.

Dispersion games are generalization of 2x2 dispersion games for an arbitrary numbers of agents and actions. However, we restrict the problem here to N agents, each of which has a binary choice. In these games agents prefer outcomes in which the agents are maximally dispersed across the set of possible actions. For instance, each agent chooses a resource to utilize, and her utility depends on the number of other agents who try to utilize the same resource. In this case, the capacity of a resource is limited.

The *El Farol* bar problem and the minority game have a common feature. Agents are rewarded a unitary payoff whenever the side chosen happens to be chosen by the minority of the population. There are many ways to generalize the solution to these dispersion problems. For instance, different people have different tolerances for what constitutes a crowd or an unacceptable delay. Each agent could also have a parameter that represents her tolerance for congestion. These observations motivate us to extend the *El Farol* bar problem as one-shot simultaneous games under several different payoff schemes.

The El Faro bar problem and its variant, the minority game, are formulated as follows. Consider a collective of N agents. Each agent has to choose between S_1 or S_2, and those on the minority side win. More specifically, at each period of the stage game, N agents must choose privately and independently between two strategies:

S_1: go to the bar,

S_2: stay home.   (8.1)

The payoff function of each agent depends on the actions of all agents. The payoff to each agent is declared after all agents have chosen independently, those who are in the minority win and receive payoffs The payoff function to an agent i is formally defined as follows:

<A Basic Payoff Scheme>

(i) $U_i(S_1) = 1$,   if $p(t) = \sum_{1 \le i \le N} a_i(t)/N \le \theta$,

(ii) $U_i(S_1) = -1$,   if $p(t) > \theta$,   (8.2)

(iii) $U_i(S_2) = -1$ if $p(t) < \theta$,

(iv) $U_i(S_2) = 1$ if $p(t) > \theta$.

We represent the choice of agent i at time t by $a_i(t) = 1$ if she chooses S_1, and $a_i(t)=0$ if she chooses S_2. The total attendance at t is denoted by $A(t) = \sum a_i(t)$, and therefore the ratio of agents that choose S_1 is $p(t)=A(t)/N$. The value of θ is the capacity rate of the bar and is set as $\theta=0.6$ in the *El Farol* bar problem and $\theta=0.5$ in the minority game.

Let us analyze the structure of this minority game to see what to expect. Consider the extreme case, in which only one agent chooses S_1, and all of the others choose S_2. This lucky agent gets a reward point, and there is no reward for the others, and there is a huge waste of the resource. An equally extreme example occurs when $N/2$ agents choose S_1 and $N/2$ agents choose S_2. From a social point of view, the second situation is preferable since all of the agents can get an equal payoff. In this perfect coordination, the average gain (efficiency) per agent would also be maximized. Therefore, waste is proportional to the amplitude of fluctuation, and the average gain is usually far from this desirable outcome.

The generalized story of the *El Farol* bar problem and the minority game is as follows. N agents in total decide independently each night whether to go to a bar. Going is enjoyable if the bar is not crowded, otherwise the agents would prefer to stay home. Crowded is defined by the capacity C ($0 < C < N$), according to which the bar is crowded if more than C people attend, whereas it is not crowded, and thus enjoyable, if the number of attendances is C or less. Let agents have the identical payoff functions, and a is the positive payoff for attending an under-crowded bar, and $-b$ is the negative payoff for attending a crowded bar.

Without loss of generality, the payoff received for staying home is set to be zero.

With the above generalization, the payoff function for each agent is defined as follows:

<Payoff Scheme 1>

(i) $U_i(S_1) = a$,   if $p(t) = \sum_{1 \le i \le N} a_i(t)/N \le \theta$,

(ii) $U_i(S_1) = -b$,   if $p(t) > \theta$,   (8.3)

(iii) $U_i(S_2) = 0$.

where $\theta = C/N$ is the capacity rate of the bar.

Let us consider another payoff scheme in which the payoff is defined as a linearly decreasing payoff function the proportion of the agents that make the same choice.

<Payoff Scheme 2>

$$U_i(S_1) = a - (a+b)p(t),$$
$$U_i(S_2) = 0$$ (8.4)

In this payoff scheme, agents that choose S_1 (going to the bar) are rewarded with a payoff that is a linearly decreasing function of the ratio of the attendance, $p(t)$. On the other hand, the payoff for choosing S_2 (staying home) is linearly increasing with respect to the proportion of the attendances, $p(t)$. That is, more payoff is awarded to every agent choosing the minority side. Clearly, this structure favors the smaller minority. This is similar to a lottery in that we would like to win, but it is even better if we are the only winner.

With the basic payoff scheme described by (8.2), whenever the side an agent chooses happens to be chosen by the minority of the agents, they receive an award. That is, the agents in the minority receive the payoff +1 and agents in the majority receive -1 as penalty. For instance, for the *El Farol* bar problem, if the bar is not crowded, agents who go the bar enjoy themselves and receive the payoff, and agents who stay home receive the penalty since they lose the opportunity for enjoyment.

However, if the bar is crowded, agents who attend the bar will suffer miserably and will receive the −1 penalty, and agents who stay home will receive the +1 payoff as a bonus for making the right decision.

With Payoff Scheme 1 described by (8.3), agents who stay home receive nothing and agents who go to the bar receive either a payoff or a penalty. If the *El Farol* bar is not crowded, then agents who go to the bar enjoy themselves and receive the payoff *a* (*a*>0). However, if the bar is crowded agents who attend the bar will suffer miserably and will receive a negative payoff -*b* (*b* > 0). The payoff to each agent under this payoff scheme is shown in Figure 8.1(a).

As we noticed before, the dispersion problem with Payoff Scheme 1 shown in (8.3) contains a knife-edge response to increased attendance, and the analysis of equilibrium depends crucially on how the agent accounts for her own behavior. A formal treatment of the knife-edge case can be remedied with Payoff Scheme 2 described by (8.4). With this payoff scheme, agents who stay at home receive nothing and those agents who go to the bar receive payoff or penalty that is proportional to the level of the crowdedness. The payoff to each agent under this payoff scheme is illustrated in Figure 8.1(b).

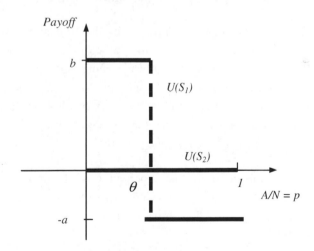

(a) Payoff functions for Payoff Scheme 1 (8.3)

Figure 8.1 Payoff functions: (a) unitary award (Equation (8.3)), (b) proportional award (Equation (8.4))

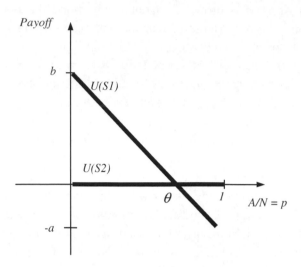

(b) Payoff functions for Payoff Scheme 2 (8.4)

Figure 8.1 (*Continued*)

8.3 The Price of Anarchy of Uncoordinated Collective Decisions

The *El Farol* bar problem is a type of congestion game in which each agent's payoff depends on the number of other agents who choose the same action. In a deterministic setting where agents utilize only pure deterministic strategies, it is easy to see that Nash equilibrium occurs for the payoff functions shown in (8.2), (8.3) or (8.4) when there is no difference between the two choices for each agent i:

$$U_i(S_1) = U_i(S_2), \quad 1 \leq i \leq N. \tag{8.5}$$

This condition implies that the expected payoff for the pure strategy of S_1 (attending the bar) is exactly equal to the expected payoff for the pure strategy of S_2 (staying home). This must hold for all agents simultaneously.

The condition in (8.5) is satisfied at the intersection of the two utility functions in Figure 8.1. Therefore, it is easy to see that Nash equilibrium occurs when exactly C (the capacity of the bar) agents attend. In addition, this condition also determines a mixed equilibrium strategy that depends on the distribution of total attendance, which, in general, depends on the probabilities for individual agents. A dispersion game also presents a unique symmetric mixed strategy Nash equilibrium, in which each agent chooses S_1 and S_2 with the probabilities $x = C/N = \theta$ and $1-x = 1-\theta$ respectively. However this symmetric mixed strategy Nash equilibrium is not Pareto optimal. Any attendance outcome that falls short of the maximum capacity of an under-crowded bar can be improved by increasing attendance, and vice versa. In contrast, the mixed strategy Nash equilibrium is fair, since the expected payoffs to all individual agents are equal and are 0. In addition, the randomness in agents' choices of strategy will generate fluctuations in attendance.

We can measure the level of efficiency by the average payoff per agent over a long period of time. Consider the extreme case in which only one agent attends the bar and all of the other agents stay home for each time period. Only this lucky agent gets the reward, and the others get nothing. Therefore, the average payoff per agent is $1/N$ in Payoff scheme 1 in (8.3). An equally extreme situation is that when $N\theta$ agents attend the bar and $N(1-\theta)$ agents stay home. In this case, the average payoff per agent is θ. From a collective efficiency point of view, the latter situation is preferable.

Let us suppose that there exists some central authority that causes a slightly larger number of agents than $N\theta$ to choose S_1 when $\theta \geq 0.5$. In this case, those who stay at home are rewarded, and the average payoff per agent is $1-\theta$. Similarly, if slightly fewer agents than $N\theta$ choose S_1 when $\theta < 0.5$, those who attend the bar are rewarded and the average payoff per agent is θ. Therefore, the average payoff per agent is given as $Max(\theta, 1-\theta)$. Similarly, if the central authority causes slightly fewer agents than $N\theta$ to choose S_1 if $\theta \geq 0.5$, and a slightly larger number of agents than $N\theta$ to choose S_1 if $\theta < 0.5$, then the average payoff per agent is $Min(\theta, 1-\theta)$. Therefore, the best-case and worst-case average payoffs are as follows:

<Best-case average payoff>

$$\underset{0 \leq \theta \leq 1}{Max}(\theta,\ 1-\theta) \tag{8.6}$$

<Worst-case average payoff>

$$Min_{0 \le \theta \le 1} (\theta, \ 1-\theta) \tag{8.7}$$

The best-case and worst-case average payoffs become the same when θ = 0.5.

The average payoff (efficiency) under Payoff Scheme 1 in (8.2) is obtained as follows. Let us suppose slightly fewer agents than the capacity $C = N\theta$ choose S_1. In this case, agents who choose S_1 receive the payoff, and the average payoff per agent is $a\theta$. On the other hand, if a slightly larger number of agents than $N\theta$ choose S_1, these agents receive negative payoff -b and the average payoff per agent is $-b\theta$. Therefore, when the payoff function has the property of a knife-edge, as shown in Figure 8.1(a), there is a fluctuation of the average payoff.

<Best-case average payoff>

$$a\theta \tag{8.8}$$

<Worst-case average payoff>

$$-b\theta \tag{8.9}$$

The average payoff per agent under the payoff function 2 is obtained as follows.

<Best-case average payoff>

$$Max_{0 \le \theta \le 1} \theta\{a - (a+b)\theta\} \tag{8.10}$$

<Worst-case average payoff>

$$Min_{0 \le \theta \le 1} \theta\{a - (a+b)\theta\} \tag{8.11}$$

The dispersion problem formulated as an N-person game can be decomposed into a 2x2 game, and then the Nash equilibrium strategy and collective efficiency (the average payoff per agent) can be obtained by analyzing the underlying game. In the dispersion game with Payoff Scheme 1, shown in (8.3), agents are rewarded a unitary payoff whenever their choice happens to be in the minority. Let us suppose each agent plays with all other agents individually under the payoff matrix in Table 8.1. The payoff to agent i obtained by playing with all other agents by choosing S_1 or S_2 is:

$$\overline{U}_i(S_1) = -n(t) + (N - n(t) - 1),$$

$$\overline{U}_i(S_2) = n(t) - (N - n(t) - 1). \tag{8.12}$$

where n represents the number of agents that choose S_1. The average payoff from play with one agent is obtained as

$$U_i(S_1) = \overline{U}_i(S_1)/N \cong 1 - 2p(t),$$

$$U_i(S_2) = \overline{U}_i(S_2)/N \cong 2p(t). \tag{8.13}$$

Then, we have the same payoff functions as shown in (8.4). Therefore, the dispersion problem with N agents can be decomposed into a 2x2 game with the payoff matrix shown in Table 8.1. With this decomposition, each agent is modeled to interact with all other agents under this payoff matrix.

Suppose each agent interacts with all other agents under the payoff matrix shown in Table 8.2. The payoff to agent i obtained by choosing either S_1 or S_2 is given as

$$\overline{U}_i(S_1) = a(N - n - 1) - bn,$$

$$\overline{U}_i(S_2) = 0. \tag{8.14}$$

Dividing by N, the average payoff per agent is obtained as

$$U_i(S_1) = \overline{U}_i(S_1)/N \cong a - (a+b)p(t),$$

$$U_i(S_2) = \overline{U}_i(S_2)/N = 0. \tag{8.15}$$

Then, we have the same payoff functions as in (8.4), and thus minority games can be decomposed into 2x2 games. The payoff matrix in Table 8.2 is equivalently transformed into the payoff matrix shown in Table 8.3 by setting $\theta = a/(a+b)$.

Note that the payoff matrix in Table 8.3 is a *dispersion game*. As shown in Chapter 3, the coordination game and the two-agent dispersion game differ only by the renaming of one agent's actions. However, with arbitrary numbers of agents and actions, these two games diverge.

We now evaluate the collective performance under the mixed *Nash equilibrium strategy*. Here, all agents choose the mixed strategy in which an agent assumes that each other agent is also choosing a fixed mixed strategy. In each round, each agent selects a strategy randomly from the probability distribution that represents the mixed Nash equilibrium. We consider a population of agents with $N=2{,}500$ for which the capacity rate is set to $\theta = 0.5$. In this case this dispersion game has a unique mixed

Nash equilibrium in which each agent selects the two strategies with equal probability.

We represent the mixed strategy $RND(x) = (x, 1-x)$ of choosing S_1 with the probability x and S_2 with $1-x$. If all agents adapt the mixed Nash equilibrium strategy, $RND(0.5)$, each agent can expect a payoff of 0.5 for each time period, and the distribution of the total payoffs follow a binomial distribution with a mean of $N/2$ and a variance of $N/4$. The variance is also a measure of the degree of social efficiency. If the variance is high, the magnitude of the fluctuations of approximately $N/2$ also becomes high, implying the loss of aggregated welfare.

Table 8.1 Underlying payoff matrix of the minority game

Own strategy \ Strategy of others	S_1 (Go)	S_2 (Stay home)
S_1 (Go)	-1 / -1	1 / 1
S_2 (Stay home)	1 / 1	-1 / -1

Table 8.2 Underlying payoff matrix of the minority game

Own strategy \ Strategy of others	S_1 (Go)	S_2 (Stay home)
S_1 (Go)	$-b$ / $-b$	0 / a
S_2 (Stay home)	a / 0	0 / 0

Table 8.3 Payoff matrix of general minority games

Own strategy \ Strategy of others	S_1 (Go)		S_2 (Stay home)	
S_1 (Go)		0		$1 - \theta$
	0		θ	
S_2 (Stay home)		θ		0
	$1 - \theta$		0	

8.4 Learning Models in Dispersion Games

The alternative to the assumption of the rational-choice model in which agents behave to maximize their payoff is a form of adaptation. The adaptation may be at the individual level through learning or it may be at the collective level through the survival and reproduction of the more successful individuals or strategies. Either way, the consequences of adaptive processes are often very hard to deduce from the collective behavior of agents who follow specific learning models since they usually generate a chain of the reactions.

An important issue in multi-agent environments is the learning model adapted by each agent. In Chapter 2, we specified several learning models that have been discussed in the literature of game theory. Arthur modeled the *El Farol* bar problem, where the individual agents in creative ways try to forecast the next attendances and correspondingly decide to attend or stay at home. Agents may behave differently because of their personal beliefs on the outcome of the next time period, which only depends on what agents do at the next time period and the past history. Therefore, each agent is modeled to learn the successful prediction rule. Arthur believes that any solution to the *El Farol* bar problem would require heterogeneous agents who pursue different prediction rules, and the heterogeneity in agents' actions arises from the heterogeneity in predicted attendance. Arthur's solution, in which each agent maintains a collection of heterogeneous prediction rules, leads to patterns of attendance that fluctuate considerably above and below the capacity level.

Challet and Zhang (2005) take a different approach in modeling heterogeneous agents. Agents make decisions based on the common knowledge of the past history, which can be represented by a binary sequence, and each bit indicates whether an agent is on the winning side. The past history available at time t is represented by $\mu(t)$. The heterogeneity in agents arises from the collection of the heterogeneous action rules, and they investigate how agents choose different actions with the common information $\mu(t)$.

If the size of the past history $\mu(t)$ is M, then the size of the strategy space is 2^M. Each agent has a finite set of randomly drawn S strategies out of the strategy space. Some strategies maybe shared by multiple agents, however, if the size of the past history is moderately large, the chance of repetition of a single strategy is exceedingly small. All S strategies at an agent's disposal can collect points if they win based on the past $\mu(t)$ and on the actual outcome of the next play. However, these points are only virtual points as they record the merit of a strategy as if it were used each time. The agent uses the strategy having the highest accumulated points for her action and gets a real point only if the strategy used happens to win in the next play.

The interesting result by Challet and Zhang is that there is some critical parameter defined by the ratio of the number of agents N and the size of the strategy space, 2^M. This critical parameter determines the collective performance, and the fluctuations show an interesting pattern, which is basically classified into the three regimes: (1) if the number of agents is small with respect to the number of the strategy space, then the outcome is seemingly random, which very similar to what we would expect if agents were just tossing coins to decide whether to go (this is the mixed Nash equilibrium strategy), (2) when the number of agents is greater than the strategy space, they enter the herding phase, resulting in big fluctuations, and (3) in all other cases, the minority game fluctuates between either a crowded phase or a random phase.

Suppose that agents use predictive rules like those suggested by Arthur and that attendance at *El Farol* for the last Thursday night has been exactly the capacity C. How should an individual agent decide whether or not to attend in this case? Common sense suggests that agents who have attended the bar should continue to attend next Thursday night. On the other hand, agents who have not attended should continue to remain at home because the addition of another agent will result in attendance of $C+1$ and result in penalty.

Reinforcement learning is the learning model based on the above observation in agents' behaviors. Reinforcement learning takes place in the context of iterated choice problems, which asserts that choices that have led to good outcomes in the past are more likely to be repeated in the future. With reinforcement learning, agents need not form explicit expectations, but their actual behavior is described on the basis of probability for their action. Reinforcement learning is then modeled as an updating of probability, where the agents make use of their personal experience only. The updating rule of probability relies explicitly on the payoff.

Bell (2003) proposes a model of reinforcement learning based on *habit formation*. The incentives are in agreement with the common sense idea that people tend to minimize bad experiences and maximize good ones. By developing certain habits, agents may send signals to others to avoid conflicts.

Agents are consistent in their desire to maximize pleasure and minimize painful experiences. Therefore, an agent goes to the bar more often if the bar is under-crowded but prefers to go less often if the bar is crowded. Over time, an agent gathers information about the state of the bar and remembers this in the form of the parameter. This rule can be interpreted as a kind of habit formation through reinforcement learning. Not everyone can attend an under-crowded bar. Neither can everyone be in the minority. By the final iteration, the agents have divided themselves into two groups: agents who always attend the bar and agents who always stay at home. This division of the agents appears nowhere in the algorithm statement rather it is an emergent property of the solution based on reinforcement learning or individual habit formation.

However, the type of equilibrium that is actually realized when agents follow reinforcement learning depends on the nature of the information available to them. In particular, Franke and Bell show that limiting the information available to agents leads agents to successfully coordinate on an efficient equilibrium, while providing more information leads to an inefficient outcome. By changing the information structure in the algorithm so that agents adapt their probabilities of choosing either strategy at each play causes the algorithm to no longer converge to such an optimal situation, rather the attendance patterns continue to fluctuate wildly.

Thus, Bell points out that the information structure becomes crucial. When agents each receive or utilize a subset of total information, then the overall performance is far better behaved than when all agents act on complete information. In other words, homogeneity of information may be the key ingredient driving the dispersion game. With more heterogeneous information among agents, however, the congestion problem may vanish.

The adaptive solution proposed by Bell thus provides a simple mechanism whereby a large collection of decentralized agents, each acting in their own best interest and with only limited knowledge, drives a solution to many social congestion problems.

8.5 The Principle of Give-and-Take in Dispersion Games

Since the class of dispersion games displays interesting properties, we need to explore the learning models that may work effectively. The specialized learning model for the specific learning environment generally exhibits better performance than generic and representative learning models.

In this section, we propose a new behavioral rule based on the principle of give-and-take. This behavioral rule departs from the conventional assumption in learning models such that agents adapt their behavior in the direction of improving their payoff. We usually assume that an agent is guided by self-interest, and therefore tends to choose the action that yielded a higher payoff, and to avoid action with a lower payoff. The principle of give-and-take, on the contrary, is based on the following behavioral rule: an agent yields to others by changing her action if she can receive the payoff by choosing the minority side.

We formalize the behavioral rule based on the principle of give-and-take. The state variable $\omega(t)$ denotes the following collective outcomes:

(i) $\omega(t) = 0$ if $A(t)/N \le \theta$ (not crowded),   (8.16)

(ii) $\omega(t) = 1$ if $A(t)/N > \theta$ (overcrowded).

Each agent has common information on the state variable $\omega(t)$, and decides whether to choose S_1 ($a_i = 0$) or S_1 ($a_i = 1$) at the next time period $t+1$ depending on whether she is rewarded or not. The action $a_i(t+1)$ of agent i at $t+1$ is then determined by the following rule. At the current period

(i) $(\omega(t) = 0) \wedge (a_i(t) = 1) \Rightarrow a_i(t+1) = 0$

(ii) $(\omega(t) = 1) \wedge (a_i(t) = 0) \Rightarrow a_i(t+1) = 1$

(iii) $(\omega(t) = 1) \wedge (a_i(t) = 1) \Rightarrow a_i(t+1) = RND(x)$ (8.17)

(iv) $(\omega(t) = 0) \wedge (a_i(t) = 0) \Rightarrow a_i(t+1) = RND(y)$

where $RND(x)$ represents the mixed strategy $x = (x, 1-x)$, in which S_1 is chosen with the probability x and S_2 is chosen with the probability $1-x$.

We need to specify how an agent decides the mixed strategy $RND(x)$ when she is in the majority side by choosing S_1, and $RND(y)$ when she is in the majority side by choosing S_2. The expected number of agents who choose S_1 at $t+1$ when all agents follow the rule in (8.17) is

$$A(t+1) = xA(t) + N - A(t) \qquad (8.18)$$

$RND(x)$ in (8.17) is determined in order to satisfy the following condition:

$$A(t+1) = N\theta . \qquad (8.19)$$

Therefore, the probability x to choose S_1 is set as

$$x = \{N\theta - (N - A(t))\} / A(t).$$ (8.20)

We assume that the condition $N - A(t) \leq N\theta$ is satisfied. That is, if the attendance is greater that the capacity (overcrowded), then the number of agents who stay home should be smaller than the capacity. This assumption is satisfied if $\theta = 0.5$.

Similarly, we specify the mixed strategy $RND(y)$. The expected number of agents who choose S_1 at $t+1$ is given as

$$A(t+1) = y(N - A(t)).$$ (8.21)

Then, $RND(y)$ is set to satisfy the following condition:

$$A(t+1) = N\theta.$$ (8.22)

The probability y of choosing S_1 is then set as

$$y = N\theta / (N - A(t))$$ (8.23)

Here, we also assume that the condition $N - A(t) \geq N\theta$ is satisfied. That is, if the total attendance is below the capacity, then the number of agents who stay home should be greater than the capacity. This assumption is satisfied if $\theta = 0.5$.

We consider a population of agents with $N = 2{,}500$ and the capacity rate $\theta = 0.5$. Figure 8.2 shows the simulation result when all agents follow the behavioral rule of give-and take in (8.17). Figure 8.2(a) shows the ratio of attendance over time, and it is shown that the average number of agents who attend, by choosing $S_1 (Go)$, converges to the capacity rate. Figure 8.2(b) shows the distribution of the cumulative payoff of the population. All agents receive the same average payoff 0.5. This result indicates that high collective efficiency and equity are achieved when all agents behave under the principle of give-and-take.

Ratio of attendance

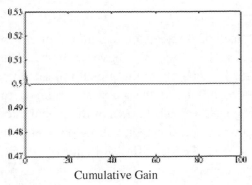

Cumulative Gain

Generation

(a) Ratio of attendance over time

Cumulative payoff

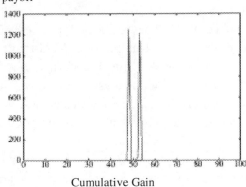

Cumulative Gain

(b) Distribution of the cumulative payoffs over 100 iterations

Figure 8.2 Simulation result under give-and-take (θ = 0.5)

8.6 Localized Dispersion Games and Emergence of Dynamic Orders in Harmony

The matching methodology also plays an important role in the outcome of social games. Thus far, we have assumed that agents play the dispersion game by adapting to the global information of the population. The basic model thus far is the same as assuming that agents interact with all other agents, which is known as the global interaction model. We refer to this type of dispersion game as a global minority game (*GMG*).

On the other hand, the idea of local minority game (*LMG*) is that each agent play the minority game with their nearest neighbors. In many situations, agents are not assumed to be knowledgeable enough to correctly guess or anticipate all other agents' actions in the collective. The hypothesis of local interaction reflects the limited ability of agents to receive, decide, and act based upon aggregated information they receive in the course of interaction.

Consider a collective of agents located in a two-dimensions lattice who interact with their nearest neighbors. We arrange these agents in a 50 x 50 area with no gaps, and the four corners and edges of the area connect with those on the opposite side, as shown in Figure 6.2. We consider the two cases of localized minority games, in which each agent interacts with her four neighbors and eight neighbors with the payoff matrix in Table 8.4.

In an LMG, we aim at discovering fundamental local or micro mechanisms that are sufficient to generate the desirable macroscopic structures. The main concern in a GMG was to show how interacting agents self-organize into a desirable collective behavior in time. In an LMG, however, they have to self-organize their behavior in both time and space.

We now define the behavioral rule of give-and-take in an LMG by modifying the rule in (8.17). We denote the ratio of the neighbors of agent i who chooses S_1 at t by $p_i(t)$, and define the following local state variable $\omega_i(t)$:

Table 8.4 Underlying payoff matrix of the local minority game

Own strategy \ Strategy of others	S_1 (Go)		S_2 (Stay home)	
S_1 (Go)		0		0.4
	0		0.6	
S_2 (Stay home)		0.6		0
	0.4		0	

(i) If $p_i(t) \le \theta$, $\omega_i(t) = 0$ (locally crowded),

(ii) If $p_i(t) > \theta$, $\omega_i(t) = 1$ (locally overcrowded). (8.24)

We set the capacity rate at $\theta = 0.6$, and the agents play the minority game with the payoff matrix given in Table 8.4. Agent i decides whether to choose S_1 ($a_i = 0$) or S_1 ($a_i = 1$) at $t+1$ as follows:

(i) $(\omega_i(t) = 0) \wedge (a_i(t) = 1) \Rightarrow a_i(t+1) = 0$

(ii) $(\omega_i(t) = 1) \wedge (a_i(t) = 0) \Rightarrow a_i(t+1) = 1$

(iii) $(\omega_i(t) = 1) \wedge (a_i(t) = 1) \Rightarrow a_i(t+1) = RND(x)$ (8.25)

(iv) $(\omega_i(t) = 0) \wedge (a_i(t) = 0) \Rightarrow a_i(t+1) = RND(x)$

where $RND(x)$ represents the mixed strategy $x = (x, 1-x)$. We set $x=0.5$, and S_1 and S_1 are chosen with equal probability.

The efficiency of the LMG depends on the number of neighbors with which to interact. Let us consider the configuration shown in Figure 8.3, in which each agent plays with four neighbors. In this configuration, agents who choose S_1 (white) interact only with agents who choose S_2 (black), and agents who choose S_2 interact only with agents who choose S_1. Since each agent interacts with the matrix in Table 8.4, an agent who chooses S_1 (white) receives a payoff of 0.6 per neighbor. However, an agent who chooses S_2 receives a payoff of 0.4. This inequality between agents who choose S_1 and agents who choose S_2 will be diminished if all agents alternate their choice, so that agents who choose S_1 become agents who choose S_2, and vice versa, in the next round. If all agents take turns in their independent choices, then they receive the same average payoff of 0.5. Therefore, the desirable collective behavior of the most efficiency and equity is achieved if they take turns and realize the two patterns shown in Figure 8.3 alternatively.

We now investigate the case in which each agent plays a minority game with eight neighbors. The most desirable configuration achieved with four neighbors in Figure 8.4(a) is no longer desirable when agents interact with eight neighbors. Let us consider the configuration in Figure 8.6(b), agents who choose S_1 (white) receive an average payoff of 0.45 per neighbor, and agents who choose S_2 receive an average payoff of 0.3. This inequality between agents who choose S_1 and agents who choose S_2 will be diminished if all agents alternate their choices, so that agents who choose S_1 become agents who choose S_2, and vice versa, in the next round. If all agents take turns, then they receive the same average payoff of 0.375.

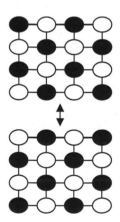

Figure 8.3   Configuration of S_1 choosers (white) and S_2 choosers (black): Interaction with four neighbors

We show the simulation results in Figure 8.5. Figure 8.5(a) shows the numbers of agents who choose S_1 (attend) and S_2 (stay at home) over time when each agent plays the minority game with four neighbors. Figure 8.5(b) shows the results with eight neighbors. These results show that when agents play with four neighbors, they quickly converge to the situation where and half of the agents attend and the other half stay at home. However, if they play with eight neighbors, a longer time is required but there is a sudden convergence to the situation in which the agents split into two groups based on their choice of S_1 or S_2.

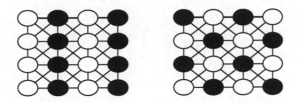

Figure 8.4 Configuration of S_1 choosers (white) and S_2 choosers (black): Interaction with eight neighbors

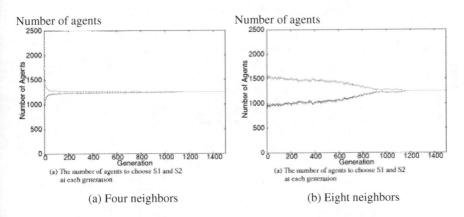

(a) Four neighbors   (b) Eight neighbors

Figure 8.5 Number of agents to choose S_1 and S_2 at each iteration

Figure 8.6 shows the maximum, average and minimum payoff per neighbor over time. When the agents play the minority game with four neighbors (Figure 8.6(a)), they converge into two groups. In one group each agent receives a payoff of 0.6, and an agent in the other group receives a payoff of 0.4. Then, the average payoff per agent converges to 0.5.

Figure 8.7 shows the payoff distribution for the final two plays of the game. It is shown that all agents receive the same payoff at the final stages for both cases.

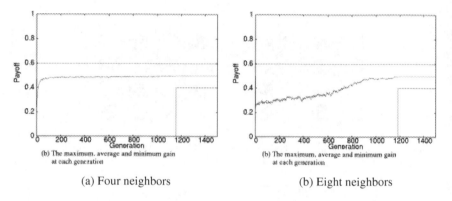

(a) Four neighbors　　　　　　(b) Eight neighbors

Figure 8.6 Maximum, average, and minimum payoff per agent over time

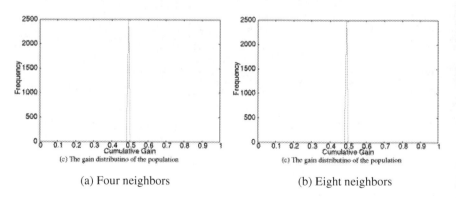

(a) Four neighbors　　　　　　(b) Eight neighbors

Figure 8.7 Distribution of the average payoff of the last two periods

Figure 8.8 and Figure 8.9 show the configuration of agents who choose S_1 and agents who choose S_2. The white cells denote the agents who choose S_1, and the black cells denote the agents who choose S_2. In the case in which each agent interacts with four neighbors, they generate two meshed patterns, as shown in Figure 8.8. When each agent interacts with eight neighbors, however, they generate stripe patterns, as shown in Figure 8.9. In the beginning, all agents choose independently, and their collective outcome is far from desirable. However, if they repeatedly adjust their behavior based on the rule of give-and-take, then the agents self-organize themselves into the most desirable behavior by taking turns choosing S_1 and S_2, alternately. We can characterize such desirable collective behavior as *interactive synchrony*.

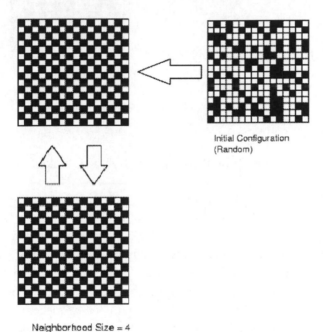

Initial Configuration
(Random)

Neighborhood Size = 4

Figure 8.8 Interactive synchrony produced starting from randomly chosen initial strategies (LMG with four neighbors)

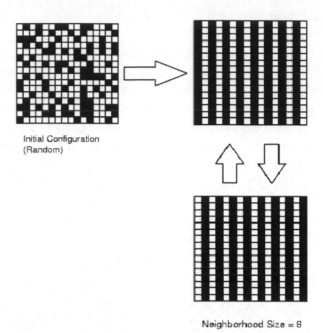

Figure 8.9 Interactive synchrony produced starting from randomly chosen initial strategies (LMG with eight neighbors)

8.7   Interpretation of the Principle of Give-and-Take

The theory of self-organization has grown out of many disparate scientific fields, including physics, chemistry, biology, cybernetics, computer modeling, and economics. Self-organization is basically the spontaneous creation of a globally coherent pattern out of uncoordinated decentralized behaviors. However, the overall collective behavior is self-organized as a function of its own maintenance, and thus tends to resist perturbations. Local interaction of large numbers of decentralized agents produces synchronized behavior. This surprising finding appears consistently in the emergence of macro-structure from the bottom up, according to the principle of give-and-take, which outwardly appears quite different from the collective phenomena the agents generate.

Solving a congestion problem from the bottom up, rather than by centralized planning and control, depends deeply on socially intelligent behavior of individuals. A rational approach based on the individual preference maximization will be useless in solving complex social congestion problems. Preferences, motives, or beliefs of agents can only provide a necessary but not sufficient condition for the explanation of socially intelligent behavior. Although, the basic mechanisms underlying human behavior are still far from clear, the different approaches need to be better integrated. For future development in the study of self-organization in collective systems, we may need to focus on the aspect of collective intelligence that will emerge beyond an individual's optimization behavior.

Humans are social creatures that learn to engage extensively in social exchange. We trade services and goods and information among friends and associates. Those who fail to develop social relationships will face many hardships. Although this observation might involve some altruistic elements, it appears to be largely based on reciprocity. If some people fail to reciprocate your favors and assistance, you stop the relationship This is judged to be why people are cooperative and trusting. In long-term social relationships, the norm of reciprocity seems to be the most widespread and persistent norm that regulates behavior (Gouldner, 1960). Relationships that go well seem to be almost always be characterized by a pattern of reciprocal solidarity, i.e., both agents repeatedly act to some extent in solidarity with their partner and as a result receive reciprocation. In order to solve social conflicts with others, we may need to change ourselves and alter our behavioral rules. The principle of give-and-take is very important in human society.

There are two contradictory views in answering the basic question as to why we support others or why should we always be kind to others. One is the idea of support out of pity (altruistic interpretation), and the other is the idea of support in expectation of returns (selfish interpretation) (Morioka, 1995).

The former, the altruistic idea of support, states that we sometimes help others in trouble because we want to ease their hardship. For instance, many volunteers may not support others in expectation of returns. The essential motivating factor here is a *feeling of pity*. We are living an enjoyable peaceful life because of a lot of people's assistance. We feel good even when we do a small kindness for others, such as just giving directions to someone who is lost. We may be happy if we win a lottery or if others accept your opinion after pushing very hard, but these are not true joys. The joy of being kind to others can not be taken away by anyone. However, the joy of accumulating money or having people accepting our opinion can be taken away from us. We may work hard to gain money and material possessions, but these things can easily be destroyed.

The latter, the selfish idea of support, states that the reason why a person helps others in trouble is that the person expects the same in return. In other words, a person expects to be helped by someone in return (not necessarily by the exact person whom she helped) if the norm of mutual support has taken root in her society.

Simulation results based on the principle of give-and-take shown in this chapter support an old saying, *"Those who are kind to others are sure to be rewarded."* (In Japanese, "nasake wa hito no tamenarazu".)

Chapter 9

Collective Evolution of Behavioral Rules

We have observed that the performance of the collective system heavily depends on how agents' behaviors are properly coupled. This chapter explores an alternative learning model, coupled learning, and focuses on coupling dynamics that may change in time according to coupled behavioral rules. We show that collective evolution serves to secure desired outcomes by establishing sustainable behavioral rules. This chapter also presents a comparative study of two evolving collectives, one in a spatial structure, and the other in a small-world network structure. The small-world environment is shown to encourage desirable collective evolution more than the spatial environment.

9.1 Repeated Interactions on Social Networks

This chapter and the next chapter are devoted to the issue of *emergence* of desired collective behaviors through collective evolution in the context of iterated social games. The study on the emergence of a desired collective from the bottom up is the complementary approach to the evolutionary approach in which variation and selection are important considerations. A growing interest in this approach comes not only from evolutionary computation, but also from other scientific disciplines.

In Chapter 2, we classify social interactions formulated as non-cooperative games into four categories: prisoner's dilemma games, coordination games, hawk-dove games, and dispersion games. It is shown that equilibrium situations led by natural selection are far from efficient.

Prisoner's dilemma games are stylized situations that capture the logic of a spectrum of social disasters that we bring upon ourselves if we seek our own self-interest. In a situation such as prisoner's dilemma games, individuals to detect (D) will always be favored by natural selection, even though the average payoff in a population of defectors is less than in a population of cooperators. In terms of evolutionary game theory, to defect is the unique evolutionary stable strategy (ESS).

Two different types of solutions to this conflict between equilibrium and efficiency have been proposed. First, the *Iterated Prisoner's Dilemma* (IPD) was made popular by the work of Axelrod (1980). Axelrod did computer and human experiments on the repeated prisoner's dilemma. The most successful strategy is the *Tit-For-Tat* (TFT) strategy, which starts by playing C (Cooperate) and then the agent plays whatever its opponent played in the previous round. In repeated games, there is a probability that two agents will meet again, and the agents can remember how they played in previous encounters. This allows more complicated strategies than the binary choice of C or D. Axelrod conducted a computer tournament with 62 different strategies submitted by scientists from all around the world. The most successful strategies among them are, (i) nice: the agent never defects first, (ii) forgiving: the agent restores cooperation after an accidental defection, and (iii) retaliatory: the agent reacts by playing the same strategy as the opponent.

An important feature of the strategy choice in the real world is that strategies cannot be implemented without error. Since the other agent does not necessarily know whether a given action is an error or a deliberate choice, a single error can lead to significant complications. The effects of error have been treated under the rubric of noise. The issue of how to cope with noise has become an important research question among many scientists. Clearly, when noise is introduced, some unintended defections will occur, and this may undercut the effectiveness of those successful strategies.

Two different approaches to coping with noise in the context of the IPD have been proposed. (i) Generosity, in which some percentage of the other agent's defections are allowed to go unpunished, has been widely advocated as a good way to cope with noise. A generous version of TFT, called GTFT is also known to prevent a single error from echoing indefinitely. (ii) Contrition, in which a reciprocating strategy such as TFT can be modified to avoid responding to the other agent's defection after her own unintended defection, allows a quick way to recover from error. It is based upon the idea that one shouldn't be provoked by the other agent's response to one's own unintended defection.

Axelrod and Yin (1997) conducted a powerful test by taking into account that rules that are unsuccessful in a noisy environment are less likely than are relatively successful rules to be used again. The fraction of the population represented by a given rule in the next generation of the tournament is proportional to that rule's tournament score in the previous generation. When this evolutionary process is repeated over many generations, the proportion of the various rules changes, and the environment faced by each rule tends to emphasize those rules that have been doing relatively well in the noisy setting.

The basis of the analysis by Axelrod and Yin is the global environment, where the average score of each rule when paired with all other rules is compared. Other situations where cooperative behavior can be spread out are models that introduce some kind of spatial structure so that all interactions are local. Nowak and Sigmund (1993) showed that cooperation survives if agents in a population locally interact with each other and learning is driven by imitation of successful behavior. Agents play against their nearest neighbors and not against random opponents or against all other agents of the population. The introduction of spatial interaction may affect the evolutionary dynamics in various ways. The possibility of spatial structures may also allow for stability where the global or random matching model would be unstable.

The introduction of spatial dimensions is shown in Figure 9.1. Agents allocated to each cell of a *nxn* lattice play an underlying game against their nearest neighbors. The summed payoff of each game provides the agent's fitness. After every individual has played the game with her neighbors, each rule of the agents is updated according to the general evolutionary rules based on the principle of natural selection. Each agent is replaced by an offspring of the highest scoring individual of the nearest neighbors. These offspring play the same strategy as their ancestors, unless a mutation occurs, which happens at a small mutation rate. If a mutation occurs, the offspring's strategy is not its parent's

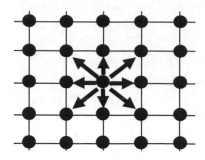

Figure 9.1 Games on a grid. Each agent interacts with her nearest neighbors

strategy but a new strategy chosen randomly. The main effect of the spatial structure in the IPD is that cooperative strategies can build clusters in which the benefits of mutual cooperation can outweigh losses against defectors. Thus, clusters of cooperators can invade groups of defectors that prevail in non-spatial populations.

The evolutionary dynamics described above could also be interpreted as a learning process. In the random interaction model or mean-field model, we could say that each agent checks to see if another randomly chosen agent in the population gets a higher payoff, and, if so, switches to that strategy with a probability proportional to the payoff difference.

In the lattice model each agent may choose the strategy of the most successful agent among her immediate neighbors. This may not be the most successful strategy in the position of this agent, since her neighbors may interact with different neighbors. The introduction of spatial interactions leads to the development of spatial games in which agents are located in the nodes of a fixed regular network of interaction, displaying rich spatio-temporal dynamics.

Recent studies on the structure of social, technological, and biological networks have shown that they share salient features that situated them far from being completely regular or random. Social interactions are rarely well described by random or regular networks. Therefore, we also need to study the influence of the topological aspects of networks by exploring the different network topology.

The topology of social networks is much better described by what has been called a *small-world network*, as shown in Figure 9.2. In a regular lattice model, agents interact with the nearest neighbors. In the version of a small-world network, a fraction of the neighborhood is replaced by breaking interactions. An equal number of new agents are selected from outside of the current neighborhood. These new agents for interaction are selected randomly from the rest of the population.

Kuperman and Abramson (2000) studied an evolutionary version of the prisoner's dilemma game, played by agents placed in a small-world network. Agents are able to change their strategy, imitating that of the most successful neighbor. They found that collective behaviors corresponding to the small-world network enhances defection where cooperation is the norm in the fixed regular network.

Another important issue to consider is that networks are dynamic entities that evolve and adapt driven by the actions of agents that form a network. Zimmermann and Eguíluz (2004) studied the evolution of the social network. Initially, each agent plays a prisoner's dilemma game with fixed neighbors. The network of interaction links evolves, adapting to the outcome of the game. They analyzed a simple setting of such an

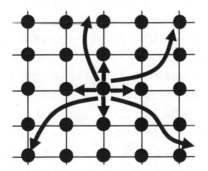

Figure 9.2 Games on a small-world network. Each agent interacts with her four nearest neighbors and four other agents randomly chosen from the population

adaptive and evolving network, in which there is co-evolution of the state of the agents and the interaction links defining the network. The network of interaction evolves into a hierarchical network structure that governs the global dynamics of the system. However, the resulting network has the characteristics of a small-world network when a mechanism of local neighbor selection is introduced.

Various studies have examined the impact of different network structures on equilibrium selection in the context of iterated coordination games. If agents can choose the partners with which to interact, then they will form networks that lead to efficient Nash equilibrium play in the underlying coordination game. Ellison (1993) analyzed the role of local interactions for the spread of particular strategies in coordination games, showing how play converges to risk-dominant equilibrium if agents are located on a circle and interact with their two nearest neighbors. Similarly, Blume (1993) and Kosfeld (2002) proved the convergence to the risk-dominant equilibrium in a population of agents located on a two-dimensional lattice.

Goyal and Vega-Redondo (2005) study the formation of networks among agents who are bilaterally involved in coordination games. In addition to specifying which pairs of agents in the population play the game, the network structure also determines how strategic information diffuses among the agents and how coordination among the agents is found. They showed that once agents are allowed to choose their partners, the situation is very different. They introduce a number of locations where agents can meet and play the coordination game with each other. Thus, at any time, agents choose both a location and a strategy in the game. Under these conditions they showed that risk dominance looses its selection force and that the population is most likely to coordinate on the Pareto efficient equilibrium. Since agents can freely choose their interaction partners, they are able to find partners that choose the Pareto efficient equilibrium strategy, and at the same time they can avoid agents that choose the risk-dominant inefficient strategy. The latter condition, i.e., the ability to avoid bad matches, is crucial in social interactions, as we discussed in Chapter 7.

9.2   Repeated Interactions with Bounded Memory

In our social life, we have to make our decisions based on our bounded capability. However, these restrictions may be improved through learning that utilizes past experiences. Interesting phenomena have also been observed using repeated games played by agents who choose their strategy based on a *behavioral rule*, which may be improved through learning.

Most models of game theory deal with specific social interaction between individuals who adapt their behavior (strategy) in order to maximize their gains within the prescribed underlying game. The situation changes abruptly when interactions are repeated, depending on the outcomes of the previous interaction, or past results. There is no doubt that we learn from our past successful and unsuccessful attempts to improve our behaviors.

In this section, we consider repeated games with some memories, in which agents are modeled to play infinitely many rounds of the underlying 2x2 game. In the framework of iterated games, a type of behavioral rule that should be considered is the deterministic strategy choice based on finite memory. This type of behavioral rule may take into account the actions that occur in a finite number of past rounds and then choose a certain strategy. A behavioral rule can then be viewed as a look-up table, in which each entry corresponds to each of the possible finite-length histories that can be memorized. The number of possible behavioral rules in the context of repeated games depends on the agent's memory size.

For instance, we consider the following cases.

(1) An agent chooses her strategy without any memory. This case is denoted as $m = 0$, or a memory of zero.

(2) An agent chooses her strategy based on the last choice of her opponent. This case is denoted as $m = 1$, or a memory of one.

(3) An agent chooses her strategy based on the outcome of the previous round, the previous join actions of herself and her opponent. This case is denoted as $m = 2$, or a memory of two,

(4) An agent chooses her strategy referring to the previous two rounds. This case is denoted as $m = 4$, or a memory of four.

When agents decide their strategy based on their memories of past rounds, the strategy choice becomes quite different. Here, we consider the IPD as an illustration. A strategy choice with memories allows more complicated interactions than the simple strategy choice of either C (Cooperate) or D (Defect).

In the case of a memory of zero ($m = 0$), there are two possible rules of the strategy choices: "always chooses D" (which is denoted as All-D) and "always chooses C" (which is denoted as All-C).

In the case of $m = 1$, we can denote a rule of the strategy choice as "$p_0 p_1$" (p_0, p_1 ε [0, 1]), where p_0 (p_1) is the probability of choosing S_2 when the opponent's last choice was S_1 (S_2). In this case, there are four behavioral rules: "00", "01", "10", and "11". For example, "11" (i.e., $p_0 = 1$, $p_1 = 1$) means always chooses S_2 (All-D) and "00" ($p_0 = 0$, $p_1 = 0$) means always chooses S_1 (All-C).

In the case of $m = 2$, a rule of the strategy choice is described as "$p_0 p_1 p_2 p_3$" (p_i ε [0, 1]), where p_0, p_1, p_2 and p_3 represent the probability of choosing S_2 when the agent's choice and the opponent's choice in the previous round are (S_1, S_1), (S_1, S_2), (S_2, S_1) and (S_2, S_2), respectively. There are $2^4 = 16$ possible rules to represent "$p_0 p_1 p_2 p_3$".

In research regarding the IPD, some special names are used for the strategy choice rules with the memory size of $m = 2$. That is, 0000 means All-C, "1111" means All-D, "0101" corresponds to TFT, and "1010" corresponds to ATFT (Anti-TFT). Here, "0111" is defined as FRIEDMAN (which plays S_1 (Cooperate) only when the previous choices of both agents were S_1), and "0110" is defined as PAVLOV.

Nowak and Sigmund (1993) found a very successful strategy choice, *win-stay and lose-shift*, which is the same as PAVLOV. With the principle of win-stay and lose-shift, if both choose S_1 (win) then they also choose S_1. If the opponent chooses S_1 and the agent chooses S_2 (win), then she also chooses S_2. On the other hand, if both choose S_2 (lose), then they change and choose S_2. If the opponent chooses S_2 and the agent chooses S_1, then she loses. Therefore, she changes and chooses S_2.

Here, the effective memory size of agents to remember past experiences is of interest. Some interesting results were obtained by Lindgren (1991). He studied this issue in the IPD by changing the memory size from a memory of 1 to a large memory. The average score for each agent is calculated, and this determines which individuals will be allowed to reproduce. Among nearest neighbors, the individual with the highest score reproduces offspring, which inherits the parent's strategy, possibly altered by mutations.

There is a small chance that the action is altered by mistake. When the memory of the rules has evolved to a longer size, agents remember their own past strategies as well as their opponents' past strategies, which corresponds to the memory size of the rules. If the memory has evolved to a greater length, more complicated rules are developed. We can easily observe open-ended evolution with the increase in the memory size in the simulations. If there exist rules of the effective memory size that realize an efficient equilibrium, then the simulation cannot be invaded by any agents with longer memory size.

9.3 A Strategy Choice with a Coupling Rule

The literature on learning in the game theory is mainly concerned with the understanding of learning procedures that if adopted by interacting agents will converge in the end to the Nash equilibrium of the underlying game. The main concern is to show that adaptive dynamics lead to a rational behavior, as prescribed by a Nash equilibrium strategy. The learning algorithms themselves are not required to satisfy any rationality requirement. Instead, they converge to a rational behavior if it is adopted by all agents. Another basic research agenda is to explore non-equilibrium explanations of equilibrium in repeated games to view equilibrium as the long-run outcome of a dynamic learning process.

Many learning models have been proposed, such as best-response learning dynamics as individual payoff improving. However, it is difficult to formulate learning dynamics that guarantee convergence to Nash equilibrium. We call a dynamical system *uncoupled* if an agent's learning model does not depend on the payoff functions of the other agents. Hart (2003) proved that there are no uncoupled dynamics that are guaranteed to converge to Nash equilibrium. Therefore, a coupling between agents, that is, the adjustment of an agent's strategy depends on the payoff functions of the other agent, is a basic condition for convergence to Nash equilibrium.

In addition, Nash equilibrium cannot make precise predictions about the outcome of repeated games. Nor can it tell us much about the dynamics by which a collective of agents moves from an inefficient equilibrium to a better outcome. These limitations, along with concerns about the cognitive demands of forward-looking rationality, have motivated many researchers to explore alternatives backward-looking learning models. Most of these efforts have been invested in evolutionary dynamics.

In this section, we will take a different approach by focusing on collective evolution of coupled rules. This approach differs from the common use of the genetic algorithm, in which the goal is to optimize a fixed fitness function. In the genetic algorithm, the focus is also on the best final result or on a good solution. In collective evolution, we are interested in better coupling among agents, which leads to desirable joint actions.

The first question we must address is what individuals know and what it is that they are learning about. In repeated games, agents repeatedly play an underlying game, each time observing their payoff and other agents' strategies. In the classic work on learning in game theory, the agents select their strategy in the next iteration of the game based on the result of the previous play using some updating rule. In the repeated model, agents engage in a series of games with different rules at each stage. In fact, the nature of each game depends on the results of the pervious game, and this means the strategy choice depends on agents' joint action in the previous rounds of games.

An important aspect of iterated games is the introduction of a coupling rule by which an agent can decide her strategy. We will shift attention to coupling dynamics with coupling rules. We make a distinction between adaptive or evolutionary dynamics and coupling dynamics. In an adaptive dynamics, other mechanisms are allowed as well, e.g., modifications of strategies based on the strategy distribution of the population. But, such adaptive dynamics do not necessarily improve the outcome to which the individual belongs in the long run. Evolutionary dynamics, on the other hand, refer to the systems based on the basic mechanisms of biological evolution, that allows, inheritance, mutation, and selection. However, as we observed in Chapter 2, evolutionary dynamics based on natural selection also converge to an inefficient outcome. Coupling dynamics differ, in this sense, from evolutionary dynamics, in which a fixed goal is used in the fitness function and where there is no coupling between agents.

The essence of various social interactions among agents can be modeled by the underlying games describing pair-wise interactions between agents with two strategies to choose from. Depending on their joint choices, they obtain a certain payoff. Therefore, a better method of coupling between agents may be key in improving an outcome. In the models we discuss here, an agent is locally coupled to her neighbor. The success or failure for a certain behavioral rule depends on how agents are coupled each other.

We consider the prisoner's dilemma game as an illustration. Each agent has a coupling rule to decide the action in the next game based on the joint actions in previous round. That is, a strategy choice for repeated games uses the memory of the previous rounds to choose one of the two strategies for the next play.

Let assume that each agent remembers the past h outcomes. At time t, therefore the history would be the outcomes at $t-h$, $t-h+1$,..., $t-1$. A coupling rule must specify, for each history, what strategy the agent should choose. A quick calculation shows that the number of possible coupling rules with the outcome of only the previous round (the memory of $m=2$) is 2^4 and with the previous two rounds (the memory of $m=4$) is 2^{16}. Therefore, with the increase of the memories of the past rounds, there are a huge number of coupling rules. The hope is that agents would find a better coupling rule out of the overwhelming number of possible rules after a reasonable number of repeated games.

We assume that each agent has a coupling rule for a memory of two, which means that the outcome of the previous move is used to make the next choice. Each coupling rule is represented as a binary string so that genetic operators can be applied. We represent S_1 (Cooperate) by 0 and S_2 (Defect) by 1. In Table 9.1, we show all possible coupling rules for the memory of two. There are four possible outcomes for each move between two agents: $(S_1, S_1)=(0, 0)$, $(S_1, S_2)=(0, 1)$, $(S_2, S_1)=(1, 0)$, and $(S_2,$

S_2)=(1, 1). Each coupling rule specifies the strategy choice based on the outcome of the previous round. Agent strategies are restricted to those employing only the previous move with the other agent to determine the next choice.

As discussed in the previous section, the well-known rules are: ALL-C= "0000", ALL-D="1111", TFT="0101" and PAVLOV="0110". These are the rules with no probabilistic strategy choice. The main difference between PAVLOV and TFT is the value of p_4. While both strategies cooperate with each other, PAVLOV readily exploits unconditional cooperators, but is more heavily exploited by unconditional defectors.

Nowak *et al* (1992), and Grim (1995) also worked on the spatial IPD by considering stochastic strategies that depend only on the last play. Such strategies are referred to as *Markov strategies*. This rule is defined by the four probabilities (p_1, p_2, p_3, p_4) given the outcome of the previous round, which is also shown in Table 9.1.

In populations of such Markov strategies, in which interactions between individuals are in the form of an IPD, they examined how spatial structure influences the evolution of cooperation and what impact it has on the evolutionary dynamics. Comparing the spatial model with a randomly mixed model, they also showed that, PAVLOV and generous variants thereof are very successful strategies in the stochastic environment, where agents sometimes make mistakes in implementing rules.

Table 9.1 Some well-known rules for strategy choices in the IPD

(p_i, i=1, 2, 3 and 4 represent the probability of choosing S_2)

Previous strategy		Rules of strategy choices				
Own	Opponent	ALL-C	ALL-C	TFT	PAVLOV	MARKOV
0	0	0	1	0	0	p_1
0	1	0	1	1	1	p_2
1	0	0	1	0	1	p_3
1	1	0	1	1	0	p_4

We now consider a learnable behavioral rule. Although the coupling rules in Table 9.1 are fully specified before interactions start, instead we consider that agents can learn each content of the rule. They learn which strategy they have to choose for each of the four different outcomes that can arise in the iterated game. Specifically, each agent has a learnable coupling rule, as shown in Table 9.2, in which the # symbol represents either 0 or 1.

We can fully describe a coupling rule of a deterministic strategy choice by recording what the strategy will do in each of the four different outcomes that can arise in the underlying game. There are $2^4=16$ possible coupling rules, as shown in Figure 9.3. We investigate what types of coupling rules are generated and spread out the population through the iteration of the underlying games.

An agent having an internal model with a 7-bit string, as shown in Figure 9.4, constitutes the coupling rule with the memory size, $m=2$. At each generation, agents repeatedly play the underlying game for T rounds. One generation corresponds to the repetition of a game for T rounds.

Each coupling rule is represented by bit-strings in Figure 9.4. Each position of a binary string represents the following strategy. The first position encodes the strategy that an agent takes at each generation. Since no memory exists at the start, an extra bit is needed to specify a hypothetical history. A position j, $j\in[2,3]$, encodes the memory that an agent and her opponent choose at the previous round. The strategy site j, $j\in[4...7]$, encodes the coupling rule in Table 9.2, which specifies the strategy choice corresponding to the memories stored at the site $j\in[2,3]$.

Table 9.2 A learnable coupling rule (# represents 0 or 1)

Strategy site in Figure 9.4	Previous strategies		Next strategy
	Own	Opp	
4	0	0	#
5	0	1	#
6	1	0	#
7	1	1	#

The first process that comes to mind for behavioral rule generation is to carry out a kind of random trial-and-error, making limited random changes in the rules that are already in place. However, the process of population-based search with random variation and selection is often insufficient to create desirable rules of interest. Selection is required because without the fitness criterion and a procedure for eliminating poor solutions, the search would degenerate into a purely random walk. In genetics an interaction called *crossover* causes the characteristics of the parents to appear in new combinations in the offspring. Crossover is the mechanism that breeders exploit when they crossbreed superior behavioral rules. This recombination of set of alleles is most interesting from the point of view of rule discovery.

The crossover operator is used to evolve coupling rules. The average payoff per generation (per T iterations of the underlying game) is calculated, and this determines which agents succeed. Each agent compares her average payoff with those of all agents who interact. Unsuccessful agents will replace part of their poor coupling rule as follows: half of the coupling rule in Figure 9.4 (including the first strategy site representing the initial strategy choice) is replaced with the rule of the most successful neighbor who gains the highest average payoff.

Agents mimic their most successful neighbor to improve their coupling rule. Their success depends in large part on how well they learn from their neighbors. If an agent gains a better payoff than her neighbor, there is a chance that her coupling rule will be imitated by others. In the collective evolution approach, there is no need to assume a rational calculation to identify the effective rule. Instead, analysis of what is chosen at any specific time is based on an implementation of the idea that effective rules are more likely to be retained than ineffective rules.

Moreover, collective evolution allows the introduction of a new rule as occasional random mutations of old rules. It could be that the more successful agents are more likely to survive and reproduce effective coupling rules. A second interpretation is that agents learn by trial and error, keeping effective rules and altering rules that give a low payoff. A third interpretation is that agents observe each other, and those with poor performance tend to imitate the rules of those that they see doing better.

Type 1: 0 0 0 0 (ALL-C)   Type 9: 0 0 0 1
Type 2: 1 0 0 0   Type 10: 1 0 0 1
Type 3: 0 1 0 0   Type 11: 0 1 0 1 (TFT)
Type 4: 1 1 0 0   Type 12: 1 1 0 1
Type 5: 0 0 1 0   Type 13: 0 0 1 1
Type 6: 1 0 1 0   Type 14: 1 0 1 1
Type 7: 0 1 1 0 (PAVLOV)   Type 15: 0 1 1 1 (FRIEDMAN)
Type 8: 1 1 1 0   Type 16: 1 1 1 1 (ALL-D)

Figure 9.3 All possible coupling rules with the memory size of m=2

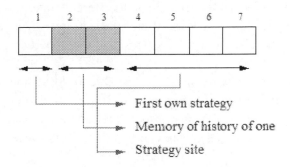

Figure 9.4 A coupling rule with the memory size of m=2

9.4 Iterated Prisoner's Dilemma Games on Social Networks

The IPD has become the standard model for the study of the evolution of cooperative behavior within a population of self-interested agents. We have observed that cooperation in the prisoners' dilemma game can survive if agents in a population locally interact with each other and adaptation is driven by the imitation of the most successful neighbor. The crucial effect of local interaction in this model is that it allows cooperative agents to cluster together. Since the positive externalities from cooperation are locally restricted, local interaction reduces the possibility for defectors to exploit cooperators. As a consequence, cooperators that are surrounded by other cooperators can earn higher payoffs than defectors who are primarily surrounded by other defectors. Together with the imitation of successful agents this gives cooperators a chance to survive.

However, suppose that every agent comes to use the same strategy. Is there any reason for some agent to use a different strategy, or would the native strategy remain the choice of all? We will investigate this issue by considering a population of agents who play the underlying game based on a coupling rule.

An agent with a new rule is said to be able to invade the population if she can get a higher payoff than agents with the native rule. In this case a new rule is said to invade a native rule. Axelrod defines such a rule to be *collectively stable* if no other rule can invade it. This concept is basically the same as the evolutionary stable strategy (*ESS*). The motivation behind applying collectively stability to the analysis is to discover which kinds of rules can be sustained in the face of any possible alternative rule. If everyone is using a native rule and some other rule gives a better payoff, then some agents are sure to find this better rule sooner or later. Thus, only a rule that cannot be invaded can maintain the population as the rule used by many agents.

A typical example of a collectively stable rule is TFT. A population of agents using TFT will cooperate with each other, and each will get the payoff at Pareto efficiency every iteration. If another rule is to invade this population, it must offer a higher expected payoff. However, no such rule exists, and therefore TFT is collectively stable. Any rule is defined to be *nice* if it starts to cooperate. Nice rules are also collectively stable. On the other hand, ALL-D is also collectively stable. If all other agents defect, then there is no point for any agent to cooperate.

As we discussed in Section 9.2, the introduction of spatial interactions leads to the development of spatial games in which agents are located in the nodes of a fixed network of interaction. For example, in Axelrod's work (1984), it was found that the most successful rule in spatial populations was a rule that ranked only 31st of 62 in his round robin tournament.

A more ambitious objective is to find a learning procedure that will enable the agents to obtain the Pareto efficient payoff. We say that a set of rules is *Pareto efficient* if the total payoff for all agents is maximized. It is easy to see that there is no general way to guarantee that agents will learn such an efficient rule.

We arrange agents for a 20×20 area (N = 400 agents) with the lattice model shown in Figure 9.1 with no gaps, and the four corners and sides of the area connect to the opposite sides. All agents of the 20x20 lattice play the dilemma games in Table 9.3 against their eight neighbors. They repeat interaction for a certain number of rounds (T=20), defined as one generation, based on learnable coupling rules. The payoffs of the repeated game are summed and the average payoff per generation provides the individual's score. The strategy choice for each agent is driven by a coupling rule that improves over several generations.

In the beginning, 400 agents have different coupling rules, which are randomly generated by specifying the values of # in Table 9.2. A part of

Table 9.3 Payoff matrix of the underlying dilemma game

Own strategy \ Strategy of the other agent	S_1	S_2
S_1	3 / 3	5 / 0
S_2	0 / 5	1 / 1

the coupling rule is replaced with the rule of the highest scoring agent among her eight neighbors (*crossover*). Since no memory exists at the start, one extra bit is needed in order to specify the initial strategy to start the game at each generation.

We consider two cases to specify the initial strategy:
(1)   The initial strategy is chosen randomly.
(2)   The initial strategy of the most successful neighbor is mimicked.

(Case 1)   *The initial strategy used to play the game is chosen randomly*

In this case, the average payoff per agent was approximately 1.8, and both the cooperative and defect strategies coexist by making clusters. However, the coupling rules learned by all 400 agents were aggregated into two types, "1011" and "0011", as shown in Table 9.4(a). Approximately 60% of the learned rules were 1011, which is an All-D-like rule, and the remaining 40% of the learned rules were "0011", which is a TFT-like rule.

(Case 2) *The initial strategy used to play the game is copied from the most successful neighbor*

Figure 9.5(a) shows the average payoff per agent over generations. The average payoff was increased to 2.87. Initially both agents who defect and agents who cooperate were present. However, this situation quickly disappeared and the ratio of agents who choose the cooperative strategy increased and the population obtained higher payoffs by exhibiting a cooperative population.

In the beginning, most agents have different coupling rules, however, the coupling rules learned by all 400 agents were aggregated into two types, "0111" and "0101", as shown in Table 9.4(b). Approximately 97% of agents learned the coupling rule of 0111. The rest of the agents (3%) learned the rule of "0101", which is TFT.

There are a couple of important differences between Case 1 and Case 2. It is actually *easier* for cooperation to evolve if agents also mimic the initial strategy to invoke the game of each generation from the most successful neighbor. As a result, the coupling rule to sustain the cooperative outcome is realized after a few generations. As shown in Table 9.4(b), all agents learned to start to play with 0 (cooperate) at each generation, and the cooperation is clearly more stable in this case.

The coupling rule 0111, which is learned by most agents can be interpreted as follows. If both agents decide to cooperate, then they cooperate. However, if one of the agents defects, then the other agent defects as well. This rule of the strategy choice is similar to FRIEDMAN and TFT in Axelrod's tournament (1980). FRIEDMAN is a totally unforgiving rule that employs permanent retaliation. It is never the first to defect, but once the other agent defects even once, FRIEDMAN defects from then on. In contrast, the learned rule "0111" is unforgiving for one generation, but thereafter is forgiving of that defection, since the agent starts over with cooperate at the next generation.

TFT is unforgiving for only one move, but thereafter is forgiving of that defection. TFT is also characterized as reciprocity, since if one agent defects and the other cooperates, then the first agent cooperates during the next round and never tries to exploit agent the other again, even if she wins the game. On the other hand, rule "0111" exploits the other agent if it brings a higher payoff.

Here, evolutionary dynamics refer to the movement of the population average in the four-dimensional coupling rule space as shown in Table 9.2. The proportion of each rule in the population may be changed by crossover, and fitter rules increase their share in the population. The game between two agents with a coupling rule becomes a kind of the stochastic process on a finite automaton representing the state diagram of the outcomes. This game automaton has as its internal states, the pairs of possible internal states for the two agents, and the transitions are determined as the phase diagram of the two coupling rules.

The game between two coupling rules with finite memory can be described as a stationary stochastic process. The state transition of the outcomes when both agents choose their strategies according to the learned coupling rule is illustrated in Figure 9.6 as a state transition diagram. The outcomes "00" and "11" are perfect absorbing states. Once the process enters such a state, it tends to stay there, unless occasional randomness creates noise in the system. Since each agent also learns to cooperate in the first round of each generation, as shown in Table 9.4(b), they remain at the absorbing state at "00".

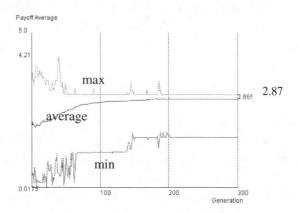

(a) Repeated games on the fixed local network: each agent interacts with eight fixed neighbors

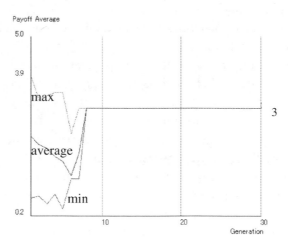

(b) Repeated games on the small-world network

Figure 9.5 Payoffs per agent in iterated prisoner's dilemma games

(Case 3) *Iterated games on the small-world network: the initial strategy mimics the highest scoring agent among previous partners*

We also compare and identify the effect the method of interaction by considering the topology of a small-world network. The locally networked agents will be compared to half-mixed populations, which are again modeled by a lattice, but on which each agent interacts with four partners that are nearest neighbors and four partners that are randomly chosen on the lattice, as shown in Figure 9.2. Figure 9.5(b) shows the result of the small-world network. There is an important difference between this graph and the graph obtained using the fixed local

Table 9.4 Coupling rules learned by 400 agents (prisoner's dilemma games)

(a) Fixed local network (initial strategy: random)

Rule type	Initial strategy	Strategy site				Number of agents
	1	4	5	6	7	
14	0 or 1	1	0	1	1	330
13	0 or 1	0	0	1	1	70

(b) Fixed local network (initial strategy: mimicry)

Rule type	Initial strategy	Strategy site				Number of agents
	1	4	5	6	7	
15	0	0	1	1	1	389
11	0	0	1	0	1	11

(c) Small-world network (initial strategy: mimicry)

Rule type	Initial strategy	Strategy site				Number of agents
	1	4	5	6	7	
15	0	0	1	1	1	400

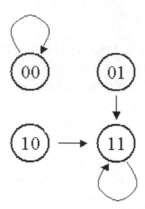

Figure 9.6 State transitions of two agents who play with the coupling rule of "0111"

network (Figure 9.5(a)). Figure 9.5(b) shows that it is actually easier for cooperation to evolve in the small-world network environment.

As a result, all agents gain the same efficient payoff 3. The cooperative strategy could be realized after a few generations, as shown in Figure 9.5(b). The cooperation is clearly more stable in the small-network environment compared with the fixed local network environment. In the beginning, each agent has a different coupling rule. The rules learned by 400 agents were aggregated into only one type "0111", as shown in Table 9.4(c).

The scope of sustainable cooperation is dependent on how agents interact. If they interact locally in a fixed lattice network, then two types of rules can coexist. The introduction of a small-world network, so that individuals interact with those in their neighborhood as well as with new partners who may not have met before, affects the collective dynamics in various ways. The possibility of space-temporal structures may allow for global stability, where the local interaction model would allow two behavioral rules coexist.

In particular, we observed the following effects of the spatial and small-world spatial structure in the IPD played with coupling rules.

(1) Small-world network structure greatly facilitates the evolution of cooperative behavior. There is more cooperation in a structured

population with a small-world network and cooperation evolves much faster.

(2) In the small-world network, a qualitatively different coupling rule, compared to the populations in the spatial context, evolves. Clustering, as it occurs in the fixed local network, is a very strong reason for the survival of the cooperative strategy. However, it permits the coexistence of two rules. On the other hand, the small-world structure has a strong stabilizing effect on collective evolution toward the most desirable outcome by spreading out the unique sustainable rule.

The problem with All-C is that it provides an incentive for the agents to defect. Unconditional cooperation places a burden on the rest of the agents. On the other hand, TFT promotes the mutual interest of all agents rather exploit the weaknesses of some agents. A better strategy would be based on reciprocity but it is a bit more forgiving than TFT. Generous tit-for-tat (GTFT), which repays cooperation with a probability of cooperation but forgives defection with some probability is successful in a stochastic environment where agents make some mistakes when implementing their strategy.

TFT does well by promoting the mutual interest of all agents rather than exploiting some agents and requires agents to help others as well as themselves by making it difficult for inferior strategies to survive. In addition, agents must help themselves no more than they help others. Therefore, TFT has the self-policing feature and gives agents an extra incentive to interact with other agents. TFT can teach reciprocity to other agents so that they can build a mutually beneficial relationship. However, the problem of TFT is that once a mutual defect is started, it can continue indefinitely. The other problem of TFT is that in the case in which TFT plays itself and an agent mistakenly defects, mutual cooperation cannot be recovered because one of the two agents will always defect.

Doebeli, Hauert and Killingback (2004) compared the spatial model with a randomly mixed model. They combined the IPD and spatial structure in a more stochastic model in which agents interact with only their neighbors and new randomly mutated strategies can appear at any time. They showed that RETALIATOR (the same as FRIEDMAN) occurs most frequently in non-spatial populations. FRIENDMAN cooperates only if both players mutually cooperate in the previous round. Therefore, FRIENDMAN is very resistant to exploitation by mutual defectors like ALL-D, but at the same time, FRIENDMAN is also very vulnerable to stochastic errors, because it has no means to reestablish cooperation once it accidentally defects.

Among spatial structures with some noise, PAVLOV is known as the most successful. One very clear advantage of PAVLOV over FRIENDMAN, for example, is its ability to return to mutual cooperation with other individuals playing the same strategy, after an occasional mistake leads to a defection. This feature is very important in the stochastic world, where occasional errors occur.

Lindgren (1997) investigated evolutionary dynamics based on the IPD with a more general set of rules by changing the memory size. They demonstrated various evolutionary phenomena by studying the behavior in two completely different worlds: the mean-field model (all interact with all) and the local interaction model. The average payoff for each agent is calculated, and this determines which agents are allowed to reproduce offspring in the next generation. The offspring inherits the parent's strategy, possibly altered by mutations to be described below in detail for the different models. The successful rules that evolve are basically more sophisticated versions of PAVLOV, which returns to cooperation only after a series of two mutual defections or when mutual defection follows mutual cooperation.

The learned coupling rule "0111" in collective evolution in the framework of this chapter is similar to FRIEDMAN. In the framework of the proposed model, the agents reevaluate their rules after repeated play for one generation, and the agents then cooperate in playing the game. Therefore, the learned rule of "0111" is unforgiving within one generation, but thereafter is forgiving of the defection since the rules start with cooperate at the next generation.

Fowler *et al.* (2005) also suggested that egalitarian motives are more important than motives for punishing non-cooperative behavior. They also argued that the desire to reduce inequality may motivate cooperators who altruistically punish defectors. This finding is consistent with evidence that humans may have an incentive to punish the highest earners in order to promote equality, rather than cooperation. The evolutionary history of humans suggests that egalitarianism shaped many human cultures and that egalitarian motives may, therefore, be a powerful force behind the punishment of defectors.

A number of questions, such as why so many different successful rules are discovered in the context of the same IPD and whether there are any better alternatives than have been already discovered, remain to be answered. In most previous research, agents behave like automata with pre-specified rules. The only way that agents modify their pre-specified rules are by mutation. If a mutation occurs, which happens at a small mutation rate, the rule of an agent is replaced with a new rule chosen randomly from the entire rule space.

One can imagine how a collection of self-interested agents with learning models might collectively evolve. However, in principle one could fold this evolutionary element into meta-learning that includes both short-term learning and long-term evolution. We emphasize the effect of learning a behavioral rule rather than a strategy. We also emphasize the effect of learnable behavioral rules rather than fixed behavioral rules.

Fortunately, there are never as many different coupling rules in a population as there are agents, because most agents mimic the most successful rule from their neighbors. However, it is doubtful whether agents succeed in exploring a superior rule and spread it to the entire population when inferior rules such as All-D are easy to exploit.

In the context of collective evolution, agents, initially endowed with randomly chosen rules, jointly improve their rules by exchanging part of their rules with the most successful neighbor. We showed that mutual cooperation in the prisoner's dilemma game is sustained if the strategy choice is driven by a coupling rule, which is also jointly improved.

The crucial effect of the local interaction model is that it allows cooperative strategies to cluster together. However, this clustering also helps to retain defects. Since cooperative behavior is exploited by defection, it cannot invade the cluster of defection. On the other hand, small-world networks solve the weakness of the local network, and a superior rule that sustains mutual cooperation is discovered and spreads to the entire population.

What is the motive for cooperation? What in society makes us help or support each other? As discussed in the previous chapter, there are two contradictory views in answer to the basic question of why we should cooperate or be kind to others. One is idea of cooperation in expectation of returns (selfish interpretation). The latter point is that those who are kind to others are sure to be rewarded. The other is the idea of sympathy (altruistic interpretation).

Social norms are self-enforcing patterns of social behavior. It is in everyone's interests to conform given the expectation that others are going to conform. Many spheres of social interactions are governed by social norms such as reciprocity. We can likely understand now that harmony in a society is based on the balance between selfish and altruistic motivations. The desired outcome is a condition in which there is a perfect balance in the society.

9.5 Iterated Coordination Games on Social Networks

In this section, we consider cases in which pair-wise interaction between agents is formulated as a coordination game. The coordination game with the payoff matrix in Table 9.5 has two strict Nash equilibria, (S_1, S_1) and (S_2, S_2), and one mixed strategy equilibrium. The most preferable Pareto-efficient equilibrium is (S_1, S_1), which dominates the other equilibria. There is another equilibrium solution, risk- dominance, in which (S_2, S_2) risk-dominates (S_1, S_1). How do agents choose their strategy when Pareto-efficient equilibrium and risk-dominant equilibrium are different?

Table 9.5 Payoff matrix of the underlying game: coordination game

Own strategy \ Strategy of the other agent	S_1	S_2
S_1	1 / 1	0 / -9
S_2	0 / -9	0 / 0

(Case 1) The initial strategy of each generation is chosen randomly

The average payoff per agent was approximately 0.3, which is far from the Pareto-efficiency, in which all agents could gain 1. The coupling rules learned by 400 agents were aggregated into only type, "0111", which is interpreted as follows. If agent A chooses the Pareto-efficient strategy S_1 (0), then agent B also chooses S_1 (0), and if agent A chooses risk-dominant strategy S_2 (1), then agent B also chooses the same risk-dominant strategy S_2 (1).

(Case 2) The initial strategy of each generation mimics the highest scoring agent among her neighbors.

Figure 9.7(a) shows the average generation payoff per agent. After a few generations the average payoff was increased to 1. Initially there were two types of agents: agents who gained a high payoff of 1 and agents who gained a lower payoff below 1. However, this changed quickly, and the ratio of agents who choose the Pareto-efficient strategy increased and the entire population obtained the same payoff at Pareto-efficiency. In the beginning, each agent had different behavioral rules that were chosen randomly. The coupling rules learned by all 400 agents were aggregated into two types, "0111" and "0101", as shown in Table 9.6. Approximately 90% of the agents learned behavioral rule "0111", and the remaining 10% of the agents learned rule "0101".

Most agents learned the same coupling rules in both Case 1 and Case 2. However, the average payoffs per agent of are quite different for each case, which reflects the difference in strategy at the beginning of each generation.

(Case 3) Iterated games on a small-world network: the initial strategy mimics the highest scoring agent among her neighbors.

Figure 9.7(b) shows the same experiment in a small-world network framework. The coupling rules learned by all 400 agents were aggregated into only one type, "0111", as shown in Table 9.6(c). There are a couple of important differences in this graph and the graph obtained using the fixed spatial environment (Figure 9.7(a)). Figure 9.7(b) shows that it is easier for the Pareto-efficient strategy to evolve in a small-world network environment. As a result, the rule that sustains the Pareto-efficient outcome could be spread out more quickly in a small-world network environment.

The game between two coupling rules with finite memory can be also described as a stationary stochastic process. The state transition of the outcomes when both agents decide their strategies according to the learned coupling rule is illustrated in Figure 9.8 as the state transition diagram. Outcomes "00" and "11" are perfect absorbing states. Once the process enters such a state, it tends to stay there, unless occasional randomness creates noise in the system. Since each agent also learns to start the game by choosing the Pareto-efficient strategy $S_1(0)$, at each generation, they remain in the absorbing state "00". However, in Case 1, in which all agents choose their first strategy randomly, there are two types of clustering in the population. Clusters of agents who always play the Pareto-efficient strategy $S_1(0)$, and clusters of agents who always play the risk-dominant strategy $S_2(1)$, result in a lower average payoff.

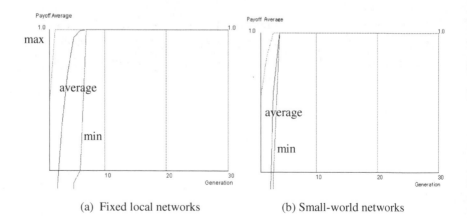

(a) Fixed local networks   (b) Small-world networks

Figure 9.7 Average payoff per agent in iterated coordination games

Table 9.6 Coupling rules learned by 400 agents in coordination games

(a) Fixed local network (initial strategy: random)

Rule type	Initial strategy	Strategy site				Number of agents
	1	4	5	6	7	
15	0 or 1	0	1	1	1	400

(b) Fixed local network (initial strategy: mimicry)

Rule type	Initial strategy	Strategy site				Number of agents
	1	4	5	6	7	
15	0	0	1	1	1	361
11	0	0	1	0	1	39

(c) Small-world network (initial strategy: mimicry)

Rule type	Initial strategy	Strategy site				Number of agents
	1	4	5	6	7	
15	0	0	1	1	1	400

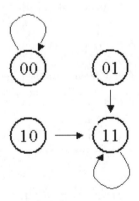

Figure 9.8 State transitions of two agents who play with the coupling rule of "0111"

9.6 Iterated Hawk-Dove Games on Social Networks

In this section, we consider social interaction in which a pair-wise interaction between agents is formulated as a hawk-dove game with the payoff matrix in Table 9.7. In this game, there is the unique symmetric Nash equilibrium in mixed strategies with this game: both agents use the strategy S_1 (hawk) with probability $p=5/6$ and the strategy S_2 (dove) with probability $1-p=1/6$. At the mixed strategy equilibrium, the expected payoff is 5/6. If each agent chooses strategy S_2 (dove), (not equilibrium) each agent can receive 5. This implies that the mixed-strategy results in inefficient equilibrium. Evolutionary dynamics based on natural selection also selects this mixed Nash equilibrium.

It was found that if the hawk-dove game is played in spatially structured populations, there are more cooperative individuals (dove) than in non-structured populations (Killingback and Doebeli,1996). The main effect of spatial structure is that, in structured populations, the dove strategy can build clusters in which the benefits of mutual doves outweigh losses with respect to hawks. Thus, clusters of doves can invade populations of hawks that constitute an ESS in non-spatial populations.

As discussed in the previous section, we also consider the following two cases:

(1) The initial strategy is randomly chosen.

(2) The initial strategy of an agent mimics the highest scoring agent among her neighbors.

Table 9.7 Payoff matrix of the underlying game: hawk-dove game

Own strategy \ Strategy of the other agent	S_1 (Hawk)	S_2 (Dove)
S_1 (Hawk)	-1 -1	0 10
S_2 (Dove)	10 0	5 5

(Case 1) *The initial strategy of each generation is randomly chosen.*

The average payoff per agent was approximately 0.7, which is far from the Pareto-efficiency of 5. The coupling rules learned by 400 agents were aggregated into two types, "1011" and "0010", as shown in Table 9.8(a). Approximately 60% of the agents learned "1011" and the remaining 40% of the agents learned "0010".

(Case 2) *The initial strategy of each generation mimics the highest scoring agent among her neighbors.*

Figure 9.9(b) shows the average generational payoff per agent. After a few generations, the average payoff was increased to 5. Initially there are agents who gain high payoffs and agents who gain low payoffs. However, this changed quickly, and the ratio of agents who chose the dove strategy increased, and the entire population came to obtain the same payoff.

Table 9.8 shows the rules learned by 400 agents, which are aggregated into three types. After a few generations, 400 different rules were aggregated into three types. The learned coupling rules in Table 9.8 have the form of "##01", where # represents either 0 or 1. This type of coupling rule can be interpreted as follows. If both agents decide to choose the dove strategy, then they choose the dove strategy. However, if one of the agents decides to choose the hawk strategy, then the other agent chooses the hawk strategy as well.

The state transition of the outcomes when both agents choose their strategies according to the learned coupling rule "0001"is illustrated in Figure 9.10 as a state transition diagram. The outcomes "00" and "11" are perfect absorbing states. Once the process enters such a state, it tends to stay there, unless occasional randomness creates noise in the system. Since each agent also learned a rule to choose the dove strategy (1), at the first play of each generation, as shown in Table 9.8, the agents remain in the absorbing state at "11".

The outcome "11" is both equitable and efficient; however, it is not Nash equilibrium. The implication being that, while there is one desirable outcome, it may be difficult for decentralized agents to reach this equitable and efficient outcome if they learn their best-response strategies rather than the coupling rules.

(Case 3) *Iterated games on a small-world network: the initial strategy mimics the highest scoring agent.*

Figure 9.9(b) shows the same experiment on a small-world network framework. The coupling rules learned by 400 agents were aggregated into only one type, "0001", as shown in Table 9.8(c). There are a couple of important differences between the small-world environment (Figure

Table 9.8 Coupling rules learned by 400 agents in hawk-dove game

(a) Fixed local networks (initial strategy: random)

Rule type	Initial strategy	Strategy site				Number of agents
	1	4	5	6	7	
14	0 or 1	1	0	1	1	220
5	0 or 1	0	0	1	0	80

(b) Fixed local networks (initial strategy: mimicry)

Rule type	Initial strategy	Strategy site				Number of agents
	1	4	5	6	7	
9	1	0	0	0	1	320
10	1	1	0	0	1	76
11	1	0	1	0	1	4

(c) Small-world network (initial strategy: random)

Rule type	Initial strategy	Strategy site				Number of agents
	1	4	5	6	7	
9	1	0	0	0	1	400

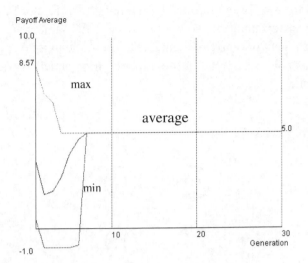

(a) Repeated games on fixed local networks: each agent interacts with eight fixed neighbors

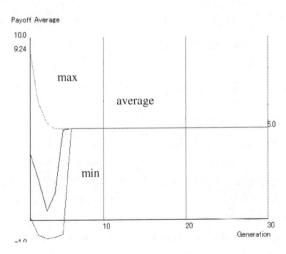

(b) Repeated games on small-world networks

Figure 9.9 Average payoff per agent in iterated hawk-dove games

9.9(b)) and the spatial environment (Figure 9.9(a)). Figure 9.9(b) shows that it is easier for all agents co-evolve to share the same coupling rule in a small-world network environment. As a result, the unique coupling rule "0001" was able to spread more quickly in a small-world network environment.

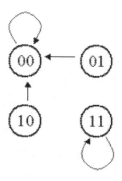

Figure 9.10 State transitions of two agents who play with the coupling rule of "0001"

9.7   Sustainable Coupling Rules

Most game theory models deal with specific social interactions between individuals who adapt their behavior (strategy) in order to maximize their gains within the prescribed underlying game. The situation changes abruptly when games are repeated and agents behave based on past experiences and choose their strategy depending on past outcomes.

We find that the structure of the underlying payoff matrix determines which equilibrium is played, independently of the specific payoff. This contrasts with the play of games between individuals, where payoffs play an important role in determining equilibrium.

There is no doubt that people learn from past successful and unsuccessful attempts to improve their behaviors. Most learning models apply when agents learn or adapt based on losses or gains. On the other hand, meta-learning applies to improving behavioral rules.

In particular, we focus on the coupling rules that provide the guidance to choose their strategy. This means that agents attempt to realize a better outcome for both agents rather than to get a good payoff. We have studied the dynamics of an ensemble of locally coupled agents that attempts to drive the collective system from an incoherent behavior to a desirable behavior.

Agents constantly improve their behavioral rules. Thus, an important requirement for an efficient behavioral rule is that it should be robust. That is, it may not to be replaced by other rules. Significantly, if a rule achieves Pareto-efficiency, then it is robust. Therefore, we can conclude that sustainable behavioral rules are also robust.

In this section, we develop the definition of a sustainable coupling rule that serves to secure sustainable relationships among agents in an attainable manner. The coupling rule specifies the strategy choice at each play of the underlying game. After playing the games several times, which is defined as one generation, they review their current rules and update their incumbent rule with the new rule if their average payoff is poor compared with their neighbors. This character of collective evolution may allow for the possibility of escalating the conventional co-evolutionary path with no end. That is, agents might continually adapt to each other in more and more specialized ways, never stabilizing at a desirable behavioral rule.

We define a set of behavioral rules to be *efficient* if the total payoff for both agents is maximized when they follow these rules when choosing a strategy for each iterated game. An ambitious objective is then to find a learning procedure that will enable the agents to obtain such efficient rules, then the mission of collective evolution is to harness the collective systems in which interacting agents attempt to explore a better behavioral rule.

We also define a set of coupling rules to be *sustainable* if they are not to be replaced by other rules. In this case, the payoffs to both agents should be maximized and equitable when the agents follow these sustainable coupling rules in choosing their strategy. An ambitious objective of collective evolution is also to find a learning procedure that will enable the interacting agents to obtain such sustainable coupling rules through repeated play of the underlying games.

We consider the case in which a collection of agents plays a given underlying *2x2* game with the payoff matrix *G*. By playing the games several times, each agent receives the appropriate payoff, as dictated by the payoff matrix *G*. A strategy choice for repeated play of the game uses the recent outcomes of play to choose one of the two strategies for the next play.

The coupling rule r_i of agent *i*, *i=1*, *2*, determines the particular strategy choice for each possible outcome. The memory $m \, \varepsilon M$ at time *t* consists of the history of outcomes that have occurred thus far. Given the underlying game *G*, a coupling rule for an agent is a mapping from the set of memory *M*, the set of possible outcomes, to the set of possible strategies. A quick calculation shows that the number of possible couplings becomes huge. The hope is that agents would find a better coupling among the overwhelming number of possible rules after a reasonable number of generations.

We define a desired outcome and denote it by $V_i(G)$, which is the payoff obtained by agent *i* at Pareto-efficiency of the underlying game *G*.

Definition 9.1   *A pair of coupling rules (r_1, r_2) of agent i, i=1, 2, is defined as sustainable if they cannot be replaced by other coupling rules.*

Given an underlying game *G* and the number of iterations *T* in repeated games, we denote the expected *T*-iteration average payoff of agent *i* when both agents follow a set of coupling rules (r_1, r_2) as $U_i(r_1, r_2)$, *i = 1;2*.

Lemma 9.1 *If the set of coupling rules (r_1, r_2) is sustainable for agent i, i = 1, 2, then the sum of the average payoff per iteration should be Pareto efficient by satisfying*

$$U_1(r_1, r_2) + U_2(r_1, r_2) = V_1(G) + V_2(G) \qquad (9.1)$$

This lemma implies that if both agents *i*, *i = 1*, *2*, play with a pair of sustainable coupling rules (r_1, r_2), then their average payoff per iteration is Pareto-efficient.

Lemma 9.2 *If agent i plays with a sustainable coupling rule r_i and the other agent plays with some other rule r, which is not a sustainable coupling rule, then her average payoff is worse than $V_i(G)$, i.e.,*

$$U_i(r_i, r) < V_i(G) \tag{9.2}$$

This requirement is that if an agent plays with another coupling rule that is not sustainable, the average payoff per iteration becomes worse than the desired value at Pareto efficiency.

We now obtain sustainable coupling rules in the context of repeated games with the memory size of 2 ($m=2$). In this case, each coupling rule needs 4 bits to represent the strategy choices, as shown in Table 9.2. In this chapter, we have investigated the prisoner's dilemma game, the coordination game and the hawk-dove game. We will continue our discussion on the dispersion game in the next chapter.

Here, we characterize the sustainable coupling rules when the underlying game is one of four different types.

(1) *The underlying game is the prisoner's dilemma game in Table 9.3.*

A sustainable coupling rule should be of the form "0##1". That is, a sustainable coupling rule implies that if the outcome is (S_1, S_1), both agents cooperate. However, if the outcome is (S_2, S_2), both agents defect, and one of the agents defects in the next round. In other outcomes, one agent cooperates and the other defects, and so the other agent might cooperate or defect, which is represented by #∈ (0,1).

(2) *The underlying game is the coordination game in Table 9.5*

A sustainable coupling rule should be of the form "0##1". This rule implies that if the outcome is (S_1, S_1), both agents choose the Pareto-strategy (S_1), and so the agents also choose $S_1(0)$ next time. On the other hand, if the outcome is (S_2, S_2), both agents choose the risk-dominant strategy $S_2(1)$. For all other outcomes, she might choose either S_1 or S_2, which is denoted by #∈ (0,1).

(3) *The underlying game is the hawk-dove game in Table 9.7.*

A sustainable coupling rule should be of the form "###1". This rule implies that if the outcome is (S_2, S_2), both agents choose S_2 (dove), and so one agent chooses $S_2(1)$ next time. For all other outcomes, she might choose either S_1 (hawk) or S_2 (dove), which is denoted by #∈ (0,1).

(4) *The underlying game is a dispersion game in Table 10.1.*

When the underlying game is the dispersion game in Table 10.1, there are two types of sustainable coupling rules. One type is of the form "#01#". This rule implies that if the outcome is (S_1, S_2), both agents choose distinct strategies, and one agent chooses $S_1(0)$, the same strategy as was chose in the previous round. In the case in which the outcome is (S_2, S_1), one agent should choose $S_2(1)$, which is the same strategy as in the previous round. For all other outcomes in which both agents choose the same strategy, an agent might choose either S_1 or S_2, which is denoted by #∈ (0, 1).

There is another type of sustainable coupling rule "#10#" when the underlying game is a dispersion game. This rule is completely opposite to the coupling rule "#01#". If the outcome is (S_1, S_2), an agent changes her strategy by choosing $S_2(1)$. In the case in which the outcome is (S_2, S_1), the other agent also switches to $S_2(1)$.

Browning and Colman (2004) investigated how alternating coordination can evolve without any communication between agents who play the asymmetric dispersion game. Using a genetic algorithm incorporating mutation and crossing-over, they showed that coordinated turn-taking can evolves in games with asymmetric Nash equilibria. By alternating coordination the agents benefit from it. The asymmetry in payoffs from interaction induces agents to learn the behavioral rule, so-called give-and-take to break the asymmetry. However, how agents evolve alternating coordination without communication is not fully explained. We will investigate this issue in the next chapter.

Chapter 10

Collective Evolution of Synchronized Behavioral Rules

In the previous chapter, we focused on the role of the coupling rule in the context of repeated games. The term coupling dynamics refers to systems that exhibit a time evolution in which the characteristics of the internal dynamics of agents change by introducing plasticity into the coupling rules. In this chapter, we consider another type of social interaction in which agents should be dispersed. In particular, we focus on the emergence of synchronized behavioral rules that sustain efficient and equitable outcomes.

10.1 Dispersion Games on Social Networks

Dispersion games are clearly important role and deserve a great deal of discussion and scrutiny. We view the approach of this chapter as opening the door to substantial additional work on this exciting class of games. Unfortunately, the analysis is not a simple one. The gap between underlying games, treated in the previous chapter, and dispersion games requires further simulation works.

The dispersion game with the payoff matrix in Table 10.1 has two pure Nash equilibria, (S_1, S_2) and (S_2, S_1). There is another equilibrium with mixed strategies. If both agents choose S_1 with probability θ and S_2 with probability $1-\theta$, they also reach a Nash equilibrium. At the two pure equilibria (S_1, S_2) and (S_2, S_1), the agents receive different payoffs if $\theta \neq 0.5$. In this case, one agent receives 2θ and the other agent receives $2(1-\theta)$. However, in an equilibrium situation involving mixed strategies both agents receive the same payoff $2\theta(1 - \theta)$. Therefore, this mixed

Nash equilibrium situation seems fairer than the first two asymmetric pure Nash equilibria. However, this mixed Nash equilibrium is inefficient because the payoff to both agents is lower than in the first two cases. The sum of the payoffs at the pure equilibria is 2 and that at the fair mixed Nash equilibrium is $4\theta(1-\theta)$, which is less than 2. We thus observe that the criterion for efficiency contradicts that for equity.

The number of possible coupling rules in the repeated games depends on the agents' memory size. We can observe open-ended evolution with the increase of the memory size in computer simulation. If there exists a rule of the effective memory size to realize the Pareto-efficient outcome, then the outcome cannot be altered by any rule with a longer memory size. As we have shown in the previous chapter, when the underlying game is a prisoner's dilemma game, a coordination game, or a Hawk-Dove game, the effective memory size is $m=2$.

However, when the underlying game is a dispersion game, agents may need longer memories. We assume that each agent remembers the past outcomes of two rounds and that the memory size is $m=4$. A quick calculation shows that the total number of coupling rules with the memory size $m=4$ is 2^{16}. A coupling rule specifies, for each history, what strategy the agent should choose, as shown in Table 10.2. The hope is that agents would find a better coupling rule from among the overwhelming number of possible rules after a reasonable number of repeated interactions.

Table 10.1 Underlying game: dispersion game ($0 < \theta < 1$)

Own choice \ Choice of opponent	S_1	S_2
S_1	0 / 0	2θ / 2(1−θ)
S_2	2(1−θ) / 2θ	0 / 0

Agents repeatedly play the dispersion game in Table 10.1 for T (=20) iterations based on the rule represented by a binary string in Figure 10.1. The values of the first two strategy sites, p_1 and p_2, encode the strategies that the agent chooses at $t=0$ and $t=1$. The strategy sites p_j, $j \in [3,...,6]$, encode the memories of the strategies chosen by the agent and her opponent at the previous round, $t - 1$. The strategy sites p_j, $j \in [7,...,23]$, encode the strategy that the agent should choose at the next round t, corresponding to the values at the strategy sites p_j, $j \in [3,...,6]$. We also assume that each agent occasionally makes a mistake with some probability ε in implementing the strategy specified by the coupling rule.

Table 10.2 Coupling rules with the memory size of four (m=4)

(own: one's own strategy, opp: opponent's strategy, S_1=0, S_2=1, #: 0 or 1)

Strategy site in Figure 10.1	Past strategies				Next strategy
	t-2		t-1		
	own	opp	own	opp	
7	0	0	0	0	#
8	0	0	0	1	#
9	0	0	1	0	#
10	0	0	1	1	#
11	0	1	0	0	#
12	0	1	0	1	#
13	0	1	1	0	#
14	0	1	1	1	#
15	1	0	0	0	#
16	1	0	0	1	#
17	1	0	1	0	#
18	1	0	1	1	#
19	1	1	0	0	#
20	1	1	0	1	#
21	1	1	1	0	#
22	1	1	1	1	#

An agent mimics the coupling rule of the most successful neighbor as a guide for improvement of her rule. The success depends in large part on how well the agents learn from each other, and if some agents are doing well, their effective rules have a chance to be imitated by others.

(Case 1) *Symmetric dispersion game*

First of all, we consider the case in which all agents repeatedly play the symmetric dispersion game with the payoff matrix in Table 10.3. The average payoff per agent at each generation is shown Figure 10.2. The highest and lowest payoffs per agent are also shown. There exist lucky agents, who receive the maximum payoff of 1, and unlucky agents, who receive a lower payoff.

Figure 10.2(a) shows the result when there is no implementation error. The average payoff per agent was gradually increased to 0.78. Figure 10.2(b) shows the result with the implementation error rate of 5%. Consequently, collective evolution leads to a more desirable outcome when agents have a little chance of making mistakes in implementing rules. Furthermore, the difference between the highest and lowest payoffs becomes small, and the equity of the population is also improved.

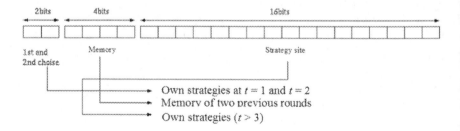

Figure 10.1 Representation of a coupling rule of the memory size, *m=4*

Table 10.3 Symmetric dispersion game with $\theta=0.5$ in Table 10.1

Own choice \ Opponent's choice	S_1		S_2	
S_1		0		1
	0		1	
S_2		1		0
	1		0	

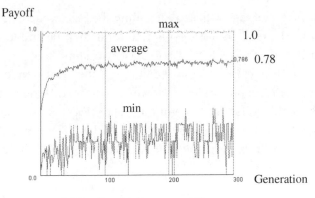

(a) Implementation error: 0%

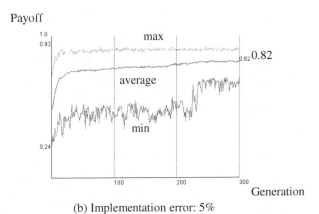

(b) Implementation error: 5%

Figure 10.2 Simulation results with the fixed local network

We also compare and identify the effect of the manner of interaction by considering the small-world network. The locally networked agents will be compared to a half-mixed population in which a half of the population is again modeled by a lattice, but in this case each agent interacts with four partners that are nearest neighbors and four partners that are randomly chosen from the population. Figure 10.3 shows the result of the small-world network. There is an important difference in this graph and the graph obtained using the fixed local network (Figure 10.2). Figure 10.3 shows that it is actually easier for desired outcomes of efficiency and equity to evolve in the small-world network environment.

The advantage of agent-based modeling is that we can investigate coupling rules learned by all agents that lead to a desirable collective outcome at the macro level. In Table 10.4, we show the coupling rules learned by 400 agents. In the beginning, they are endowed with randomly chosen coupling rules. However, these different rules were updated through collective evolution. The 400 rules were finally aggregated into 15 types, as shown in Table 10.4. The numbers in the right-hand column represent the number of agents who share the same rule.

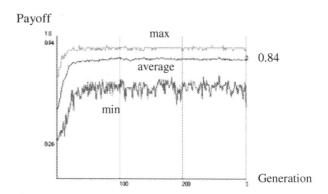

Figure 10.3 Simulation result with the small world network

Collective Evolution of Synchronized Behavioral Rules

293

These 15 aggregated rules also have the same values at the following strategy sites: #8, #9, #11, #12, #14, #15, #17, #18, #19, #20, #21, and #22. The values of the strategy sites are also summarized in Table 10.5. From this table, we can imply the following two interesting properties. Firstly, although each agent has a memory of four ($m=4$) and her coupling rule depends on the outcomes of the two previous rounds, her strategy choice is made depending on the previous round. Secondly, if an agent chooses $S_1(0)$ and her opponent chooses $S_2(1)$ (in this case both agents gain the payoff), she repeats the same strategy $S_1(0)$. Similarly, if she chooses $S_2(1)$ and her opponent chooses $S_1(0)$ (in this case both gents also gain the payoff), then she also repeats the same strategy $S_2(1)$.

Table 10.4 Learned coupling rules with the error rate of 5%

Rule type	Initial Strategy		Strategy site																Number of agents
	1	2	7	8	9	10	11	12	13	14	15	16	17	18	19	20	21	22	
1	0	0	1	0	1	0	0	0	1	1	1	0	1	0	0	0	1	0	36
2	0	0	0	0	1	0	0	0	1	1	1	0	1	0	0	0	1	0	31
3	0	0	1	0	1	1	0	0	1	1	1	0	1	0	0	0	1	0	30
4	0	0	1	0	1	0	0	0	0	1	1	1	1	0	0	0	1	0	30
5	0	0	1	0	1	1	0	0	0	1	1	1	1	0	0	0	1	0	25
6	1	1	1	0	1	0	0	0	0	1	1	1	1	0	0	0	1	0	22
7	1	1	1	0	1	1	0	0	0	1	1	1	1	0	0	0	1	0	18
8	1	1	0	0	1	0	0	0	0	1	1	1	1	0	0	0	1	0	18
9	0	0	0	0	1	1	0	0	1	1	1	0	1	0	0	0	1	0	17
10	0	0	0	0	1	0	0	0	0	1	1	1	1	0	0	0	1	0	16
11	1	1	1	0	1	0	0	0	1	1	1	0	1	0	0	0	1	0	14
12	0	0	1	0	1	1	0	0	1	1	1	1	1	0	0	0	1	0	14
13	1	1	0	0	1	0	0	0	1	1	1	0	1	0	0	0	1	0	13
14	1	1	1	0	1	1	0	0	1	1	1	0	1	0	0	0	1	0	12
15	1	1	1	0	1	0	0	0	1	1	1	1	1	0	0	0	1	0	11

All other rules are interpreted as follows. If both agents choose the same strategy (in which case they do not gain the payoff), cases in which they may choose the same strategy as in the previous round or change their strategy are equally likely to occur. Therefore, we can observe that learned coupling rules have the following common feature. If they gain the payoff (success), then they repeat the same strategy, and if they cannot gain (fail), then they change their strategy. This common feature is the same as the principle of reinforcement learning.

In Table 10.6, we show the coupling rules learned by 400 agents in the small-world network architecture without any implementation error. All learned rules were aggregated into 15 types. The numbers in the right-most column represent the number of agents who learned the same type of rules.

Table 10.5 Characteristics of the learned coupling rules in Table 10.4

Strategy site in Figure 10.1	Past strategies				Strategy at t
	t-2		t-1		
	own	opponent's	own	opponent's	
7	0	0	0	0	0 or 1
8	0	0	0	1	0
9	0	0	1	0	1
10	0	0	1	1	0 or 1
11	0	1	0	0	0
12	0	1	0	1	0
13	0	1	1	0	0 or 1
14	0	1	1	1	1
15	1	0	0	0	1
16	1	0	0	1	0 or 1
17	1	0	1	0	1
18	1	0	1	1	0
19	1	1	0	0	0
20	1	1	0	1	0
21	1	1	1	0	1
22	1	1	1	1	0

These 15 aggregated types also have common values at the strategy sites except at #7, #10, #19, and #22. The features of the learned rules are summarized in Table 10.7. The common values at the strategy sites at #8, #9, #11, #12, #13, #14, #15, #16, #17, #18, #20, and #21 imply the following property. If they gain the payoff (success), then they repeat the same strategy, and if they cannot gain (fail), then they change the strategy.

When agents interact with fixed neighbors (local interaction), a mistake in implementing the strategy plays an important role in helping agents to learn coupling rules that realize efficient outcomes. However, if agents interact in the small-world network environment, they succeed in learning coupling rules that realize the most efficient outcomes without any mistake.

Table 10.6 Learned coupling rules on the small-world networks with the error rate of 0%

Rule type	Initial Strategy		Strategy site																Number of agents
	1	2	7	8	9	10	11	12	13	14	15	16	17	18	19	20	21	22	
1	0	1	1	0	1	0	1	0	1	1	0	0	1	0	0	0	1	0	64
2	0	0	1	0	1	1	1	0	1	1	0	0	1	0	1	0	1	0	58
3	0	0	1	0	1	1	1	0	1	1	0	0	1	0	0	0	1	0	47
4	0	0	1	0	1	0	1	0	1	1	0	0	1	0	1	0	1	0	31
5	0	1	0	0	1	1	1	0	1	1	0	0	1	0	0	0	1	0	27
6	1	1	1	0	1	0	1	0	1	1	0	0	1	0	0	0	1	0	23
7	0	1	0	0	1	1	1	0	1	1	0	0	1	0	1	0	1	0	20
8	1	1	1	0	1	1	1	0	1	1	0	0	1	0	0	0	1	0	18
9	0	0	0	0	1	0	1	0	1	1	0	0	1	0	0	0	1	0	17
10	1	1	0	0	1	1	1	0	1	1	0	0	1	0	0	0	1	0	15
11	1	1	1	0	1	1	1	0	1	1	0	0	1	0	1	0	1	1	12
12	1	1	1	0	1	1	1	0	1	1	0	0	1	0	1	0	1	0	9
13	1	1	0	0	1	0	1	0	1	1	0	0	1	0	0	0	1	0	9
14	0	1	0	0	1	0	1	0	1	1	0	0	1	0	1	0	1	0	8
15	1	1	1	0	1	0	1	0	1	1	0	0	1	0	0	0	1	1	5

By comparing the results shown in Table 10.5 and Table 10.7, we can conclude that the scope of emergence of an efficient coupling for realizing perfect coordination is dependent on how agents interact. If they interact locally in a lattice network, then perfect coordination does not occur because they may choose two possible strategies at the outcomes specified at strategy sites #13 and #16 in Table 10.5. However, the introduction of a small-world network, so that individuals interact with those in their neighborhood as well as new partners who may not have met before affect the collective dynamics, which greatly facilitates the collective evolution of perfect coordinated behavior.

Table 10.7 Characteristics of the learned coupling rules in Table 10.6

Strategy site	Past strategies				Strategy at t
	t-2		t-1		
	own	opponent's	own	opponent's	
7	0	0	0	0	0 or 1
8	0	0	0	1	0
9	0	0	1	0	1
10	0	0	1	1	0 or 1
11	0	1	0	0	1
12	0	1	0	1	0
13	0	1	1	0	1
14	0	1	1	1	1
15	1	0	0	0	0
16	1	0	0	1	0
17	1	0	1	0	1
18	1	0	1	1	0
19	1	1	0	0	0 or 1
20	1	1	0	1	0
21	1	1	1	0	1
22	1	1	1	1	0 or 1

(Case 2) *Asymmetric dispersion game*

Next, we investigate the case in which the underlying game is the asymmetric dispersion game with the payoff matrix in Table 10.8. Figure 10.4(a) shows the average payoff per agent and the highest and lowest payoffs in the population when there is no implementation error. The average payoff per agent was gradually increased to 0.75. However, the difference between the highest and lowest payoffs is large, and there are lucky agents who received the maximum payoff of 1 and unlucky agents who received almost nothing. Figure 10.4(b) shows the simulation result with the implementation error of 5%. From this simulation result, mistakes in implementing a strategy for a specified a coupling rule are also important in helping agents to learn more desirable coupling rules.

In Table 10.9, we show the coupling rules learned by 400 agents. These rules were aggregated into 15 types. The right-most column shows the number of agents who learned to share the same rule. These aggregated rules have common values at the strategy sites #8, #9, #11, #13, #14, #15, #16, #17, #18, #20, #21, and #22. These commonalities are summarized in Table 10.10. The common values at the strategy sites among the learned coupling rules imply the following interesting properties. Although the agents have a memory of four ($m=4$) and learn to choose their strategies based on the choices made during the previous two rounds, they learn to make their decisions depending on only the previous round.

Table 10.8 Asymmetric dispersion game with $\theta = 0.2$ in Table 10.1

Own choice \ Opponent's choice	S_1		S_2	
S_1		0		0.4
	0		1.6	
S_2		1.6		0
	0.4		0	

Secondly, and more interestingly, if each agent chooses $S_1(0)$ and her opponent chooses $S_2(1)$ (in this case both agents gain the payoff), she changes her choice to $S_2(1)$. On the other hand, if she chooses $S_2(1)$ and her opponent chooses $S_1(0)$ (in this case both agents also gain the payoff), then she also changes to $S_1(0)$. In all other cases, that is, if both agents choose the same choices (in which case they do not gain the payoff), the likelihood of choosing the same strategy as in the previous round is equal to that of choosing the other strategy.

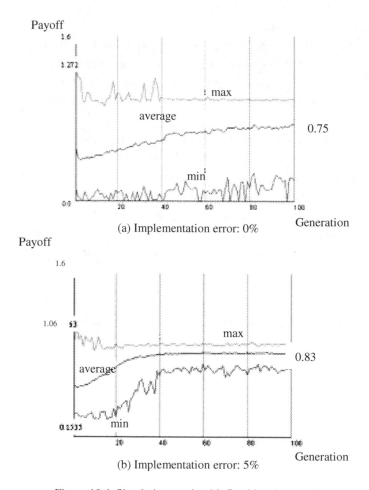

Figure 10.4 Simulation result with fixed local networks

Most agents succeeded in learning the coupling rules that have the following property. If the agent gains the payoff (success), then they change their strategies. We define this behavioral rule based on the principle of *give-and-take,* as discussed in Chapter 7. In Chapter 7, we showed that the rule of give-and-take is effective for realizing efficient and equitable outcomes when the underlying social interaction is modeled as a minority game. However, we did not discuss the background or derivation of this rule. A central authority may force its members to follow such a rule. However, our interest is to show how the agents could evolve such behavioral rules based on the principle of give-and-take rule without any control from the outside When agents face symmetric dispersion games with the payoff matrix in Table 10.3, there is no difference in the payoff under outcome (S_1, S_2) or (S_2, S_1).

Table 10.9 Learned coupling rules for a fixed local network with an error rate of 5%

Rule type	Initial Strategy		Strategy site																Number of agents
	1	2	7	8	9	10	11	12	13	14	15	16	17	18	19	20	21	22	
1	0	0	1	1	0	0	1	1	0	0	0	1	0	1	0	1	0	0	72
2	1	0	0	1	0	0	1	1	0	0	0	1	0	1	0	1	0	0	61
3	1	0	1	1	0	0	1	0	0	0	0	1	0	1	0	1	0	0	43
4	0	1	0	1	0	0	1	0	0	0	0	1	0	1	0	1	0	0	40
5	0	1	1	1	0	1	1	1	0	0	0	1	0	1	0	1	0	0	37
6	1	1	1	1	0	1	1	0	0	0	0	1	0	1	0	1	0	0	35
7	0	1	0	1	0	1	1	1	0	0	0	1	0	1	0	1	0	0	31
8	1	1	0	1	0	1	1	0	0	0	0	1	0	1	0	1	0	0	31
9	0	0	1	1	0	0	1	1	0	0	0	1	0	1	1	1	0	0	13
10	1	0	1	1	0	1	1	1	0	0	0	1	0	1	1	1	0	0	12
11	1	1	0	1	0	1	1	1	0	0	0	1	0	1	1	1	0	0	10
12	0	0	0	1	0	0	1	1	0	0	0	1	0	1	1	1	0	0	10
13	1	1	0	1	0	0	1	0	0	0	0	1	0	1	1	1	0	0	2
14	0	0	1	1	0	0	1	1	0	0	0	1	1	1	0	1	0	0	2
15	1	1	0	1	0	1	1	0	0	0	0	1	0	1	1	1	0	0	1

Table 10.10 Characteristics of learned coupling rules in Table 10.9

Strategy site	Past strategies				Strategy at t
	t-2		t-1		
	own	opponent's	own	opponent's	
7	0	0	0	0	0 or 1
8	0	0	0	1	1
9	0	0	1	0	0
10	0	0	1	1	0 or 1
11	0	1	0	0	1
12	0	1	0	1	0 or 1
13	0	1	1	0	0
14	0	1	1	1	0
15	1	0	0	0	0
16	1	0	0	1	1
17	1	0	1	0	0 or 1
18	1	0	1	1	1
19	1	1	0	0	0 or 1
20	1	1	0	1	1
21	1	1	1	0	0
22	1	1	1	1	0

Therefore, they learn the coupling rules to continue the same strategy if they gain. On the other hand, when they face asymmetric dispersion games with the payoff matrix in Table 10.8, the payoffs to both agents at the two pure Nash equilibria (S_1, S_2) and (S_2, S_1) become asymmetric. Therefore, they learn to realize efficient and equitable outcomes by visiting the two pure Nash equilibria alternatively.

Social norms are self-enforcing patterns of social behavior. It is in everyone's interests to conform given the expectation that others are going to conform. Many spheres of social interactions are governed by social norms. We have showed that the agents collectively evolve such social norms. The introduction of genetic algorithms enabled researchers to investigate the natural selection of social norm using sophisticated computer simulations. The evolutionary problem is to explain how such social behaviour could have evolved, given that natural selection operates at the individual level. Computer simulations have shown that, after thousands of repetitions of social interactions, social norms such as such as reciprocity, give and take, and so forth.

In an evolutionary approach, there is no need to assume a rational calculation to identify the effective rule. Instead, the analysis of what is chosen at any specific time is based upon an implementation of the idea that effective rules are more likely to be retained than ineffective ones. Furthermore each agent mimics the most successful neighbor as guidance of improving her coupling rule. Their success depends in large part on how well they learn from their neighbors. If an agent gains more payoff than her neighbor, there is a chance her coupling rule will be imitated by others. The more successful agents are more likely to survive and reproduce effective coupling rules. However, agents also observe each other, and those agents with poor performance tend to imitate the rules of those they see doing better. This mechanism of collective evolution tends to evolve to both efficient and equitable outcomes. Furthermore, the asymmetry in payoffs from interaction induces agents to learn the behavioral rule, so-called give-and-take to break the asymmetry.

A major shortcoming of this influential research is its focus on games in which cooperation or coordination involves the agents acting similarly. There are games in which favourable payoffs are possible only if one player acts one way while the other acts the opposite way. To cooperate successfully, the agents have to alternate or *take turns*, out of phase with each other. A typical example is the dispersion game. If this type of interaction is repeated, then the agents benefit, in terms of natural selection, by *coordinated alternation* by taking turns in choosing one of the two strategies and there is evidence to show that this type of *turn-taking* occurs quite commonly in nature. Give and take or alternation is a strategy that is intuitive and simple, but even so it is beyond the scope of most traditional learning models.

Hanaki (2006) used adaptive models to understand the dynamics that lead to efficient and fair outcomes in the repeated battle of sexes game with the payoff matrix in Table 2.4 in Chapter 2. He develops a model that not only uses reinforcement learning but also the evolutionary learning that operates through evolutionary selection. He found that the efficient and fair outcome emerges relatively quickly through turn taking. However, his model requires a long run pre-experimental phase before it is ready to take turn. Turn taking in the battle of the sexes game is just one of many game theoretic phenomena, and it raises an important general point for further studies.

Browning and Colman (2004) investigated how this type of coordinated, *alternating cooperation* can evolve without any communication between agents who play the dispersion game. Using a genetic algorithm incorporating mutation and crossing-over, they showed that coordinated turn-taking can evolves in games with asymmetric Nash equilibria. The procedure followed Wu and Axelrod (1997). For each outcome of the game, each agent receives one of four payoffs, and she remembers three past outcomes. Since there are 4^3 different three-move histories, each string of 64 binary digits suffices to specify a choice for every three-move history. The offspring rules that played in each subsequent generation were formed from the most successful rule of the previous generation, using a genetic algorithm. The algorithm implemented the following five steps: (1) The payoff values were assigned according the underlying game. (2) An initial population was for each of the 20 randomly chosen rules. (3) In each generation, each of the 20 rules was paired with each of the others for the fixed number of repetitions with every other rule in the population (global interaction). (4) At the end of each generation, after each rule had played with each of the others, each rule's mean payoff was computed, and it was as signed a mating probability proportional to its fitness score. (5) For each offspring strategy, two rules were randomly selected as parents, selection being proportional to mating probability scores.

They showed that about 85% of the plays in the population are characterized by coordinated turn taking. They study the nature, properties and phenomena of coordinated alternating cooperation in a range of dispersion games with asymmetric equilibria. By alternating coordination the agents benefit from it, however, how agents evolves alternating coordination without communication is not fully explained.

10.2 Generalized Rock-Scissors-Paper Games

The hand game "Rock-Scissors-Paper (RSP)", which is also known as "*Janken*" in Japan, has been played world-over for a long time. It is most often used to solve small conflicts between people but it can also be played to decide more serious matters. We should recognize that such a simple game is not only a children's game and that there are actually organizations dedicated to this game, as evidenced by the home page of the World RSP Society.

The RSP game consists of each player shaking a fist a number of times and then extending the same hand in one of three configurations: a fist (rock), two fingers extended (scissors), or flat (paper). Each of these is referred to as a strategy, and the winning strategy is dependent upon the opponent's strategy. Rock wins against scissors, scissors wins against paper, and paper wins against rock. If each player chooses the same strategy, the round is a stalemate, and must be replayed. This RSP game is formulated with the payoff matrix in Table 10.11, which is a zero-sum game.

Table 10.11 Payoff matrix of the rock-scissors-paper game

Own choice \ Opponent's choice	S_1 (Rock)	S_2 (Scissors)	S_3 (Paper)
S_1 (Rock)	0 / 0	-1 / 1	1 / -1
S_2 (Scissors)	1 / -1	0 / 0	-1 / 1
S_3 (Paper)	-1 / 1	1 / -1	0 / 0

The RSP game is also important in many scientific disciplines. For instance, one of the central aims of ecology is to identify mechanisms that maintain biodiversity. Numerous theoretical models have shown that competing species can coexist if ecological processes such as dispersal, movement, and interaction occur over small spatial scales. In particular, this may be the case for non-transitive communities, that is, communities without strict competitive hierarchies. The classic non-transitive system involves a community of three competing species satisfying a relationship similar to the RSP game. Such relationships have been demonstrated in several natural systems. Some models predict that local interaction and dispersal are sufficient to ensure the coexistence of all three species in such a community, whereas diversity is lost when the ecological processes occur over larger scales.

Kerr *et al.* (2002) set out to investigate the mechanisms that maintain biodiversity in ecosystems. The study of three bacterial strains engaged in an interaction that mimics the RSP game shows the importance of localized interactions in maintaining biodiversity. Understanding the processes that maintain and generate biodiversity is crucial to conserving biodiversity. They explored whether genetic diversity can persist over the long time scales required for evolution. They found that the triangular relationship among rock, scissors, and paper, alone is not sufficient to preserve biodiversity. Biodiversity disappeared when the strains were grown in environments that allowed them to interact globally and more thoroughly. On the other hand, localizing the interactions preserves genetic diversity.

Their work also has the potential to help answer one of the biggest questions in evolution such as why so many different types of organisms exist. The localization of dispersal and interaction with RSP games is an example of one process that might prove important in maintaining all that diversity. Although Kerr and colleagues are not the first to show that localized interactions can turn into a dynamic coexistence of many types, endlessly chasing each other. However, their approach offers new ideas to understand how biological communities are built, which is one of the most intriguing aspects of the study of biodiversity.

We can extend the zero-sum RSP game to a non zero-sum game with the generalized payoff matrix in Table 10.12. The situation of the non-zero-sum game is very different from that of the zero-sum game. In the zero-sum game situation with the payoff matrix in Table 10.11, the sum together of all wins and losses is 0. If someone wins, the other has to lose. In the zero-sum game situation, each agent has strong incentive to win. But in the non zero-sum game situation, agents do not compete only to win or lose, since the sum of all wins and losses is not zero. Since profits can be increased by cooperating with the opponent, implicit coordination between the agents may occur.

We consider a population of agents located a lattice network, as shown in Figure 9.3 in Chapter 9. The agents repeatedly play the generalized RSP game with the payoff matrix in Table 10.12. Agents play with their nearest eight neighbors based on the coupling rules. The coupling rules of the agents are updated using the crossover operator. Each agent mimics part of the coupling rule of the most successful neighbor.

If we set $\lambda = 2$ in Table 10.12, this game becomes strategically equivalent to the zero-sum game in Table 10.11. In this case, this payoff matrix has the unique mixed Nash equilibrium strategy such that each strategy (rock, scissors or paper) is chosen with the same probability. The expected payoff to each agent under this mixed Nash equilibrium is $(\lambda + 1)/3$.

If the payoff parameter λ is increased and becomes greater than 2, then the Pareto-efficient outcome is achieved when both agents choose distinct strategies. However, under these asymmetric situations, one agent receives the payoff λ, and the other agent receives nothing, then the problem of fairness may arise. The sum of the payoff to both agents at the Pareto-efficient outcome is λ. Therefore, the price of anarchy, the ratio of the average payoff at Nash equilibrium to that of at the Pareto-efficient outcome is about 2/3.

Adaptation and Evolution in Collective Systems

Table 10.12 Generalized payoff matrix of a rock-scissors-paper game ($\lambda \geq 2$)

Own choice \ Opponent's choice	S_1 (Rock)	S_2 (Scissors)	S_3 (Paper)
S_1 (Rock)	1 \ 1	0 \ λ	λ \ 0
S_2 (Scissors)	λ \ 0	1 \ 1	0 \ λ
S_3 (Paper)	0 \ λ	λ \ 0	1 \ 1

10.3   A Coupling Rule with a Memory of Two

A coupling rule uses the past outcomes of play to choose one of the three strategies for the next round. Here, we assume that each agent can remember the last round of play (memory of $m=2$). There are nine possible outcomes, (S_1, S_1), (S_1, S_2), (S_1, S_3), (S_2, S_1), (S_2, S_2), (S_2, S_3), (S_3, S_1), (S_3, S_2), and (S_3, S_3) for each round of the repeated RSP game with three strategies.

We can fully describe a rule of the deterministic strategy choice by recording what the strategy will do in each of the nine different outcomes. The number of possible rules with the memory size $m=2$ is 3^9. A three-bit string is used, and we represent "rock (S_1)=0", "scissors (S_2)=1" and "paper (S_3)=2". Each coupling rule is represented as a binary string in Figure 10.3, and the genetic operators can be applied. The first strategy site p_1 encodes the initial strategy that the agent takes at each generation. The strategy sites p_j, $j \in [2,3]$ encode the history of the last round. The strategy sites p_j, $j \in [4,...,12]$ encode the strategy that the agent takes corresponding to the values at the strategy sites p_j, $j \in [2,3]$.

Each agent plays the RSP game T times (T=20) with the eight nearest-neighbor agents and attains a success score measured by her average payoff per neighbor. The 20 repetitions compose one generation.

A crossover technique form a genetic algorithm is used to evolve coupling rules. The hope is that agents find a better coupling rule from among the overwhelming number of possible rules after a reasonable number of generations. Unsuccessful agents update their coupling rules according to the crossover operator, in which half of the coupling rule in Figure 10.3 (including the first strategy site representing the initial strategy) is replaced with the rule of the most successful neighbor who gains the highest average payoff. The neighbors also serve another function. If the neighbor is doing well, she is also protected from adopting a selfish rule, and thus more effective rules can spread throughout the population from neighbor to neighbor.

We also consider the effect of implementation error in collective evolution. That is, there is a small probability of choosing a different strategy from that specified by the rule. Significant differences will also be observed when agents make small mistakes in implementing their rules.

The simulation results when agents repeated play RSP games with the payoff matrix in Table 10.12 ($\lambda = 2$) are shown in Figure 10.4. This figure shows, (i) the average payoff per agent, and (ii) the ratio of each strategy over the generation. Figure 10.4 shows the case without any implementation error. It is shown that all agents succeed in gaining the same payoff of 1.

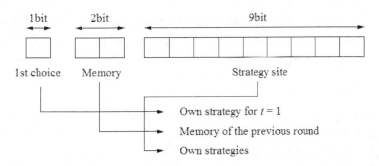

Figure 10.5 Architecture of the coupling rule with the memory size of m=2

Figure 10.5 shows the results with the implementation error of 10%. In this case, almost all agents succeed in gaining the payoff of 1. In addition, a few agents gain payoffs of slightly higher than 1, and some agents receive payoffs of less than 1. Figure 10.6 (b) and Figure 10.7(b) show the strategy distributions over the generation. Without any mistakes, all agents come to choose "scissors" (S_2) and realize the Pareto-optimal outcome by causing the game to end in a tie. However, some agents choose "rock" (S_1) instead of "scissors" (S_2) by mistake.

In the beginning, 400 agents have different coupling rules. These rules were aggregated into 20 types, as shown in Table 10.13, without any mistakes. These 20 rule types also have common values at the strategy sites #5="10", #6="11" #7="12", and #9="21".

The game between two coupling rules with finite memory can also be described as a stationary stochastic process. The state transition of the outcomes when both agents choose their strategies according to the same coupling rule of type 1 is illustrated in Figure 10.18(a) as the state transition diagram. If two agents with the same coupling rule interact, there exist multiple absorbing states. However, they also learn to initiate the game by taking the same strategy "rock (0)" and therefore are absorbed into the outcome with back-to-back scissors strategies, "11".

The state transition of the outcomes when both agents choose their strategies according to the distinct coupling rules (type 6 vs. type 10) is illustrated in Figure 10.8(b) as the state transition diagram. In this case of heterogeneous interaction, there exists only one absorbing state, and starting from the initial pair of strategies of "20", their strategy choices are absorbed into the outcome of "11".

On the other hand, with the implementation error of 10%, the initial 400 different coupling rules were aggregated into one type, as shown in Table 10.14. The state diagram of the play by two agents with the same coupling rule, given in Table 10.14, is shown in Figure 10.9. There are two absorbing states at "11" and "00". The agents also learned to initiate the game by taking the same strategy "rock (0)", and therefore they are eventually absorbed into the outcome of "00". However, with some mistakes, there are some chances to move to other outcomes by choosing different strategies, and so the agents eventually reach the other absorbing state of "11".

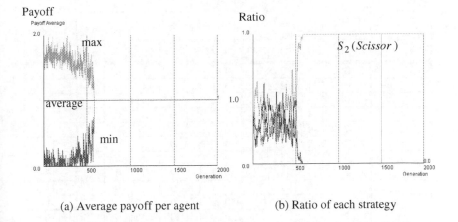

(a) Average payoff per agent   (b) Ratio of each strategy

Figure 10.6 Simulation results with $\lambda = 2$ (implementation error: 0%)

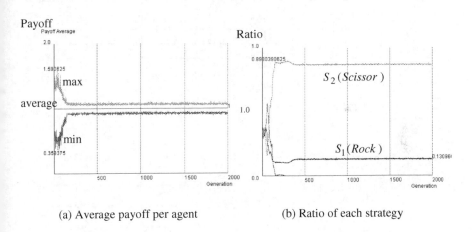

(a) Average payoff per agent   (b) Ratio of each strategy

Figure 10.7 Simulation results with $\lambda = 2$ (implementation error: 10%)

Table 10.13 Learned coupling rules with $\lambda = 2$ (implementation error: 0%)

Rule type	Initial strategy 1	2	3	4	5	6	7	8	9	10	Number of agents
1	0	1	2	0	0	1	0	2	0	1	46
2	0	1	2	0	0	1	0	2	0	0	42
3	0	1	2	0	0	1	0	2	0	2	28
4	0	1	0	1	0	1	0	2	0	2	28
5	0	1	0	1	0	1	0	2	0	1	27
6	2	2	2	0	0	1	0	2	0	1	16
7	0	2	2	0	0	1	0	2	0	1	15
8	2	1	2	1	0	1	0	1	0	2	13
9	0	0	2	0	0	1	0	2	0	0	11
10	0	2	2	1	0	1	0	1	0	1	10
11	2	1	2	0	0	1	0	2	0	1	10
12	0	1	0	0	0	1	0	2	0	0	9
13	0	2	2	0	0	1	0	2	0	2	8
14	2	2	2	1	0	1	0	1	0	1	8
15	0	2	0	1	0	1	0	2	0	1	8
16	0	2	2	1	0	1	0	2	0	1	7
17	0	2	2	0	0	1	0	2	0	0	7
18	2	1	2	1	0	1	0	2	0	2	6
19	0	1	2	1	0	1	0	2	0	1	5
20	0	1	2	0	0	1	0	1	0	0	5

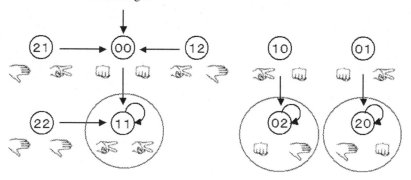

Figure 10.8(a) State diagram of the strategy choices of two agents who have the same coupling rule (rule type 1). There are three absorbing states. If the choices are (1,1) then the game is a tie, and if the agents choose (0,2) or (2,0) one agent wins and the other loses.

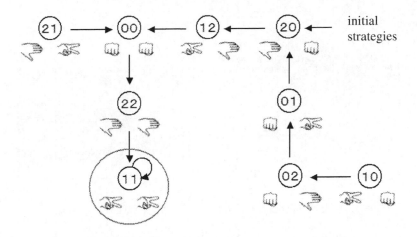

Figure 10.8(b) State diagram of the strategy choices of two agents who have different rules (rule type 6 vs. rule type 10)

Table 10.14 Learned coupling rules in with $\lambda = 2$ (implementation error: 10%)

Rule type	Initial strategy	Strategy site										Number of agents
	1	2	3	4	5	6	7	8	9	10	
1	0	0	1	1	1	1	2	1	2	0	400

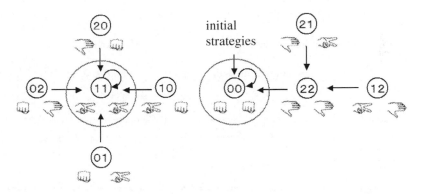

Figure 10.9 State diagram of the strategy choices of two agents. There are two absorbing states at (0,0) and (1,1), in which the result is a tie

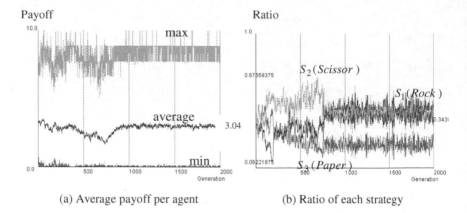

(a) Average payoff per agent   (b) Ratio of each strategy

Figure 10.10 Simulation result with $\lambda = 10$ (implementation error: 0%)

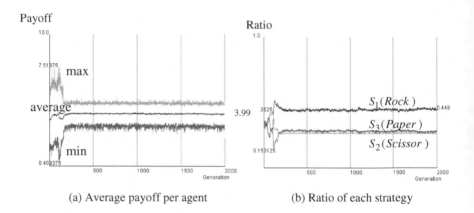

(a) Average payoff per agent   (b) Ratio of each strategy

Figure 10.11 Simulation result with $\lambda = 10$ (implementation error: 10%)

Table 10.15 Learned coupling rules with $\lambda = 10$ (implementation error: 0%)

Rule type	Initial Strategy	Strategy site									Number of agents
	1	2	3	4	5	6	7	8	9	10	
1	1	0	0	0	1	1	0	2	1	1	166
2	1	0	0	0	1	2	0	2	1	1	145
3	1	0	0	0	1	0	0	2	1	1	89

We now investigate the strategic situation by increasing the payoff of winning the game by setting $\lambda=10$ in Table 10.12. Figure 10.10 shows the simulation results without any implementation error. Figure 10.10(a) shows the payoff per agent at each generation, and there exit lucky agents who gain the highest payoff, which is close to 10, by always winning the game and also unlucky agents who gain almost nothing by always losing the game. The average payoff per agent is approximately 3.04, which is lower than the expected payoff at Nash equilibrium, which is approximately 3.7. In the beginning, 400 different coupling rules were aggregated into three types, as shown in Table 10.15. Figure 10.10(b)

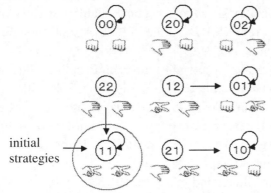

Figure 10.12 State diagram of the strategy choices of two agents who have the same rule (Rule type 1). There are two absorbing states. Since they learn to start the play with Scissors (1) the play results in a tie at "11"

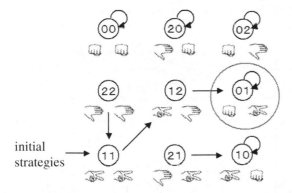

Figure 10.13 State diagram of the strategy choices of two agents who have different rules (Rule type 1 vs. Rule type 2). There is a unique absorbing state at "01", and one agent continues to win while the other loses

shows the strategy distributions, in which some fluctuations are observed.

As we discussed in Chapter 9, when the underlying game is a dispersion game, collective evolution leads to a more equitable situation when agents have little chance to make mistakes in implementing strategies specified by a coupling rule. Figure 10.11 shows the simulation results with the implementation error of 10%. With some implementation errors, the payoff difference between lucky agents who gain the highest average payoff and unlucky agents who gain the lowest average payoff become small, as shown in Figure 10.11(a). The average payoff per agent is increased to approximately 4. Figure 10.11(b) show the strategy distributions over generations, which become stable. Slightly more agents come to choose "rock (S_1)", and the two other strategies are less utilized in the population.

Without any implementation error, 400 different coupling rules in the beginning were aggregated into three types as shown in Table 10.15. The state transition of the outcomes when both agents choose their strategies according to the same coupling rule of type 1 is illustrated in Figure 10.12 as the state transition. The state transition of the outcomes when both agents choose their strategies according to the distinct coupling rules (type 1 vs. type 2) is illustrated in Figure 10.13.

With the implementation error of 10%, 400 different coupling rules in the beginning were aggregated into eight types as shown in Table 10.16. As shown in Table 10.16, 400 rules in the primitive generation are aggregated into eight types, which also have common values at the

Table 10.16 Learned coupling rules with $\lambda = 10$ (implementation error: 10%)

Rule type	Initial Strategy 1	Strategy site									Number of agents
		2	3	4	5	6	7	8	9	10	
1	2	0	1	0	2	0	2	1	0	0	149
2	2	2	1	0	2	0	2	1	0	0	102
3	2	0	1	0	2	2	2	1	0	0	58
4	2	2	1	0	2	2	2	1	0	0	41
5	2	2	1	0	2	0	2	1	0	2	20
6	2	0	1	0	2	0	2	1	0	2	15
7	2	0	1	0	2	2	2	1	0	2	9
8	2	2	1	0	2	2	2	1	0	2	6

strategy sites #3="01", #4="02", #5="10", #7="12", #8="20" and #9="21". The state diagram of the play by two agents can be analyzed in the following two cases.

(Case 1) *Agents who have the same coupling rule*

The strategy choices between two agents with the same coupling rule type i, $i=1,2,...,8$, are shown in Figure 10.14. In this figure, there is one absorbing state at "00" and one limiting cycle. The state diagram contains two paths, one for moving towards to the absorbing state and one for the limiting cycle, and there is no path between the two cycles. As shown in Table 10.16, agents also learn to initiate the play by choosing paper (2) and strategy choices eventually converge to 00. This means that if an agent plays with other agents of the same rule, they converge to the state of a tie, and receive the lower payoff of 1.

(Case 2) *Agents who have different coupling rules*

We now investigate the state diagrams of plays by two agents who have different coupling rules in Table 10.6. The state diagram is shown in Figure 10.15. In this case there is no absorbing state and there is one limit cycle. Starting from any state, it eventually converges to an efficient cycle such that agents win three times and lose three times. With some mistakes, some interesting properties emerge. If an agent A chooses rock (0) and her opponent B chooses "scissors (1)" (in this case she wins and her opponent loses), then in the next round agent A chooses "scissors (1)" and agent B chooses "paper (2)". In the following round agent A chooses "paper (2)" and agent B chooses "rock (0)". Therefore, agent A wins three times and agent B loses three times.

However, after these games, the two agents completely reverse roles, and the winning agent thus far, agent A, chooses "scissors (1)" and the losing agent thus far, agent B, chooses "rock (0)". After these three one-sided games, they trade places. The winner thus far chooses "scissors (1)" and loser thus far chooses "rock (0)". The winner then becomes the loser, and vice versa. In total, her opponent wins three times. Both agents are eventually absorbed into the limit cycle of the three-wins and three-losses. Thus far, this agent wins three times and her opponent loses three times. Therefore, the two agents switch roles as winner and loser. Since both agents win three times and lose three times, on the average, they gain the payoff at Pareto-efficiency.

If the system were to start from the set of the states, it would evolve to an attractor. These are known as the basin of attraction. In this case, the point attractor for the state of the systems is replaced by a circle, and in the limit, the system moves endlessly around this circle.

The coexistence of multiple attractors constitutes the natural mode of systems capable of performing regulatory tasks. We would expect to see the system staying within one basin of attraction and then at some point switching between different attractors as we add some noise.

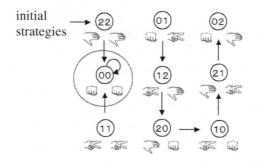

Figure 10.14 State diagram of the strategy choices of two agents who have the same rule (Rule type 1). There is a unique absorbing state at (0,0), and both agents continue to reach a tie

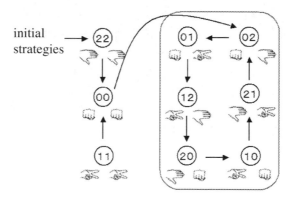

Figure 10.15 State diagram of the strategy choices of two agents who have different rules (Rule type 1 vs. Rule type 2). There is a unique limit cycle that visits the state: (0,1), (1,2), (2,0), (1,0), (2,1) and (0,2). Both agents continue to win three times and loose three times

A number of studies have examined the dynamics of an ensemble of globally coupled components with the aim of driving the system from incoherent collective evolution to a state of spontaneous full synchronization. Synchronization is a form of macroscopic evolution observed in a wide class of complex systems. Typically, it appears when the range of the interactions inside the system is of same order as the system size. Mechanical and electronic devices, as well as certain chemical reactions are known to exhibit synchronized dynamics.

We have observed that a collective of locally coupled agents who play the three-strategy game, Rock-Scissors-Paper, drives the collective from incoherent collective behavior to a state of spontaneous full synchronization, and they can sustain dynamic orders of efficiency and equity. Therefore, collective evolution of coupled rules has been proven to be an appropriate paradigm for such kinds of emerging desired collectives.

If the generalized RSP game has the same payoff structure as the original RSP game, formulated as the zero-sum game, each agent learns to enter into a tie. If the payoff for winning the game increases, agents learn to win and lose in a coordinated way. That is, if one agent wins three rounds, then the previously winning agent loses the next three rounds. If all agents repeat this coordinated behavior, they can realize the most efficient and equitable outcomes.

We have also found that, under suitable conditions, the collective system evolves from completely uncoordinated behavior to a state of full synchronization of coordination. Bearing in mind the role of synchronization as a collectively desired behavior, we incorporated an additional evolutionary mechanism. Concretely, each agent is allowed to vary her coupling rule according to a given criterion.

In this case, inefficient and unsynchronized rules are eliminated and replaced by slightly modified rules produced by crossover with more successful rules. Thus, the collective system may be able to learn to perform a specific collective task, and in particular, to evolve towards a coherent synchronized outcome. However, as shown in Figure 10.9, the average payoff per agent is slightly lower than the value at Pareto-efficiency. Therefore, we may need to investigate some obstacles of the perfect coherent synchronized outcome.

Heterogeneity turns up repeatedly as a crucial factor in complex systems and organizations. But the situation is not always as simple as saying that heterogeneity is desirable and homogeneity is not. The basic question as to the correct balance between heterogeneity and homogeneity remains in many fields. When heterogeneity is significant, we need to be able to show the gains from heterogeneity. An agent type is a category of agents within the larger population who share some characteristics. We usually distinguish types by some aspects of the agents' unobservable internal models that characterize their observable behaviors. The notion of type facilitates the analysis of heterogeneity.

Agents are categorized by location in the coupling rule space. Since the space of all coupling rules is so complex, this categorization is not trivial in the beginning. For example, we might constrain the coupling rules to be a finite number of rules. Even after these kinds of limitations, we might still be left with too large a space of rules to consider. However, there are further disciplined approaches to winnowing down the rule space. The question is how best to represent meaningful classes of agents and then use this representation to obtain effective rules.

The collection of agent types includes agent types with which the agent being designed might interact. These agent types may come with a distribution, in which case one can hope to design an agent to receive the maximum expected payoff. In either case we need a way to speak about agent types. The agents, located on the lattice, play 2x2 RSP games against their eight nearest neighbors, and all rules one for each agent are aggregated into a few types. Therefore, an agent may play with other agents with the same coupling rule or with agents with different coupling rules. They should also learn the locations of the space so that maximum number of dispersed agents with different coupling rules may play the dispersion game.

If an agent plays with another agent who has a different rule type, they can sustain the efficient cycle with three wins and three loses, and both agents obtain the equal payoff of $\lambda/2$. The sum of their payoff is also Pareto-efficient. However, this desirable situation will disappear if an agent plays with another agent who has the same coupling rule. Therefore it is a very difficult task for the agents to evolve synchronized coupling rules that satisfy coherency in both time and location.

10.4   A Coupling Rule with a Memory of Four

It is an interesting exercise to figure out the effect of the memory size of agents who remember past rounds. In this section, we consider the coupling rule with the memory size of four ($m=4$). Therefore, a strategy choice for repeated play uses the past two rounds to choose one of the three strategies for the next play. Since there are 3^4 possible distinct outcomes, we need 81 bit strings to represent a coupling rule. The number of possible rules with the memory of four ($m=4$) is increased to 3^{81}. The hope is that agents would find a better coupling rule out of the overwhelming possible rules after a reasonable number of generations.

Each coupling rule is represented as a bit string in Figure 10.16. Each value of p_j, $j \in [1,...,87]$ carries the following information. The first and second strategy sites encode the initial two strategies that the agent takes at each generation. Since no memory exists at the start of the game, an extra two bits is needed to specify the strategies at the first and second round as a hypothetical history. The strategy sites p_j, $j \in [3,...,6]$ encode the history of the strategies (rock, scissors or paper) that the agent and her opponent selected during the previous two rounds. The strategy sites p_j, $j \in [7,...,87]$ encode the strategy that the agent should take according to the past two rounds.

Figure 10.17 shows (a) the average payoff per agent and (b) the strategy distribution over the generation when the agents play the game with the payoff matrix in Table 10.12 ($\lambda=2$) without any implementation error. All agents gain the same payoff after several hundred generations. As shown in Figure 10.17(b), the ratio of "rock (S_1)" is relatively high compared with the ratios of "scissors (S_2)" and "paper (S_3)".

In the beginning, 400 agents have different coupling rules, which were aggregated into a few types. The aggregated rules also have common values at the strategy sites. Eight aggregated rules are also represented as one meta-rule, as shown in Table 10.17. Except for the strategy sites marked by #, all learned coupling rules have common values.

The state diagram of the plays between two agents with the coupling rule in Table 10.17 is shown in Figure 10.18. There is one limit cycle that visits the states "2211", "1100", "0000" and "0022". Therefore, the two agents continue to reach a tie by choosing "rock (S_1)" at a ratio of 0.5 and "scissors (S_2)" and "paper (S_3)" at a ratio of 0.25.

Figure 10.19 shows the simulation results with the implementation error of 10%. Figure 10.19(a) shows the average payoff per agent. In this case, almost all agents succeed in gaining the same payoff of 1, and a few agents gain more than 1 or less than 1. The strategy distribution in Figure 10.19(b) shows that the ratios of the three strategies are almost the same. Therefore, we can conclude that in the repeated RSP game with $\lambda = 2$, which is strategically equivalent to the zero-sum RSP game, three strategies (rock, scissors and paper) can coexist without any implementation error.

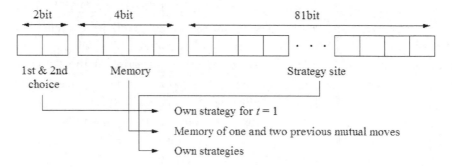

Figure 10.16   Architecture of the coupling rule with the memory size of *m=4*

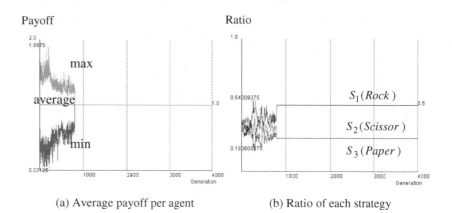

(a) Average payoff per agent   (b) Ratio of each strategy

Figure 10.17   Simulation result with $\lambda = 2$ and a memory of *m=4* (implementation error: 0%)

Table 10.17　Learned coupling rules with the memory size of $m=4$ and $\lambda = 10$ (implementation error: 0%) (The # symbol indicates the possibility of either 0 or 1)

Initial Strategy	Second Strategy	Strategy site														
1	2	3	4	5	6	7	8	9	10	11	12	13	14	15	16	17
2	1	2	#	#	#	#	2	0	#	1	#	2	1	0	0	#

Strategy site																					
18	19	20	21	22	23	24	25	26	27	28	29	30	31	32	33	34	35	36	37	38	39
1	#	2	#	0	#	2	#	2	#	#	#	0	#	#	#	0	0	#	2	#	0

Strategy site																					
40	41	42	43	44	45	46	47	48	49	50	51	52	53	54	55	56	57	58	59	60	61
#	0	#	2	1	#	#	1	#	#	#	#	0	2	#	0	#	#	0	1	0	#

Strategy site																					
62	63	64	65	66	67	68	69	70	71	72	73	74	75	76	77	78	79	80	81	82	83
#	#	0	2	2	0	#	0	#	1	1	1	2	2	0	1	1	0	2	0	1	1

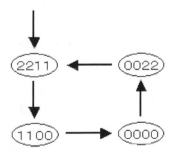

Figure 10.18　State diagram of the strategy choices of two agents. There is a unique limit cycle that visits the state: "2211", "1100", "000", and "0022". Both agents continue to reach ties choosing Rock (0) at a ratio of 0.5, and Scissors (1) and Paper (2) at a ratio of 0.25

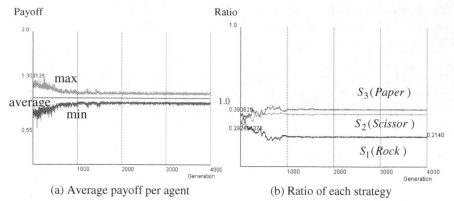

(a) Average payoff per agent   (b) Ratio of each strategy

Figure 10.19 Simulation results with $\lambda = 2$ and *m=4*, and with an implementation error of 10%

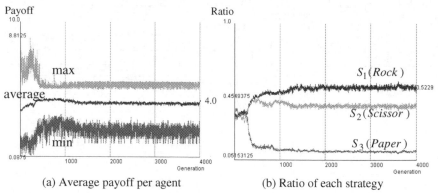

(a) Average payoff per agent   (b) Ratio of each strategy

Figure 10.20 Simulation results with $\lambda = 10$ and *m=4*, and with an implementation error of 0%

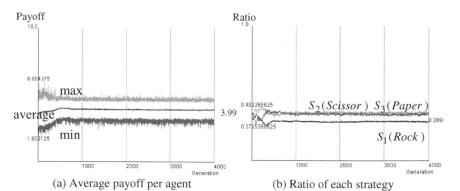

(a) Average payoff per agent   (b) Ratio of each strategy

Figure 10.21 Simulation results with $\lambda = 10$ and m=4, and with an implementation error of 10%

We show the state diagram of the strategy choices of two agents in Figure 10.16. There is the unique limit cycle that visits the state: "2211", "1100", "0000" and "0022". Both agents continue to reach ties by choosing "rock (S_1)" at a ratio 0.5 and "scissors (S_2)" and "paper (S_3)" at a ratio of 0.25.

We now show the simulation results when the payoff for winning the game is increased to $\lambda=10$ and without any implementation error. Figure 10.20(a) shows the average payoff per agent. There are lucky agents who gain the highest payoff and unlucky agents who gain almost nothing. The average payoff per agent is approximately 4, which is higher than the expected payoff at Nash equilibrium, which is approximately 3.7. Figure 10.20(b) shows the strategy distributions. The ratios of "rock (S_1)" and "scissors (S_2)" are high, and the ratio of "paper (S_3)" is relatively low.

Figure 10.21 shows the simulation results with an implementation error of 10%. The average payoff per agent (Figure 10.21(a)) is approximately 4, which is the same as the simulation result without implementation error. However, in this case, the payoff difference between the lucky agent who gains the highest average payoff and the unlucky agent who gains the lowest average payoff becomes small. The strategy distribution is shown in Figure 10.21(b) and the ratios of the three strategies become approximately the same. Therefore, we conclude that the implementation error is effective to realize efficient and equitable outcomes while sustaining the diversity of the population.

The number of possible strategies in repeated RSP games depends on the agents' memory size. It is possible, in principal, to derive an efficient behavioral rule with a finite memory size. We can observe open-ended evolution with the increase of the memory size in the simulation. It is also an interesting exercise to figure out the effective memory size of agents that is required in order to remember past outcomes.

In the previous section, we compared cases in which agents behave based the behavioral rules of agents having memory sizes of two and four. If all agents have the same memory size, the effective memory size that is required in order to realize efficient and equitable outcomes is $m=2$. However, by increasing the memory to $m=4$, dynamic coexistence of all three strategies can be realized by sustaining the diversity of the strategy population.

10.5   Effects of Implementation Error in Collective Evolution

Evolution through natural selection is often understood to imply improvement and progress. A heritable trait that confers to its bearer a higher fitness will spread within the population. The average fitness of the population would therefore be expected to increase over time. This is often pictured as a steady ascent on a *fitness landscape* (Mayley, 1997). The landscape metaphor suggests some solid ground over which the population moves. Although the environment selects the adaptations, these adaptations can also shape the environment. By moving across a fitness landscape, the population changes the landscape.

The behavior of a collective system can be characterized by the associated payoff function to each agent. The trajectory of the behavior of an agent moves from a given behavioral rule to that of the neighboring agent for which the payoff function is improved. More generally, the payoff function represents the degree to which a certain behavioral rule is preferable to the current rule. The higher the value of the payoff, the better, or the more fit, the outcome.

The payoff function determines the agent space into a *payoff landscape*, where every point in the space has a value associated with the average payoff of each agent over one generation. This payoff landscape in general has many peaks and valleys. The attractors of the collective dynamics will now correspond to a locally optimized payoff landscape (Nowark and Sigmund, 2004).

The collective system will always move upward in the payoff landscape. When it has reached a locally optimal point, some agents will not be able to leave this point. The local maximum of the payoff landscape are the points that separate the basins of the attractors that lie between the peaks. For the evolution of the systems, in general, better or fitter usually means more potential for growth. However, the collective dynamics implied by a payoff landscape does not, in general, lead to the overall optimal state. The path of the collective systems will in general end in a *local* optimal rather than in the *global* optimal.

An effective way to obtain an evolutionary system out of a locally optimal system is to add a degree of indeterminism to the system dynamics, that is, to give the system the possibility of making transitions to states other than the locally-most-fit state. This can be seen as the injection of noise or random perturbation into the evolutionary system, which makes it deviate from its preferred trajectory. Physically, this is usually the effect of outside perturbations.

Instead, we consider the role of implementation error, or *"mistakes"*, as internal perturbations that can push the collective system upwards, towards a higher potential of the landscape. This may be sufficient to allow the collective system to escape from a local optimum, after which it will again start to climb up towards a better state.

Therefore, such internal perturbations push the collective system towards a more efficient outcome, and mistakes generally increase fitness. The stronger the mistake the better the collective system will be able to escape the relatively shallow valleys, and thus reach a potentially better outcome. However, a collective system with some mistakes will never be able to truly reach a global optimum because whatever level of fitness it reaches, it will still be perturbed and pushed into less fit states.

In this section, we continue our discussion on the role of mistakes. The influence of making a mistake will be verified. Mistakes in implementing a strategy are important and their influence should be examined thoroughly. When agents occasionally make small mistakes, they collectively evolve to full coordination by realizing ideal dynamic orders of efficiency and equity. Depending on the initial strategies, agents start at inefficient cycle, but mistakes lead the agents to more efficient strategies. However, these mistakes also lead agents from efficient rules toward less efficient rules.

In order to verify the role of mistakes in collective evolution in more detail, we increase the length of the simulation and simulate up to 4,000 generations. Each agent plays the generalized RSP game in Table 10.12 with $\lambda=10$. In Table 10.18, we show how 400 different rules in the initial generation are aggregated into a few common rules. After 4,000 generations, they converge into six types when there is no implementation error. However, the convergence is much faster with an implementation error of 10%, and the behavioral rules converge into eight types after 2,000 generations.

Therefore, if we simulate a large number of generations, the coupling rules of all agents are aggregated into a few types without regarding the implementation error. However, a qualitative difference exits between the learned rules without any implementation error and those with some implementation error.

The game between two coupling rules with finite memory can be described as a stationary stochastic process. The state transition of the outcome when both agents choose their strategies according to the learned coupling rules is illustrated in Figure 10.22 as a state transition diagram with no implementation error. Either they play with the same or different coupling rules, and we have the same state diagram as that shown in Figure 10.22. There is one absorbing state at "0000" and one limit cycle that visits "1001" and "0110", alternatively. However, there is no commonality in the initial strategies at the start of the game at each generation. Therefore, there are two possibilities to be absorbed at "0000" and to reach the limiting cycle. In the former case, the two agents reach a tie and receive low payoffs, and in the latter case, they take turns winning and losing. Before they reach these cases, they visit many outcomes. This is the reason for the co-existence of the three strategies.

The state transition diagram for play under the coupling rules learned with the 10% implementation error is shown in Figure 10.23 and Figure 10.24. In this case, there are two different features. First, all agents learn to initiate the game by choosing "scissors (1)". Second, the state diagrams between the two agents are different depending on whether they have the same coupling rule type or different types. The state transition diagram when the two agents have the same rule is shown in Figure 10.23, and there are two absorbing states at "0000" and "2222". There are also two limit cycles, one of which visits "1122" and "2211"

Table 10.18 Number of common rules learned by 400 agents over various numbers of generations

Generation	Number of different coupling rules	
	Implementation error: 0%	Implementation error: 10%
500	400	400
1,000	400	250
1,500	368	30
2,000	238	8
4,000	6	8

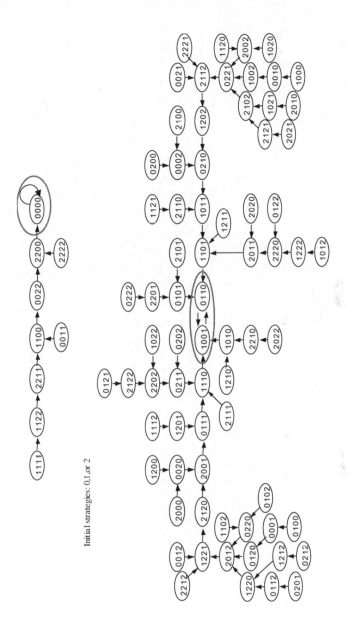

Figure 10.22 State diagram of the strategy choices of two agents who play with the same or different coupling rules learned without the implementation error

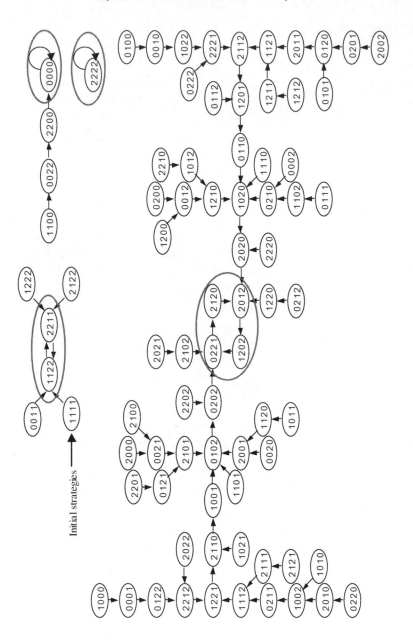

Figure 10.23 State diagram of the strategy choices of two agents who play with the same coupling rules learned with an implementation error of 10%

and the other visits "0221", "2120", "2012" and "1202". However, they learn to initiate the game with "scissors (1)" and so eventually converge to the limit cycle, visiting "1122" and "2211" alternately. By reaching this limit cycle, the two agents take turns winning and losing, which is the principle of give-and-take discussed in the Section 10.1.

The state transition diagram for the case in which the two agents have different rules is shown in Figure 10.24. There is one absorbing states at "2222", and one limit cycle that visits "0221", "2120", "2012" and "1202". However, they also learn to initiate the game with "scissors (1)" and eventually converge to the limit cycle, visiting "0221", "2120", "2012" and "1202". Before reaching this limit cycle, where they take turns winning and losing, they visit many outcomes.

In summary, whether two interacting agents play with the same rule or with different rules, they eventually reach the limiting cycle where they come to take turns winning and losing. This is the reason why they collectively realize efficient and equitable outcomes.

It is known that the most effective use of noise to maximize self-organization is to start with large amounts of noise that are then gradually decreased, until the noise disappears completely. The initially large perturbations allowing escape from local optima, while the gradual reduction will allow it to settle down in what is hopefully the deepest valley. This is the basic principle underlying *annealing*, the hardening of metals by gradually reducing the temperature, thus allowing the metal molecules to settle in the most stable crystalline configuration. The same technique is called *simulated annealing* when applied to simulation models of self-organization.

We apply the same technique of simulated annealing. In the beginning, we set the implementation error at 10% until the 1,000th generation, and then cut the error rate to 0%. The simulation results are shown in Figure 10.25, and we have two cases if we cut the error at the 1,000th generation: either efficient collective behavior will disappear (case 1) or the outcomes will remain approximately the same (case 2). Diversity is neither accidental nor random. The persistence of an individual agent depends on the context provided by the other agents as well as endogenous mistakes.

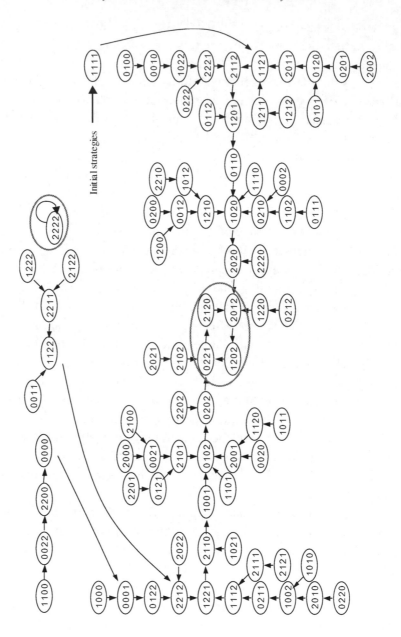

Figure 10.24 State diagram of the strategy choices of two agents who play with different coupling rules learned with an implementation error of 10%

(a) Case 1

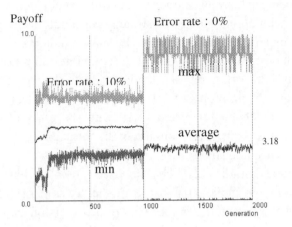

(b) Case 2

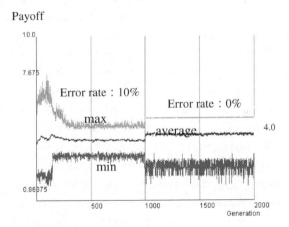

Figure 10.25   Average payoff per agent over generations. The implementation error is 10% by the 1,000th generation and is thereafter set at 0%

10.6   From Co-evolution to Collective Evolution

A reinforcement learning model successfully replicates human behavior for games with an unique mixed strategy Nash equilibrium (Erev, 1988). However, experimental studies have been accumulating evidence that the human behavior exhibited in other types of games does not coincide with the equilibrium solutions of standard game theory. Several distinct models have been proposed to account for such learning processes. Attempting to characterize and work with the class of strategies that people actually consider is an important project for behavioral game theory (Bowles, 2004).

Experimental studies have been focused to explain human behavior in such well-known games, the battle of the sexes game, the hawk-dove game, and the dispersion game. Except a dispersion game, the Pareto-efficient outcome is also fair. On the other hand, the Pareto-efficient and fair outcome of a dispersion game is achieved only if two agents alternate between the two pure strategy equilibria. It is reported that in these games, experimental subjects behave as if they are motivated by fairness and efficiency considerations. Subjects often find and coordinate their actions so that they can maximize the aggregate payoff and receive the almost the same payoff (McKelvey, 2002, Arifovic, 2005). Observations that people behave as if they are concerned about fairness and efficiency have led some researchers to develop models with a richer class of preferences in which players care not only about their own material payoffs but the payoffs to others (Fehr, 1999).

Hanaki (2005) uses adaptive models to understand the dynamics that lead to efficient and fair outcomes in repeated games. Instead of assuming that fairness and efficiency considerations are a primitive of the underlying model, he has demonstrated that a simple learning model applied to a limited set of finitely-complex repeated game strategies can generate the efficient and fair outcomes.

Experimental subjects often try to explore possible actions and decide what to do next based on the resulting outcomes. However, he developed a model of rule learning by enumerating all deterministic two-state automata (rule of memory of two), and it does not scale easily to automata with more than two states. His model not only uses reinforcement learning but also the evolutionary learning that operates through evolutionary selection. It also requires a long run pre-experimental phase before it is implemented. Furthermore, what has not been explored in his model is the underlying dynamics that lead to an efficient and fair outcome.

The most unrealistic aspect of the rule learning is the large number of rules each agent considers. A realistic model should account for the fact that the agents consider a much smaller number of rules from which they learn. The rules agents consider are often preconditioned by factors such as imitation that have evolved over the generations. The set of rules agents consider is a small subset of the possible rule space. Occasionally agents are given a chance to look for a different partner to learn if they are unhappy with the status quo. Evolutionary pressures make agents more likely to adopt the rules of successful agents with higher payoff. Over time, the majority of the population will learn about a similar subset of possible rules that may realize and sustain efficient and equitable outcomes of the underlying games.

Starting with an intuitively plausible set of assumptions, we demonstrated that collective evolution develops into the efficient and fair outcome of the underlying games, such as a prisoner's dilemma game, a coordination game, a hawk-dove game, and a dispersion game. We also investigate the dynamics behind the convergence to the efficient and fair outcome.

We conclude by summarizing what we have learned thus far in the framework of collective evolution. The mission of collective evolution is to harness collective systems and to serve to secure a sustainable relationship in an attainable manner so that a desirable outcome of the collective system could emerge. Of particular interest has been the question as to the conditions under which social interactions among agents will result in an outcome that is in some sense optimal.

Put differently, we examined how social interactions can be restructured so that agents are free to choose their own actions while avoiding outcomes that none would have chosen. This is the same as the pursuit of a Pareto-efficient outcome. Another important consideration is the principle that the collective outcome should also be fair. We can say that we are interested in determining the correct behavioral rules. It is shown that collective evolution of coupling rules between agents has proven to be an appropriate paradigm for such emerging desired collective outcomes.

We define a set of behavioral rules to be *efficient* if the total payoff for all involved agents is maximized when they follow these rules to choose a strategy for each iterated game. Then, we need to devise behavioral rules that induce self-regarding agents to learn efficient rules. The success or failure of a certain behavioral rules depends on what other rules are present. An ambitious objective is then to find a learning procedure that would enable the agents to obtain and implement such efficient behavioral rules.

The framework developed in Chapter 9 and this chapter is distinct from co-evolution in three aspects. First, there is the coupling rule, which is a deterministic or stochastic process that links past outcomes with future behavior. The second aspect, which is distinguished from individual learning, is that agents may wish to optimize the outcome realized by the joint actions. The third aspect is to describe how a coupling rule should be improved with the criterion of performance to evaluate how well the rule is doing.

In Chapter 8, we showed that, if a collective of interacting agents who repeatedly adapt their behavior to their neighbors based on the behavioral rule of give-and-take, they could realize the most desirable outcome. We define such desired collective behavior as *interactive synchrony*. In Chapter 9, we showed that agents could collectively evolve such a give-and-take rule when the underlying game is an asymmetric dispersion game with two strategies.

In this chapter, we have extended this approach further by considering the case in which the underlying dispersion game has three strategies. The Rock-Scissors-Paper (RSP) game is a typical form of representing the triangular relationship: Rock crushes scissors, scissors cut paper and paper covers rock. Rock-scissors-paper relationships are also common in many ecosystems, and this simple RSP game has been used to explain the importance of biodiversity.

Most evolutional processes are modeled based on *a mean-field model*, which posits that agents interact with each other. This is essentially assuming that the populations are mixed. Because of advances in computational ability, we are now able to consider how populations interact in space and relax this assumption. As we have briefly introduced in Section 10.3, Kerr *et al.* demonstrated the importance of the scale of interaction and dispersal on maintaining biodiversity. The scale at which organisms interact and disperse can have profound effects on the maintenance of biodiversity. Biodiversity disappeared when the organisms were grown in environments that allowed them to interact more thoroughly. They demonstrated that spatial separation might be necessary for different populations to coexist. Their work also has the potential to help answer one of the biggest questions in ecology and evolution: Why are there so many different types of organisms out there? The localization of dispersal and interaction, coupled with rock-paper-scissors, is an example of one process that might prove important in maintaining this diversity.

They also investigated basic questions such as whether genetic diversity can persist over the long time scales required for co-evolution. In terms of game theory, the spatial environment is shown to encourage the convergence to Nash equilibrium, where three strategies, rock, scissors and paper, can coexist beyond the global environment. However, Nash equilibria of the RSP game are inefficient, and the spatial environment does not encourage high performance of the whole population.

In order to clarify this issue, we generalized a basic rock-scissors-paper relationship to a non zero-sum game in which agents may benefit from achieving a sustainable relationship. In this case, diversity resulting from proper dispersal by achieving Nash equilibrium is not sufficient, and a much more deeply correlated relationship may be required. We have observed that a collective of locally coupled agents who play the generalized RSP game drives incoherent collective behavior into a state of spontaneous full synchronization by achieving full efficiency.

Bearing in mind the role of synchronization by archiving desired collective behavior, we incorporated an additional evolutionary mechanism. Concretely, each agent is allowed to vary her coupling rule according to a given criterion. Learning itself could be fully replaced by an evolutionary mechanism in the spirit of genetic algorithms. In this case, unsynchronized rules were eliminated and replaced by slightly modified copies of successful rules. Thus, the collective of agents may be able to learn to perform a specific collective task, and in particular to evolve towards a coherent synchronized state.

In summary, we have examined the problem of interactive learning in the context of repeated games. In fact, interactive learning is a feature of almost all social systems, where the intentions of the learners are at least part of what needs to be learned. The envisioned research object is quite novel, since it requires harmony with synchronized interactions among self-interested agents. Fortunately, many of the results discussed in the preceding chapters extend readily to a wider class of situations in which many agents interact.

In this way, we obtain a robust learning procedure that leads to near-optimal behavior in situations where many agents are interacting with each other. The approach of collective evolution is very much at the forefront of the general topics of designing desired collectives in terms of efficiency, equity, and sustainability. The desired collective outcome also depends increasingly on a process that encourages both diversity and commonality among behavioral rules. Calling upon both diverse and shared perspectives among relevant agents will lead to an enhanced understanding of the situation and will help agents to behave adequately in interactive environments.

Darwinian dynamics based on mutation and selection form the core of models for evolution in nature. Evolution through natural selection is often understood to imply improvement and progress. A heritable trait that confers to its bearer a higher fitness will spread within the population. The average fitness of the population would therefore be expected to increase over time. This *fitness landscape* suggests some solid ground over which the population moves.

If multiple populations of species adapt to one another, the result is a co-evolutionary process. *Co-evolution* is defined as an evolutionary change in a trait of individuals in one population in response to a trait of individuals in another population, which is followed by the evolutionary responses by other populations to the change in the first population. Co-evolution can also come in the form of local pair-wise interactions between geographically distributed populations with each population engaged in local pair-wise interactions. Since every improvement in one species leads to a selective advantage for that species, variation will normally continuously lead to increases in fitness in one species or another.

Nowark and Sigmund (2004) points that the *Darwinian paradigm*, which is also widespread in the theory of genetic algorithms, neglects half of the evolutionary mechanism. Although the environment selects the adaptations, adaptations can also shape the environment. By moving across a fitness landscape, populations change that landscape. This is particularly clear if several populations interact, because each population can be part of the fitness landscape of the other. Therefore, the fitness landscape is shaped by the strategy distributions of each of the populations. As the population moves through the fitness landscape, new peaks and valleys form, leading to further motion.

For co-evolutionary systems, fitter usually means better or with more potential for growth. However, the co-evolutionary dynamics implied by a fitness landscape does not generally lead to the overall fittest state, and the system has no choice but to follow the path of steepest descent. This path will in general end in a local optimum of the potential, not in the global optimum. Apart from changing the fitness function, the only way for the system to escape from a local optimum is to add some noise to the co-evolutionary dynamics, that is, to give the system the possibility to make it deviate from its preferred trajectory.

Another problem to contend with in co-evolution based on the Darwinian paradigm is the possibility of an escalating *arms race* with no end. Competing species might continually adapt to each other in more and more specialized ways, never stabilizing at a desirable outcome. In general, different species are coevolving, and improvement in one species implies that it will get a competitive advantage over another species, and thus be able to capture a larger share of the resources available to all. Since every improvement in one species will lead to a selective advantage for that species, variation will normally continuously lead to increases in fitness in one species or another. This means that increased fitness in one species will tend to lead to decreased fitness in another species. The only way that a species involved in a competitive environment can maintain its fitness relative to the others is by in turn improving its strategy with no end. This effect is known as an *arms race.*

The most obvious example of an arms race is co-evolution between predators and prey (for instance, foxes and rabbits) in which the only way predators can compensate for a better defense by the prey (e.g. rabbits running faster) is by developing a better offense (e.g. foxes running faster). However, the relative fitness gap remains the same. Another example is tree growth. In this example, the net effect of an arms race may be an absolute decrease in fitness. Trees in a forest are normally competing for access to sunlight. If one tree grows slightly taller than its neighbors it can capture part of their sunlight. This forces the other trees in turn to grow taller, in order not to be overshadowed. The net effect is that all trees tend to become taller and taller, still gathering on average the same amount of sunlight while spending far more resources in order to sustain their increased height. These examples of the arms race illustrate the problem of sub-optimization. For instance, optimizing access to sunlight for each individual tree does not lead to optimal performance for the forest as a whole.

The arms race in co-evolution is also referred as the *red queen principle*, which says we have to run faster and faster to survive in the face of rivals. The red queen principle was proposed by the evolutionary biologist van Valen (1973) and is based on the observation of Alice by the Red Queen in Lewis Carroll's "*Through the Looking Glass*" that "*in this place it takes all the running you can do, to keep in the same place.*" In evolutionary biology, the arms race asserts that *competitive co-evolution* of species is seen to be a spur to the evolution of complexity itself, manifesting, however, no net gains in relative fitness. In socio-economic systems, the red queen principle asserts that a continuous application of offsetting or contravening force on the micro level can maintain global stability.

Robson (2003) and Markose (2005) discussed the relevance of the red queen principle in economics. They studied the evidence for competitive co-evolution in biology to see what implications it may have for the growth of complexity in socio-economic institutions and market environments. There are deep analogies and interconnections between biology and economics. Both disciplines concern how the properties of complex systems relate to the properties of their components. In the competition that governs the fight for scarce resources or in cases of direct confrontation with zero-sum payoffs, such as in parasite-host or predator-prey situations, what matters is the relative, rather than absolute, performance capabilities of the individuals. Certain attributes of individuals have to be enhanced relative to the same in others to maintain the *status quo*.

We have stressed that co-evolutional dynamics based on the Darwinian paradigm does not necessarily lead to an optimal situation. It can be that all agents would be better off if they jointly deviated, in a correlated way, with the use of another strategy. Such a concerted action is beyond the means of co-evolution based on the Darwinian paradigm. In this sense, collective evolution is the appropriate framework.

In biology, the individual, or better yet the gene, is the unit of selection. On the other hand, collective systems are based on an analogous assumption that individuals are selfish optimizers. With competing populations continually striving to gain an upper hand, a collective evolutionary process is expected to compel agents towards ever more refined adaptation, resulting in sophisticated behavioral rules. To induce collective evolution, the behavioral rules of agents that are best able to outperform opponents are selectively biased in favor of reproduction. On the other hand, unsuccessful behavioral rules are discarded because behavioral rules are unlikely to reproduce. Furthermore, cultural interpretations of collective evolution assume that successful behavioral rules spread by imitation or learning by the agents.

Collective evolution from the bottom up is deeply related to aggregations that have strong effects on individual behaviors. Many organisms form aggregations that have strong effects on individual behaviors. The characteristics of a collective are as follows. Interactions among individual agents who comprise a collective are strong. That is internal cohesion is strong, while external interactions are weak. Furthermore, collectives have their own characteristics and processes that can be understood independently of the individuals who compromise them.

Collective evolution is a holistic, synergetic and complex evolutionary flow that cannot be split up into components. Its collective evolutionary dynamic rests not only on mutually coupled interactions, but also on our desires for realizing better outcomes by solving mutual conflicts and overcoming competition. Collective evolution is one that has an internal process for cultivating individual learning and connecting it to the learning of others. Thus, when faced with change, a collective system has the requisite energy and flexibility to move in the direction it desires. An individual's ability to survive and grow is based on advantages that stem from core competencies that represent collective evolution.

Collectives can be treated as an additional level of organization between the individual and the populations or societies. The population can only be understood by modeling both individuals and collectives and the links between all three levels. Individuals belonging to a collective may behave very differently from individuals alone, so different traits may be needed to model individuals who are not in a collective. The behavior of collectives emerges from the traits of individual agents. Collectives can also represent how individual behaviors affect the collectives and how the state of the collective affects individuals' states and their behavior. The persistence and sustainability of the collective system in turn depends on its persistent collective evolution.

Bibliography

Abramson, G. and Kuperman, M. (2000). Social games in a social network, *Phys. Rev.*, Vol. E63.

Ackley, D. and Littman, M. (1991). Interactions between learning and evolution, *Proceedings of Artificial Life II*, MIT Press, pp. 487–509.

Adamatzky, A. (2005). *Dynamics of Crowd-Minds*, World Scientific.

Alpern, S. (2001). Spatial Dispersion as a Dynamic Coordination Problem. Technical report, The London School of Economics.

Anderson, P. (1977). Local Moments and Localized States, Nobel Lecture http://www.nobel.se/physics/laureates/1977/anderson-lecture.pdf

Anderson, P. and Arrow, K. (eds.) (1988). *The Economy as an Evolving Complex System I*, Perseus Books.

Anderson, R. W. (1995). Learning and evolution: a quantitative genetics approach, *Journal of Theoretical Biology*, 175, pp. 89–101.

Angeline, P. J. (1994). An alternate Interpretation of the iterated prisoner's dilemma and the evolution of non-mutual cooperation, *Artificial Life IV*, MIT Press, pp. 353–358.

Arifovic, J. and Maschek, M. (2004). Social vs. Individual Learning -What Makes Difference a Difference? Mimeo.

Arifovic, J., McKelvey, R. and Pevnitskaya, S. (2005). An initial implementation of the turing tournament to learning in repeated two person games. Mimeo.

Arita, T. (2000). *Artificial Life*: a constructive approach to the origin/evolution of life, society, and language (in Japanese), Medical Press.

Arita, T. and Suzuki, R. (2000). Interactions between learning and evolution outstanding strategy generated by the baldwin effect, *Artificial Life VII*, MIT Press, pp. 196–205.

Arthur, W. B. (1994). Inductive reasoning and bounded rationality, *American Economic Review*, 84, pp. 406–411.

Arthur, W. B., Durlauf, S. and Lane, D. A. (eds.) (1997). *The Economy as an Evolving Complex System II*, Addison-Wesley.

Aumann, R. (1987). Correlated equilibrium as an extension of bayesian rationality, *Econometrica*, 55, pp. 1–18.

Aumann, R. and Myerson, R. (1988). Endogenous formation of links between players and of coalitions: an application of the Shapley value, *The Shapley Value*, Cambridge University Press, pp. 175–191.

Auyang, S. Y. (1998). *Foundations of Complex System Theories in Economics, Evolutionary Biology, and Statistical Physics*, Cambridge University Press.

Axelrod, R. (1980). More effective choice in the iterated prisoner's dilemma, *Journal of Conflict Resolution*, 24, pp. 3–25.

Axelrod, R. (1984). *The Evolution of Cooperation*, Basic Books.

Axelrod, R. (1987). The evolution of strategies in the iterated prisoner's dilemma, *Genetic algorithms and Simulated Annealing*, Pitman, pp. 32–41.

Axelrod, R. (1997). *The Complexity of Cooperation*, Princeton University Press.

Axelrod, R. and Cohen, M. (2001). *Harnessing Complexity*: Organizational Implications of a Scientific Frontier, Basic Books.

Axtell, R. (2003). Economics as Distributed Computation, in *Meeting the Challenge of Soical Problems via Agent-Based Simulation*, H. Deguchi, K. Takadama and T. Terano, editors, Springer-Verlag.

Axtell, R. and Epstein, M. (1999). Coordination in Transient Social Networks: An Agent Based Computational Model of the timing of retirement" Social and Economic Dynamics Working paper, No. 11.

Bala, V. and Goyal, S. (1998). Learning from neighbors, *Review of Economic Studies*, 65, pp. 595–621.

Bala, V. and Goyal, S. (2000). Self-organization in communication networks, *Econometrica*, 68, pp. 1181–1230.

Bala, V. and Goyal, S. (2000). A non-cooperative model of network formation, *Econometrica*, 68, pp. 1181–1229.

Bakhchandani, S., Hirshleifer, D. and Welch, I. (1992). A theory of fad, fashion, custom, and cultural change as informational cascades, *Journal of Political Economy*, 100, pp. 992–1026.

Baldwin, J. M. (1896). A new factor in evolution, *American Naturalist*, 30, pp. 441–451.

Banerjee, A. and Weibull, J. W. (1995). Evolutionary selection and rational behavior, *Learning and Rationality in Economics*, Oxford Press.

Batten, D. (1998). Co-evolutionar learning on networks, *Knowledge and Networks in a Dynamic Economy*, pp. 311–332.

Beckmann, M., McGuire, C. B. and Winsten, C. B. (1956). *Studies in the Economics of Transportation*, Yale University Press.

Bell, A. M. and Sethares. (2003). Coordination failure as a source of congestion, *IEEE Transaction Signal Processing*, 51, pp. 875–884.

Berninghaus, S. K., Ehrhart, K.-M. and Keser, C. (2002). Conventions and local interaction structures: experimental evidence, *Games and Economic Behavior*, 39, pp. 177–205.

Bester, H. and Güth, W. (1998). Is altruism evolutionarily stable? *Journal of Economic Behavior and Organization*, 34, pp. 193–209.

Bhaskar, V. and Vega-Redondo, F. (2002). Asynchronous choice and markov equilibria, *Journal of Economic Theory*, 103.

Bhaskar, V. and Vega-Redondo, F. (2004). Migration and the evolution of conventions, *Journal of Economic Behavior and Organization*, 55.

Binmore, K. (2001). The breakdown of social contracts, *Social Dynamics*, Brookings Institution Press.

Binmore, K. (2005). *Natural Justice*, Oxford Press.

Bisin, A. and Verdier, T. (1998). On the cultural transmission of preferences for social status, *Journal of Public Economics*, 70, pp. 75–98.

Blume, L. E. (1993). The statistical mechanics of strategic interaction, *Games and Economic Behavior*, 5, pp. 387–424.

Boerlijst, M. C., Nowak, M. A. and Sigmund, K. (1997). The logic of contrition. *Journal of Theoretical Biology*, 185, pp. 281–293.

Bonabeau, E. (2002). Predicting the unpredictable, Harvard Business Review, March, pp. 151–161.

Bonabeau, E., Dorgio, M. and Theraulaz. (1999). *Swam Intelligence*, Oxford University Press.

Borgers, T. and Sarin, R. (1994). Learning through reinforcement and the replicator dynamics, mimeo.

Bowles, S. (2004). *Microeconomics, Behavior, Institution and Evolution*, Princeton University Press.

Boyd, R. and Lorberbaum, J. P. (1987). No pure strategy is evolutionarily stable in the repeated prisoner's dilemma, *Nature*, 327, pp. 58–59.

Brandenburger. and Dekel, E. (1987). Rationalizability and correlated equilibria, *Econometrica*, 55, pp. 1391–1402.

Browning, L. and Colman, M. (2004). Evolution of coordinated alternating reciprocity in repeated dyadic games, *Journal of Theoretical Biology*, 229, pp. 549–557.

Bull, L. (1999). On the baldwin effect, *Artificial Life*, 5, pp. 241–246.

Burton-Jones, A. (1999). *Knowledge Capitalism*, Oxford University Press.

Camazine, S., Deneubourg, J., Frank, N., Sneyd, J., Theraulaz, G. and Bonabeau, E. (2001). *Self-Organization in Biological Systems*, Princeton University Press.

Carlsson, H. and Damme, E. (1993). Global games and equilibrium selection *Econometrica*, 61, pp. 989–1018.

Cassar, A. (2002). Coordination and cooperation in Local, random and small world networks: experimental evidence, *Proc. of the 2002 North American Summer Meetings of the Econometric Society.*

Casti, J. L. (1996). Seeing the light at El farol, *Complexity*, 1, pp. 7–10.

Challet, D. and Zhang, C. (1997). Emergence of cooperation and organization in an evolutionary game, *Physica*, A246.

Challet, D. and Zhang, C. (2005). *Minority Game*, Oxford University Press.

Challet, D. and Zhang, Y.-C. (1998). On the minority game: analytical and numerical Studies, *Physica A*, 256, pp. 514–518.

Chamley, C. (2003). *Rational Herd*, Cambridge Univ. Press.

Characters, M. (1999). Comparison between darwinian and lamarckian evolution. *Artificial Life*, 5, pp. 203–223.

Cohendet, P. and Llereva, P. (eds.) (1998). *The Economics of Networks*, Sprirger.

Colman, A. (1999). *Game Theory and its Applications*, Routledge.

Cooper, R. (1999). *Coordination Games*: Complementarities and Macroeconomics. Cambridge University Press.

Cowan, R. and Jonard, N. (1999). Network structure and the diffusion of knowledge technical report 99028, MERIT, Maastricht University.

Cowan, R. and Jonard, N. (2001). Knowledge creation, knowledge diffusion and network structure, *Economics with Heterogeneous Interacting Agents*, Springer.

Crutchfield, J. and Schuster, P. (Ed.) (2003). *Evolutionary Dynamics*, Oxford University Press.

Das, R., Crutchfield, J., Mitchell, M. and Hanson, J. (1995). Evolving globally synchronized cellular automata, *Proc. of the 6th International Conference on Genetic Algorithms*, pp. 336–343.

David, P. A. (1985). Clio and economics of QWERTY, *American Economics Review*, 75, pp. 332–337.

Dekel, E., Ely, J. and Ylankaya, O. (1998). Evolution of preferences, mimeo, Northwestern University.

Devaney, R. (1989). *An Introduction to Chaotic Dynamic Systems*, Addison-Wesley Publishing.

Dixit, A. and Nalebuff, P. (1991). *Thinking Strategically*: The competitive Edge in Business, Politics and Everyday Life. Norton & Company.

Doebeli, M., Hauert, Ch. and Killingback, T. (2004). The evolutionary origin of cooperators and defectors, *Science*, 306, pp. 859–862.

Doebeli, M. and Hauert, Ch. (2005). Models of cooperation based on the prisoner's dilemma and the snowdrift game, *Ecol. Lett. 8*, pp. 748–766.

Duffy, J. and Hopkins, E. (2002). Learning, information and sorting in market entry games, working paper, University of Pittsburgh.

Durlauf, S. N. and Young, H. P. (2001). *Social Dynamics*, Brookings Institution Press.

Dutta, B. and Jackson, M. O. (2000). The stability and efficiency of directed communication networks, *Review of Economic Design*, 5, pp. 251–272.

Dutta, B. and Jackson, M. O. (2001). *Introductory chapter in Models of Formation of Network Groups*, Springer-Verlag.

Ellison, G. (1993). Learning local interaction, and coordination, *Econometrica*, 61, pp. 1047–1071.

Ellison, G. and Fudenberg, D. (1993). Rules of thumb for social learning, *Journal of Political Economy*, 101, pp. 612–623.

Ellison, G. and Fudenberg, D. (1995). Word of mouth communication and social learning, *Quarterly Journal of Economics*, 110, pp. 93–126.

Ely, J. C. (2002). Local conventions, *Advances in Theoretical Economics*, 2.

Epstein, J. M. and Axtell, R. (1996). *Growing Artificial Societies: Social Science From the Bottom Up.*: Brookings Institution Press.

Erev, I. and Roth, A. (1988). Predicting how people play games: Reinforcement learning in experimental games with unique, mixed strategy equilibria. American Economic Review, 88, pp. 848–881.

Eshel, I., Samuelson, L. and Shaked, A. (1998). Altruists, egoists, and hooligans in a local interaction model, *American Economic Review*, 88, pp. 157–179.

Fehr, E. and Gachter, S. (2002). Altruistic punishment in humans, *Nature*, 415, pp. 137–140.

Fehr, E. and Schmidt, K. M. (1999). A theory of fairness, competition and cooperation, *Quarterly Journal of Economics*, 114, pp. 817–868.

Fischer, M. and Frohlich, J. (2001). *Knowledge, Complexity and Innovation Systems*, Springer-Verlag.

Fogel, D. (1993). Evolving behaviors in the iterated prisoner's dilemma, *Evolutionary Computation*, 1, pp. 77–97.

Fogel, D. (1995). On the relationship between the duration of an encounter and the evolution of cooperation in the iterated prisoner's dilemma, *Evolutionary Computation*, 3, pp. 349–363.

Fogel, D. (ed.) (1998). *Evolutionary Computation*: The Fossil Record, IEEE Press.

Fogel, D. and Chellapia, K. (1999). Inductive reasoning and bounded rationality reconsidered, *IEEE Trans. of Evolutionary Computation*, 3, pp. 142–146.

Fogel, L. (1999). *Intelligence through Simulated Evolution*: Forty Years of Evolutionary Programming, John Wiley.

Fowler, J., Johnson, T. and Smirnov, O. (2005). Egalitarian motives may underlie altruistic punishment, *Nature*, 433.

Freeman, L. C. (1980). Centrality in social networksII: experimental results, *Social Networks*, 2, pp. 119–141.

Friedman, D. (1991). Evolutionary games in economics, *Economatrica*, 59, pp. 637–666.

Fudenberg, D. (1991). *Game Theory*, The MIT Press.

Fudenberg, D. and Kreps, D. (1993). Learning mixed equilibria, *Games and Economic Behavior*, 5, pp. 320–367.

Fudenberg, D. and Levine, D. (1998). *The Theory of Learning in Games*, The MIT Press.

Gilbert, N. and Troitzsch, K. (1999). *Simulation for Social Scientist*, Open University Press.

Gintis, H. (2000). *Game Theory Evolving*, Princeton University Press.

Glance, N. S. and Huberman, B. A. (1994). The dynamics of social dilemmas, *Scientific America*, pp. 76–83.

Gode, D. K. and Shyam Sunder (1993). Allocative efficiency of markets with zero intelligence traders: market as a partial substitute for individual rationality, *The Journal of Political Economy*, 101, pp. 119–137.

Gode, D. K. and Shyam Sunder (1994). Human and artificially intelligent traders in a double auction market: experimental evidence, *Computational Organization Theory*, Lawrence Erlbaum Associates, pp. 241–262.

Gouldner, A. (1960). The norm of reciprocity: A preliminary statement, *American Sociological Review*, 25, pp. 161–178.

Goyal, S. and Vega-Redondo, F. (2005). Learning, network formation and coordination, *Games and Economic Behavior*, 50.

Granovetter, M. (1974). *Getting a Job*, University of Chicago Press.

Granovetter, M. (1978). Threshold models of collective behavior, *American Journal of Sociology*, 183, pp. 1420–1433.

Grim, P. (1995). The greater generosity of the spatialized prisonner's dilemma, *J. Theor. Biol.*, 173, pp. 353–359.

Grimm, V. and Railsback, S. (2005). *Individual-based Modeling and Ecology*, Princeton University Press.

Hamilton, W. D. (1970). Selfish and spiteful behavior in an evolutionary model, *Nature*, 228, pp. 1218–20.

Hammerstein, P. and Selten, R. (1994). Game theory and evolutionary biology, *Handbook of Game Theory with Economic Applications*, Vol. 2, Elsevier Science, pp. 931–962.

Hanaki, N. (2006). Individual and Social Learning, Forthcoming in *Computational Economics*.

Hanaki, N., Sethi, R., Erev, I. and Peterhansl (2005). Learning Strategies, *Journal of Economic Behavior and Organization*, Vol. 56, pp. 523–542.

Harrald, P. G. and Fogel, D. B. (1996). Evolving continuous behaviors in the iterated prisoner's dilemma, *BioSystems*, 37, pp. 135–145.

Harsanryi, J. and Selten, R. (1988). *A Game Theory of Equibrium Selection in Games*, MIT Press.

Hart, S. and Mas-Colell, A. (2003). Uncoupled dynamics do not lead to Nash equilibrium, *American Economic Review*, 93, pp. 1830–1836.

Hauert, C. (2002). Effects of Space in 2x2 Games, *International Journal of Bifurcation and Chaos*, 12, pp. 1531–1547.

Hauert, Ch. and Doebeli, M. (2004). Spatial structure often inhibits the evolution of cooperation in the Snowdrift game, *Nature*, 428, pp. 643–646.

Hauert, Ch. and Szabó, G. (2005). Game theory and physics, *Am. J. Phys.*, 73, pp. 405–414.

Hauk, E. and Nagel, R. (2001). Choice of partners in multiple two-person prisoner's dilemma games, *Journal of Conflict Resolution*, 45, pp. 770–793.

Helbing, D. (1995). *Quantitative Sociodynamics*, Kluwer Academic.

Hinton, G. E. and Nowlan, S. J. (1987). How learning can guide evolution, *Complex Systems*, 1, pp. 495–502.

Hofstadter, D. R. (1995). *Fluid Concepts and Creative Analogies: Computer Models of the Fundamental Mechanisms of Thought*, New York: Basic Books.

Hofbauer, J., Sigmund, K. (1998). *Ecolutionary Games and Population Dynamics*, Cambridge Univ. Press.

Holland, G. (1995). *Hidden Order*, Addison-Wesley Publishing.

Holland, J. H. (1975). *Adaptation in Natural and Artificial Systems*, The University of Michigan Press.

Holland, J. H. (1998). *Emergence*: From Chaos to Order, Addison-Wesley.

Huberman, B. and Glance, N. (1993). Diversity and collective action, *Interdisciplinary Approaches to Nonlinear Systems*, Springer.

Huberman, B. A. and Lukose, R. M. (1997). Social dilemmas and internet congestion, *Science*, 277, pp. 535–537.

Iwanaga, S. and Namatame, A. (2001). Asymmetric coordination of heterogeneous agents, *IEICE Trans. on Information and Systems*, E84-D, pp. 937–944.

Iwanaga, S. and Namatame, A. (2002). The complexity of collective decision, *Journal of Nonlinear Dynamics and Control*, 6, pp. 137–158.

Jackson, M. O. (2003). A survey of models of network formation: stability and efficiency, mimeo, California Institute of Technology.

Jackson, M. O. and Wolinsky, A. (1996). A strategic model of social and economic networks, *Journal of Economic Theory*, 71, pp. 44–74.

Johnson, C. and Gilles, R. P. (1999). Spatial social networks, *Review of Economic Design*, 5, pp. 273–300.

Kalai, E. and Lehrer, E. (1993). Rational learning leads to Nash equilibrium, *Econometrica*, 61, pp. 1019–1045.

Kandori, M. and Mailath, G. (1993). Learning, mutation and long-run equilibria in games, *Econometrica*, 61, pp. 29–56.

Kaniovski, Y., Kryazhimskii, A. and Young, H. (2000). Adaptive dynamics in games played by heterogeneous populations, *Games and Economics Behavior*, 31, pp. 50–96.

Kerr, B., Riley, M., Feldman, M. and Bohannan, B. (2002). Local dispersal promotes biodiversity in a real-life game of rock-paper-scissors, *Nature*, 418, pp. 171–174,

Keser, C., Ehrhart, K.-M. and Berninghaus, S. K. (1998). Coordination and local interaction:experimental evidence, *Economics Letters*, 58, pp. 269–275.

Kirchkamp, O. (2000). Spatial evolution of automata in the prisoner's dilemma, *Journal of Economic Behavior and Organization*, 43, pp. 239–262.

Kirley, M. (2004). Compex networks and evolutionary games, *Proc. of the 7th Asia-Pacific Conf. On Complex Networks*.

Kirman, A. (1993). Ants, rationality and recruitment, *Quarterly Journal of Economics*, 108, pp. 137–156.

Kirman, A. (1997). The economy as an evolving network, *Journal of Evolutionary Economics*, 7, pp. 339–353.

Kirman, A. and Zimmermann, J. (eds.) (2001). *Economics with Heterogeneous Interacting Agents*, Sprirger.

Kleindorfer, R. etc. (1993). *Decision Science*, Cambridge Univ. Press.

KIilllingback, T. and Doebell, M. (1996). Spatial evolutionary game theory: hawks and doves revisited, *Proc. R. Soc. B*. 263, pp. 1135–1144.

Knight, F. M. (1924). Some fallacies in the interpretation of social costs, *Q.J. Econ*, 38, pp. 582–626.

Kosfeld, M. (2002). Stochastic strategy adjustment in coordination games, *Economic Theory*, 20, pp. 321–339.

Kreps, D. (1990). *A Course in Microeconomic Theory*, Harvester Wheatsheaf.

Kreps, D., Kreps, P., Roberts, J. and Wilson, J. (1982). Rational cooperation in the finitely repeated prisoner's dilemma, *J. Econ. Theory*, 27, pp. 326–355.

Laland, N. and Brown, R. (2002). *Sense and Nonsense. Evolutionary Perspectives on Human Behaviour*, Oxford University Press.

Lieberman, E., Hauert, Ch. and Nowak, M. A. (2005). Evolutionary dynamics on graphs, *Nature*, 433, pp. 312–316.

Lindgren, K. (1991). Evolutionary phenomena in simple dynamics, *Proc. of Artificial Life II*, pp. 295–311.

Lindgren, K. (1997). Evolutionary dynamics in game-theoretic models, *The Economy As An Evolving Systems II*, Addison-Wesley.

Lloyd, A. L. (1995). Computing bouts of the prisoner's dilemma, *Scientific American*, 272, pp. 110–115.

Macy, M. and Flache, A. (2002). Learning dynamics in social dilemmas, *PNAS*, 99, pp. 7229–7236.

Manski, C. F. and McFadden, D. L. (Eds.) (1981). *Structural Analysis of Discrete Data and Econometric Applications*, The MIT Press.

Markose, S. M. (2005). Computability and evolutionary complexity: markets as complex Adaptive systems, *The Economic Journal*, 115.

Matteo, M. (2001). Toy models of markets with heterogeneous interacting agents, *Lecture Notes in Economics and Mathematical Systems*, 503, Springer, pp. 161–181.

Mayley, G. (1997). Landscapes, learning costs, and genetic assimilation, *Evolutionary Computation*, 4, pp. 213–234.

Maynard, S. (1996). Natural selection: when learning guides evolution, *Adaptive Individuals in EvolvingPopulations: Models and Algorithms*, Belew, R. K. and Mitchell, M. (Eds.), Addison Wesley, pp. 455–457.

McFadden, D. (1975). *Urban Travel Demand: A behavioral analysis*, North-Holland.

McKelvey, D. and Palfrey, R. (2002). Playing in the Dark: Information, Learning, and Coordination in Repeated Games. Caltech. Working Paper.

McMahon, C. (2003). *Collective Rationality and Collective Reasoning*, Cambridge University Press.

Minsky, M. L. (1985). *The Society of Mind*, Simon and Schuster.

Moelbert, S. and Rios, P. D. (2001). The local minority game, cond-mat/0109080.

Morioka, M. (1995). The two human natures (in a Japanese monthly magazine Chuo Koron, pp. 76–84.

Murakami, K. and Namatame (2002). A. Evolutionary earning in strategic Enviromnents. Proc. of the 6-th International Confedrence on Complex Systems, pp. 269–277.

Murchland, J. D. (1970). Braess's paradox of traffic flow, *Transportation Res*, 4, pp. 3–394.

Namatame, A. (1998). *Multi-Agents and Complexity* (in Japanese), Morikita Shuppan.

Namatame, A. (2001). *Strategical Decision Making* (in Japanese), Asakura Shoten.

Namatame, A. (2004). *Game Theory and Evolutionary Dynamics* (in Japanese), Morikita Shuppan.

Namatame, A. (2004). The design of desired collectives with agent-based simulation, *Journal of Social Complexity*, 2, pp. 123–145.

Namatame, A. (2004). Efficiency and equity in collective systems of interacting heterogeneous agents, *Collectives and the Design of Complex Systems*, K. Tumer & D. Wolpert (eds.), Springer, (Ch 11), pp. 257–276.

Namatame, A. (2004). Localized minority games and emergence of efficient dynamic order, *Lecture Notes in Economics and Mathematical Systems*, Springer, pp. 71–85.

Namatame, A. and Sato, M. (2004). Co-evolutionary learning in strategic environments, *Recent Rdvances in Simulated Evolution and Learning*, Chen Tann (Eds.) World Scientific Press, pp. 1–20.

Narendra, K. and Thatcher, M. (1974). Learning Automata: a Survey, *IEEE Transactions on Systems, Man and Cybernetics*, 4, pp. 889–899.

Nonaka, I. and Takeuchi, H. (1995). *The Knowledge-Creating Company*, Oxford University Press.

Nowak, M. A., Szamrej, J. and Latane, B. (1990). From private attitude to public opinion: a dynamic theory of social impact, *Psychological Review*, 97, pp. 362–376.

Nowak, M. A. and May, R. M. (1992). Evolutionary games and spatial chaos, *Nature*, 359, pp. 826–829.

Nowak, M. A. and Sigmund, K. (1993). A strategy of win-stay, lose-shift that outperforms tit-for-tat in the prisoner's dilemma game, *Nature*, 364, pp. 56–58.

Nowak, M. A., etc., (1995). The arithmetics of mutual help, *Scientific American*, pp. 76–81.

Nowak, M. A. and Sigmund, K. (1998). Evolution of indirect reciprocity by image scoring, *Nature*, 393, pp. 573–577.

Nowak, M. A. and Sigmund, K. (2004). Evolutionary dynamics of biological games, *Science*, 303, pp. 793–799.

Nowak, M. A. and Sigmund, K. (2005). Evolution of indirect reciprocity, *Nature*, pp. 1291–1298.

Ochs, J. (1995). Coordination Problems, *Handbook of Experimental Economics*, Princeton University Press, pp. 195–251.

Ochs, J. (1998). Coordination in market entry games, *Games and Human Behavior*, pp. 143–172.

Ok, Efe, and Vega-Redondo. (2001). On the evolution of individualistic preferences: complete versus incomplete information, *Journal of Economic Theory*, 97.

Olson, M. (1965). *The Logic of Collective Action*, Harvard University Press.

Pigou, A. C. (1920). *The Economics of Welfare*, Mamillan.

Rapoport, A. (1966). Optimal policies for the prisoner's dilemma, University of North Carolina Tech Report No. 50.

Rapoport, A., Seal, D. and Winter. (1999). An experimental study of coordination and learning in iterated two-market entry games, *Economic Theory*, 16, pp. 661–687.

Rapoport, A., Seale, D. and Winter, E. (1998). An experimental study of coordination and learning in iterated two-market entry games, Hong Kong Univ. Sci. Technol.

Resnick, M. (1999). *Turtles, Terminate, and Traffic Jams*: Explorations in Massively Parallel Microworlds, The MIT Press.

Rhode, P. and Stegeman, M. (1996). Learning, mutation, and long-run equilibria in games:a comment, *Econometrica*, 64, pp. 443–49.

Robson, A. J. (2003). The evolution of intelligence and the red queen, *Journal of Economic Theory*, 111, pp. 1–22.

Rogers, A. R. (1994). Evolution of time preference by natural selection, *American EconomicReview*, 84, pp. 460–82.

Ronald, E. M. A., Sipper, M. and Capcarrère, M. S. (1999). Design, observation, surprise! a test of emergence, *Artificial Life*, 5, pp. 225–239.

Roughgarden, T. (2005). *Selfish Routing and the Price of Anarchy*, The MIT Press.

Rubinstein, A. (1998). *Modeling Bounded Rationality*, The MIT Press.

Samuelson, L. (1998). *Evolutionary Games and Equilibrium Selection*, The MIT Press.

Schelling, T. (1978). *Micromotives and Macrobehavior*, Norton.

Schweitzer, F. (ed.) (2002). *Modeling Complexity in Economic and Social Systems*, World Scientific.

Selten, R. (1991). Evolution, learning, and economic behavior, *Games and Economic Behavior*, 3, pp. 3–24.

Sethi, R. and Somanathan, E. (1999). Preference evolution and reciprocity, mimeo, Barnard College, Columbia University.

Shoham, Y. and Powers, R. (2003). Multi-agent reinforcement learning: a critical survey (memo).

Simon, H. (1981). *The Sciences of Artificial*, MIT Press.

Simon, H. (1982). *Models of bounded rationality*, The MIT Press.

Sipper, M. (1997). *Evolution of Parallel Cellular Machines*, Springer.

Smith, J. M. (1982). *Evolution and the Theory of Games*, Cambridge University Press.

Stanley, A., Ashlock, D. and Tesfatsion, L. (1994). Iterated prisoner's dilemma with choice and refusal of partners, *Artificial Life III*, Addison-Wesley, pp. 131–175.

Subrahamanian, V. S. (etc). (2000). *Heterogeneous Agent Systems*, MIT Press.

Sundali, J., Rapoport, A. and Seale, D. (1995). Coordination in market entry games with symmetric players, *Organiz. Beh. Human Decision Process*, 64, pp. 203–218.

Surowiecki, J. (2004). *The Wisdom of Crowds*, Random House.

Suzuki, R. and Arita, T. (2000). Interaction between evolution and learning in a population of globally or locally interacting agents, *Proc. of Seventh International Conference on Neural Information Processing*, pp. 738–743.

Suzuki, R. and Arita, T. (2003). The baldwin effect revisited: three steps characterized by the quantitative evolution of phenotypic plasticity, *Proc. of Seventh European Conference on Artificial Life*, pp. 395–404.

Tennenholtz, T. (2002). Effcient learning equilibrium, *Proc. of NIPS*, pp. 214–224.

Tesfatsion, L., Ashlock, H., Smucker, S. and Stanley, A. (1996). Preferential partner selection in an evolutionary study of prisoner's dilemma, *BioSystems*, 37, pp. 99–125.

Tumer, K. and Wolpert, D. (Eds.) (2004). *Collectives and the Design of Complex Systems*, Springer.

Turney, P., Whitley, D. and Anderson, R. W. (1996). Evolution, learning, and instinct: 100 years of the baldwin effect, *Evolutionary Computation*, 4(3), pp. 4–8.

Van Huyck, J. B., Battalio, R. C. and Beil, R. O. (1990). Tacit coordination games, strategic uncertainty, and coordination failure, *American Economic Review*, 80, pp. 234–249.

Van Valen L. (1973). A new evolutionary law, *Evolutionary Theory*, 1, pp. 1–30.

Vega-Redondo, F. (1997). The evolution of walrasian behavior, *Econometrica*, 65, pp. 375–84.

Vega-Redondo, F. (2003). *Economics and the Theory of Games*, Cambridge University Press.

Wardrop, J. G. (1952). Some theoretical aspects of road traffic research, *Proc. Institute of Civil Engineers*, Part II, 1, pp. 325–378.

Watts, A. (2002). A simple model of global cascades on random networks, *PNAS*, 99, pp. 5766–5771.

Watts, A. (2001). A dynamic model of network formation, *Games and Economic Behavior*, 34, pp. 331–341.

Watts, D. (1999). *Small Worlds*, Princeton University Press.

Watts, D. and Strogatz, H. (1998). Collective dynamics of small-world networks, *Nature*, 393, pp. 440–442.

Weibull, J. (1996). *Evolutionary Game Theory*, The MIT Press.

Weibull, J. W. (2001). Testing game theory, mimeo, Stockholm School of Economics.

Wolpert, D. and Tumer, K. (2001). Optimal payoff functions for members of collective, *Advances in Complex Systems*, 3, pp. 265–20.

Wolpert, D., Wheeler, K. and Tumer, K. (2000). Collective intelligence for control of distributed dynamical systems, *Europhysics Letters*, 49, pp. 708–714.

Wu, J. and Axelrod, R. (1997). How to cope with noise in the iterated prisoner's dillema game, *Journal of Conflict Resolution*, 39, pp. 183–189.

Yao, X. and Darwen, P. (1994). The experimental study of n-player iterated prisoner's dilemma, *Informatica*, 18, pp. 435–450.

Young, H. P. (1993). The evolution of conventions, *Econometrica*, 61, pp. 57–84.

Young, H. P. (1998). *Individual Strategy and Social Structures*, Princeton University Press.

Young, H. P. (2005). *Strategic Learning and Its Limits*, Oxford Univ. Press.

Index